THE

Alchemical
IMAGINATION

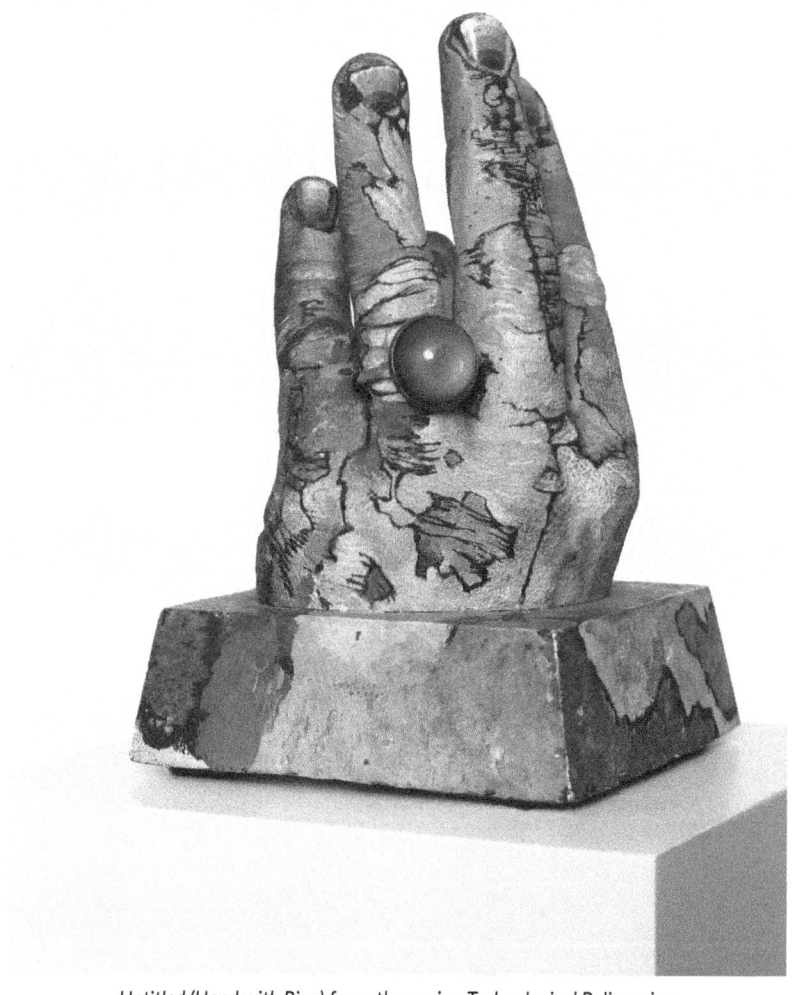

Untitled (Hand with Ring) from the series *Technological Reliquaries*,
by Paul Thek, 1967; wood, plaster, paint, and metal sculpture; 7⅜" × 4½" × 4½"
(18.7 cm × 11.4 cm × 11.4 cm). Photo by Richard Gary, courtesy of the Pace Gallery.

THE

Alchemical

IMAGINATION

Creativity as Catalyst
for Radical Transformation

ELIZA SWANN

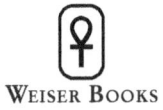

WEISER BOOKS

This book is dedicated to Angel, to our garden, and to you.

This edition first published in 2026 by Weiser Books, an imprint of
Red Wheel/Weiser, LLC
With offices at:
65 Parker Street, Suite 7
Newburyport, MA 01950
www.redwheelweiser.com

ISBN: 978-1-57863-901-4

Library of Congress Cataloging-in-Publication Data
Names: Swann, Eliza author | Aberth, Susan L. writer of foreword
Title: The alchemical imagination : creativity as catalyst for radical transformation / Eliza Swann
; foreword by Susan L. Aberth.
Description: Newburyport, MA : Weiser Books, 2026. | Includes bibliographical references and
index. | Summary: "This is the first book of its kind to address the ancient subject of alchemy
through the lens of contemporary creativity, distilling this arcane science into an accessible
series of philosophies and techniques to help readers find a deeper connection to their own
creativity. Part workbook and part historical journey, the book highlights often-overlooked
female alchemists and queer alchemical imagery and traces their many contributions to
contemporary art, handing this ancient craft to a new generation"-- Provided by publisher.
Identifiers: LCCN 2025050840 | ISBN 9781578639014 trade paperback | ISBN
9781633413979 ebook
Subjects: LCSH: Alchemy | Creative ability | BISAC: SELF-HELP / Creativity | ART / History
/ Renaissance
Classification: LCC QD26 .S88 2026
LC record available at https://lccn.loc.gov/2025050840

Cover design by Sky Peck Design
Front cover: Mixed media painting by Kathryn Sky-Peck
Back cover: Detail from the Ripley Scroll, 15th century
Interior by Brittany Craig
Typeset in Arno Pro

Printed in the United States of America
IBI
10 9 8 7 6 5 4 3 2 1

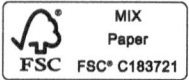

CONTENTS

FOREWORD

The very word "alchemy" can inspire trepidation for even the most ardent of esoteric seekers, calling to mind arcane chemistry and hauntingly beautiful illustrations that are frustrating to decipher. Dear reader, fear not. Eliza Swann's *The Alchemical Imagination* is going to be your golden key not only to unlocking a fundamental knowledge of alchemy's history and processes but also to harnessing its spiritual lessons. This was no easy task, although the elegance and simplicity of Swann's text might initially disguise the fact that the book is the result of many years of research, experimentation, and personal distillation.

Organized in order of distillation processes—nigredo, albedo, rubedo—each section of the book is clearly articulated yet without a loss of poetic flair, evident in such headings as "Jupiter: Tin, Liver, Zeus, and Joseph Beuys" or "Fermentation: I Am the Utterance of My Name." A judicious selection of alchemical illustrations is placed throughout the text in such a manner as to make them more understandable without losing their mysterious allure. Another great strength of *The Alchemical Imagination* is the intermingling of accounts from the author's own life experiences along with the biographical narratives of a slew of significant alchemists and artists.

As a teacher, scholar, and student of alchemy, I found myself deeply moved by this interjection of stories from Swann's journey as an artist and mystic. I was struck by how closely it resembled some of my own experiences in several uncanny details (albeit decades later). In particular, her recounting at the beginning of the book of the academy's disdain and dismissal of her work in alchemy struck an uncomfortable cord of recognition. I suspect that many readers will feel the same, so universal is the spiritual aspirant's path through the painful wilderness of isolation, alienation, and public rebuke.

Happily, Swann also provides "exercises" whereby the reader can connect to the outlined processes in a multitude of ways and hopefully begin to acquire a deeper, more embodied understanding of this occult science. Visualization, meditation, singing, writing, and poetry are some of the methods she proposes. Deceptively simple, I found these creative techniques to be highly effective and, more importantly, accessible to a modern audience with a variety of needs and approaches to this material. I can easily imagine returning to these instructions repeatedly, gaining more confidence and discovering new layers of meaning and self-expression. One of my favorites, a powerful recipe for psychic integration, is meant as preparation for discovering one's inner Philosopher's Stone. "Call yourself," Swann orders, "gather parts of yourself that may have been left behind or scattered in past moments, bringing them into the present."

My students and colleagues often ask me: How can alchemy be relevant to our times, to our lives, to the future? *The Alchemical Imagination* convincingly argues that far from being a useless relic from ages past, alchemy still has much to offer. Of certain interest to contemporary readers is what the author asserts is the gender-queer aspects of alchemical and occult philosophies. Swann is at pains to remind us that Hermes, the supernatural overlord of this sacred science, is the great disruptor of binaries, including gender. Honored as a guide for practitioners of magic (and poets), Hermes is also the patron of queer folk and, as Swann reminds us, of those who "navigate various realms and assume multiple identities."

The long-term, visionary perspective of this book may help readers to better prepare for what surely lies ahead. As I write this, the world, as we have known it, is in a profound state of change and, as with all processes of transformation, the initiate will have to endure psychic darkness, confusion, and pain before rising anew. Although apocalyptic fears and predictions have always plagued humanity, this time the ecological collapse currently being experienced is urgent. How can we move forward instead of feeling powerless and paralyzed? Swann assures us: "In the face of escalating violence, ecological collapse, and toxic systems of power, we need to return to sciences that embrace the impossible, reject greed as a driving force, and view the world as emanating from the sacred, worthy of care, attention, and devotion." I absolutely believe this to be true and, of course, *this* is the sought-after "gold" of incalculable value.

—Susan L. Aberth

ACKNOWLEDGMENTS

My thanks to every alchemist who came before me, Mom for this wild life, Susan Aberth for her wisdom and generosity, Adrian Shirk for her brilliance, Catherine Wagley for her genius, Linda Montano for all her teachings and gifts, Zeljko McMullen for teaching me to stand in my faith, Kelly Carmena and the Philosophical Research Society for their support, the Pratt Faculty Development Fund for supporting this research, David Brafman at the Getty Research Institute for his generosity and knowledge, Insight Meditation Society for the space to explore consciousness and the Hemera Foundation for supporting that research, Robert Bartlett for showing me how to make a spagyric, Diane di Prima for carrying the lantern forward, Paul Thek always and his estate for their generosity, Amy Arbus for her vision and kindness, Michael Pye and Kathryn Sky-Peck for believing in this work, and Weiser for bringing this book into being.

PART I

Nigredo

THE DARKEST HOUR OF NIGHT

On Finding Our Way
Toward Art and Alchemy

Alchemy
THE BLOOD OF THE POETS

The sun looked like a red neon eye burning through wildfire smoke, staining the city of Los Angeles a strange, sickly yellow. Ash left lacelike patterns on the dry ground like scorched fingerprints. I was in Los Angeles to examine alchemical manuscripts at the Getty Research Institute. They have a copy of the Ripley Scroll, an extraordinary, hand-painted alchemical manuscript that stretches nearly twenty-one feet long, and I had flown in especially to see it. While in town, I stopped by a professor friend's house for her kid's birthday party, where I didn't know anyone. A restless group of academics huddled under the sparse shade of a eucalyptus tree as kids tumbled around in the dry brown grass. My friend nudged me toward the group, introducing me with her elbow in my side: "This is Eliza. She's an *alchemist.*"

I mumbled that I taught alchemy at an art college in New York, trying to shield myself from being corralled into the narrow confines of "quack." But institutional shields are flimsy ones. Once, at a faculty party, someone asked what I taught, and when I said, "critical studies and alchemy," the room erupted in laughter as though these two things were an oxymoron. Here, in LA, the reaction was similar. One man choked on his cupcake and snorted, "Wait, what? Isn't that a pseudoscience? They let you teach that in college?" His words hung in the air momentarily before another man excitedly jumped in, eager to join the heckling. "You teach them to make gold? Will you teach *me*?"

The wildfire smoke was making me nauseous. Wildfires have become so extreme and unpredictable that new terms like *firenado, gigafire,* and *fire siege* have entered our vocabulary. In 2020, I had left LA after developing severe asthma during the largest wildfire season in California's history, which scorched nearly four million acres. It was the fires that compelled me to begin teaching alchemy publicly. Alchemical work offers pathways forward in the face of our ecological crisis. Alchemy weaves together the mystical, the scientific, and the philosophical to foster a more holistic, loving, and interdependent understanding of our world. As Christopher Bamford writes in *Green Hermeticism*, the alchemical worldview "seeks to understand nature in itself, for itself, out of itself, as our sacred, holy, even divine source. It is therefore a path of praise, love, and adoration" (Wilson, Bamford, and Townley 2007, 91).

I opened my mouth to say some of this, but most of the group had already dismissed the conversation and turned back to one another. Alchemy, once revered as the Divine Art, is now remembered as little more than a get-rich-quick scheme for greedy charlatans seeking gold—an image that has persisted since the Enlightenment, when science disposed of mystery in favor of mechanical philosophy. Alchemy was cultivated in temple priesthoods in the name of the divine. Ritual initiations were designed to protect its innovations from those looking to exploit the art for selfish gain; alchemists well understood that science practiced in the name of capital gain alone would become dangerous.

In any case, gold *can* be made in a laboratory—just as the alchemists foresaw. Alchemical experiments often took so long to come to fruition that they were passed down from one generation to the next, awaiting their eventual realization. Recently, while smashing lead atoms into each other at extremely high speeds to mimic the state of the universe just after the Big Bang, physicists working at the Large Hadron Collider in Switzerland incidentally produced small amounts of gold (CERN 2025).

What matters to me in the quest to make gold is that alchemists don't view themselves as separate from the metal. Alchemists believe that every external process mirrors an internal one; the transformations carried out in the laboratory are reflections of the alchemist's own inner metamorphosis. This view cultivates a deep sense of interconnection and a profound ethical responsibility. Harm done in the laboratory is not distant or abstract—it is harm done to ourselves. In many alchemical traditions, rituals of apology are offered to the earth and to the materials used, acknowledging the pain that may arise in the act of extraction. Alchemy, in this way, becomes a bridge between earth and sky, matter and spirit, body and eternity. It is a vast and integrative discipline that offers something far more precious than gold: it reveals connection and renders our interdependence acutely visible.

Earlier that weekend, in the serene, cool underground spaces of the Getty Research Institute, David Brafman, a scholar of alchemy and the curator of rare books at the Getty Museum, carefully unrolled the Ripley Scroll across a long table. There are twenty-one known versions of the Ripley Scroll, each differing in size, color, and detail, but all derived from a lost original made in the 15th century. Named after the English alchemist George Ripley, the scroll is renowned for its intricate illustrations and detailed descriptions of the twelve alchemical processes used to create the Philosopher's Stone. I adapted these twelve stages into a twelve-part course called the Alchemical Imagination, now taught at Pratt Institute, where we explore how alchemy offers radical ways of thinking about creation, transformation, and our world. I had received a grant from Pratt to visit the Getty's Ripley Scroll to experience firsthand how alchemical art lives and breathes—a return to the source.

The only sound in the room was the gentle rustle of the vellum as the scroll unrolled, slowly revealing its intricate illustrations. The first scene shows an alchemist holding a glass retort, inside which two figures are chained to an alchemical book of secrets. As the scroll unfurled further, more elaborate images emerged in brilliant golds, reds, and blues that flared against the aged parchment. A golden bird appeared perched on a planetary sphere, its feathers glowing with the light of a rising dawn. Below, crimson drops of blood fell from the planet the bird was balanced on, gently descending from a higher realm, intertwining the divine and mortal in a delicate dance of emergence and sacrifice. The scroll wasn't just beautiful—it felt like a transubstantiation through art. As I took in its imagery, I sensed the divine enter me, making me feel as though I was, as Rilke puts it, living at the limits of my longing.

From its very beginning, art has been an instrument of ritual—a way for us to sing our blood back to the divine. According to Susan Sontag in *Against Interpretation*, it wasn't until Greek philosophers began distinguishing between sacred and secular art that the idea of art as something other than an active form of prayer emerged. Sontag explains that the earliest theory of art, attributed to Plato, held that it is an artificial replica of reality: "The earliest *theory* of art, that of the Greek philosophers, proposed that art was mimesis, imitation of reality. It is at this point that the peculiar question of the *value* of art arose. For the mimetic theory, by its very terms, challenges art to justify itself" (Sontag 2001, 3).

But Plato didn't invent these ideas, nor were they connected to art criticism as we now understand it. His theories came from his time learning in Egypt, where art served a clearly defined spiritual function. In Egyptian temples, priests created images not merely to depict the divine, but to house it. Through ritual processes, sculptures and icons were ensouled, becoming vessels for spirits. Without this ritual, the image was considered "lifeless" and unfit for veneration.

Influenced by this lineage of practice, Western alchemists later adopted the distinction between eidōla (idols) and eikôn (icons). Idols were seen as mere imitations—hollow forms lacking spiritual presence. Icons, by contrast, were understood as infused with the soul of what they depicted, even if they bore no visual resemblance. A statue of Zeus might resemble the god but remain inert without divine animation; an abstract icon might appear unrelated but become a living conduit for Zeus's presence. As the Greco-Egyptian alchemist Zosimos of Panopolis wrote, objects without souls cannot "know themselves" and, therefore, cannot be truly known. To view an alchemical work of art is to witness something inspirited and alive—like the Ripley Scroll, whose intricate imagery pulses with symbolic meaning and a heartbeat all its own.

Underlying these ideas is the alchemical belief that the entire world is animated by a soul—a living, breathing essence that connects all things. To the alchemist, matter is not dead or inert but in a constant process of transformation, guided by spirit. Their task is not just physical transmutation but spiritual awakening: to bring the soul hidden within matter into conscious form.

Back at the party, I hesitated and then answered what remained of the group. "I teach alchemy at an art school because alchemists had a way of seeing our place on the planet that should never have been lost. They knew how to speak to the living soul of the world." At that, two people, who had introduced themselves as poets, moved closer, leaning in as if sharing a secret. Brian Cotnoir, a contemporary alchemist, calls alchemy "the poetry of matter." It's a perfect description. In the alchemical imagination, the world itself is an epic, ensouled poem whose words you can shape with your own tongue.

Artists of all kinds are perfectly positioned to work the magic of alchemy; they already know the magic of change-work because they turn the stuff of their imaginations into things realized. Paracelsus, a 16th-century Swiss alchemist and medical doctor, was famous not only for his early discoveries in chemistry but also for his bold criticism of the medical establishment's lack of empathy. He believed the role of alchemists was to imagine a better world into being, once writing, "Besides the stars already established, there is yet another star—Imagination—that begets a new star and a new heaven. The True Imagination leads life back to its spiritual reality" (Pagel 1982, 66).

Alchemists developed many of the materials that artists use today, such as pigments, oil paints, glass, and etching chemicals. They also uncovered and passed down techniques that allowed these materials to be infused with soul. When I encountered the Ripley Scroll, I could sense that the scroll was alive—sentient, imbued with a presence and energy that radiated its own intelligence. I could see veins of gold coursing through it, shimmering with an inner light, a living, breathing entity. While viewing the scroll in person, I realized that alchemy as a science is not focused on fixed answers or definitive truths. It values the questions more than the answers, the quest for deeper knowledge rather than the acquisition of it. What emerges from the alchemical artist's studio is never a finished "product" but mystery itself.

A violinist friend once told me that the famous violins crafted by Antonio Stradivari in the late 17th and early 18th centuries can't be replicated. These violins are renowned for their unmatched sound quality. While modern luthiers have replicated Stradivari's construction techniques, measurements, arching patterns, and varnishing methods exactly, they still can't reproduce the same sound in their instruments. When I asked why this was, he said, "Modern instrument makers have forgotten how to talk to the wood." Alchemy spans a wide range of cultural and spiritual traditions, and methods for "ensouling" art vary from group to group and from alchemist to alchemist. Standard practices include precise astrological timing, prayer, and meditation during the creation process, as well as techniques for "talking to the wood"—seeing each material as alive, imbued with a consciousness that actively participates in its transformation.

Alchemical philosophy disrupts the machine of production and challenges the fragmented, utilitarian view of the world we now take for granted. It insists that every act of creation requires an intimate, holistic engagement with the entire ecology of life. In a time when we are increasingly removed from the origins of things, when production is outsourced to systems designed to deliver results as quickly as possible, regardless of the environmental consequences, alchemy calls us to reawaken our interconnections. The alchemist is not an isolated figure working alone in a lab; they are part of an intricate, living network that extends from the inner workings of their body to the farthest reaches of the cosmos.

As Vandana Shiva says in her book *Earth Democracy: Justice, Sustainability, and Peace*, "In nature's economy, the currency is not money, it is life" (Shiva 2005, 33). In alchemical philosophy, nothing is ever truly inanimate; humanity and the Earth are viewed as integral parts of a single, dynamic, spiritual-physical organism. Alchemical knowledge cannot be standardized or mass-produced; it depends on the dynamic interplay of deeply personal relationships within an interconnected framework. This renders the mechanized production model, an assembly line focused on identical outcomes, impossible. The alchemical path rejects the efficiency-driven, replicative mindset that dominates modern life, inviting a redefinition of value that nurtures life and diversity in contrast to the death-driven logic of capitalist accumulation.

As we partygoers stood huddled beneath a darkening sky raining ash, the reasons for alchemy's resurgence after a long dormancy became clear. In the face of escalating violence, ecological collapse, and toxic systems of power, we need to return to sciences that embrace the impossible, reject greed as a driving force, and view the world as emanating from the sacred, worthy of care, attention, and devotion. I excused myself and hurried back to my hotel room. I found a message waiting for me: *The Alchemical Imagination*, a book I'd written exploring the creative possibilities within alchemy, had found its publisher. And here we are.

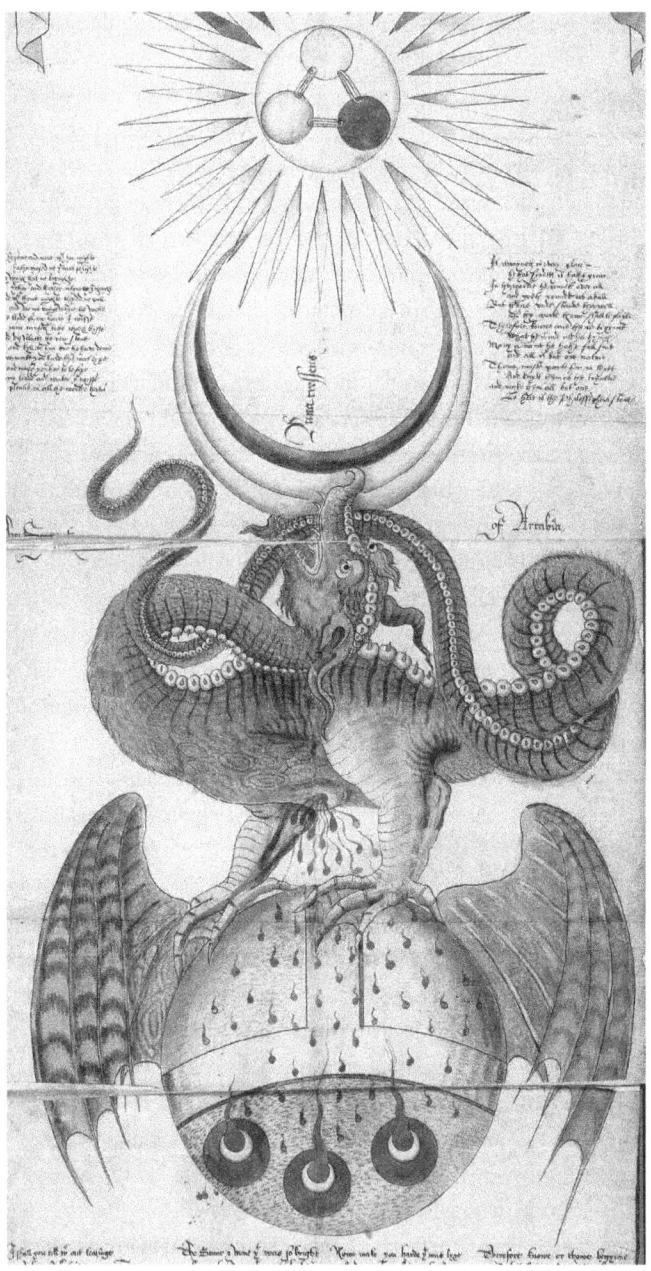

The "Serpent of Arabia" holds aloft the Philosopher's Stone. An excerpt from the Ripley Scroll, 1570. Beinecke Rare Book and Manuscript Library, Yale University.

The Book of Pearls
A BRIEF HISTORY OF ALCHEMY

In medieval Europe, alchemists referred to their blend of scientific, mystical, and creative practices as the Great Art, and for good reason. Alchemy views spiritual and material realities as deeply interconnected, allowing alchemists to approach problems as radically interdisciplinary thinkers. Their freedom of practice has led to significant technological and creative breakthroughs for millennia. This book explores alchemical principles across the natural sciences, healing arts, visual arts, and literature, providing tools to help you discover your own Great Art. Rather than presenting a single, fixed definition of alchemy, my aim is to guide you through a series of linguistic, artistic, and experiential explorations that invite a deeper engagement with the alchemical mystery, shedding light on its most significant aspects—and, if we're lucky, offering a glimpse of its elusive center.

In European alchemical philosophy, transformation unfolds in three distinct phases: nigredo, albedo, and rubedo. This book follows that progression, with each phase representing a crucial step in personal and creative development. The first phase, nigredo—the darkest hour of night—describes processes of dissolution, disintegration, and breaking apart. In the internal realm, this signifies the unraveling of old identities and outdated beliefs. Such deep questioning requires both courage and flexibility, qualities essential to any artist seeking to produce meaningful work. In part 1, our nigredo phase, I introduce the history of alchemy, share aspects of my own experiments, and invite you to explore your personal experiences through the lens of alchemical transformation.

Next is albedo, the phase of lunar illumination, when what has been broken down is filtered and clarified. In the internal laboratory, the moon's silvery light reveals new ways of perceiving, and unexpected insights emerge from turning inward. In part 2, our albedo phase, we'll explore the underlying structures of alchemical philosophy and science. The concepts introduced here provide a foundation for artists who wish to align their creative practice with the deeper mysteries of material transformation.

Following this, rubedo—the rosy dawn—represents a breakthrough. Here, the broken-down and clarified ingredients of previous phases begin to cohere into something wholly new. The dawning light reveals the world afresh, and we can start to apply the insights we've gained outwardly. In this stage, after deep reflection on the self and the nature of alchemy, the alchemist initiates the ultimate creative act: the creation of the Philosopher's Stone. In part 3, our rubedo phase, we'll walk through the twelve stages George Ripley outlined for making the Philosopher's Stone, using each stage as a point of reflection and artistic inquiry.

Alchemy is a study of the natural sciences, but it also incorporates poetry, emotion, intuition, and spiritual discipline to generate both insight and material results. The modern intellectual approach, which tends to compartmentalize knowledge into distinct categories, struggles to understand how alchemy functions as a science. Western natural sciences have separated themselves from spirituality and the creative arts for the past three hundred years, labeling science that incorporates mysticism as anti-intellectual. This division, though relatively recent in the span of human history, has been institutionalized and presented to us as the only legitimate framework for understanding reality. What began as a shift in perspective has hardened into orthodoxy, with alternative ways of knowing often dismissed as unscientific or irrational.

Alchemists engage with nature as a dynamic system, recognizing that the natural world is composed not only of tangible, sensory elements but also of intangible, unseen forces. To understand this complexity, they draw from multiple disciplines, blending science, art, and spirit. At its core, alchemy is an intensely relational practice centered on a call-and-response style of cocreating with the spirits that animate the cosmos. Because of this, I describe alchemy as "singing the world song." In learning alchemy, you learn to dialogue with the natural world and discover your place within the music, learning how to consciously contribute to its frequencies.

Before I studied it, I assumed alchemy was a quaint obsession of doddering old European men, endlessly trying—and failing—to turn lead into gold, just like the caricatures you see in children's books. How wrong I was! There are alchemists of all genders, and most are not European. Alchemy was shaped by visionaries who could see the future with clarity. Because of this foresight, they were often viewed as iconoclastic punks in their own time. As Merlin, the alchemist in T. H. White's *The Once and Future King*, complains: "I unfortunately was born at the wrong end of time, and I have to live backwards from in front, while surrounded by a lot of people living forwards from behind" (White 2011, 35).

Alchemy spans several philosophical traditions over nearly four thousand years and across three continents. Throughout its history, alchemy was banned multiple times, which led practitioners to hide their work behind cryptic language and coded messages. This, coupled with the centuries-long tendency of Western scholars to credit the Greeks as the sole inventors of philosophy and natural science, makes it hard to trace mutual influences and relationships between different groups of alchemists.

Contemporary scholars distinguish two major strands of alchemy: Eastern alchemy, which includes Chinese and Indian alchemy, and Western alchemy, whose center has shifted over millennia from Egypt to the Greco-Roman territories to the Islamic world and finally to medieval Europe. Though Eastern and Western alchemy mutually inform each other, they use different elemental and astrological systems, and we will primarily be working with the Western system here.

Chinese alchemy, with its earliest texts dating back to around the 3rd century BCE, is part of the broader Taoist tradition of mind-body-spirit cultivation, which includes practices such as qigong and neidan. In many Chinese alchemical texts, the human body is seen as a central site for engaging with cosmological forces. Material reality is shaped by the five elements, or *wuxing*, and through observing and cultivating these elements, practitioners seek to harmonize with the Tao—the underlying principle that governs the universe. Chinese alchemists developed an array of medicines, herbal preparations, and philosophical disciplines, many of which continue to shape traditional Chinese medicine and movement arts today. Chinese alchemists also explored laboratory processes such as the transmutation of base metals into gold or silver.

Indian alchemy, which flourished between 900 and 1300 CE but likely originated much earlier, spans many disciplines including metallurgy, philosophy, medicine, and hatha yoga. A key work in the Sanskrit alchemical tradition, rasaśāstra, outlines methods for preparing medicinal compounds made from herbs, metals, and minerals to promote longevity and health. The term *rasaśāstra* translates to "the science of mercury," reflecting the belief that mercury (rasa) holds transformative powers in both the physical and spiritual realms. This alchemical lineage remains alive and well today, embedded in Ayurvedic medicine and yogic practices that continue to emphasize purification, balance, and transformation.

While scholars continue to debate the precise origins of Western alchemy, there is growing consensus that it emerged from a fusion of cultures during the Hellenistic era (circa 323 to 31 BCE). This period encouraged rich cultural exchanges among Egyptian, Greek, Middle Eastern, and Indian alchemical traditions. Much of alchemy's foundation was laid by ancient Egyptian priest-alchemists who combined ritual, art, and science. For them, alchemy was a spiritual discipline in which devotional practices called upon divine powers to achieve transformations beyond ordinary human capabilities. Egyptian alchemists were incredibly skilled metallurgists, artisans, healers, and embalmers. In the vibrant intellectual atmosphere of Alexandria, Egyptian magical practices merged with Neoplatonist philosophy, giving rise to theurgy, a spiritual approach that viewed all physical matter as divine energy capable of transformation through ritual.

The Leiden and Stockholm Papyri, dating from the 3rd century CE, contain recipes for metallurgy, dyeing, and the creation of precious stones. Although these crafts had long existed in the Near East, the papyri introduced new techniques such as distillation and recognized the chemical properties of sulfur, arsenic, and mercury vapors. They also include philosophical reflections on color changes and chemical reactions, describing them as transmutations of the four elements and the death and rebirth of material "spirits."

By the 3rd century CE, Alexandria was under Roman rule. Concerned that the production of counterfeit gold by alchemists might destabilize the Roman economy, Emperor Diocletian issued an edict ordering the destruction of all alchemical texts and materials related to metal transmutation. Later, the Christian convert Emperor Theodosius enacted the Theodosian decrees, banning all religions except official forms of Christianity, which further suppressed alchemical traditions that did not conform with this orthodoxy.

Arabic alchemical scholars were instrumental in preserving and advancing the tradition, safeguarding it when much of Western alchemical literature was on the verge of being lost. After the Theodosian decrees, scholars brought alchemy to Baghdad, where it flourished within a multicultural milieu that blended Arabic, Hebrew, Christian, Zoroastrian, Greek, Indian, Mesopotamian, and later Islamic influences. Arabic alchemists excelled in practical laboratory experiments, significantly advancing the development of protochemistry and providing the first descriptions of substances still used in modern chemical processes today. Many key terms in alchemical practice, such as *alchemy* (from *al-kimya*), *alcohol* (from *al-kohl*), *elixir* (from *al-iksir*), and *alembic* (from *al-inbiq*), are of Arabic origin.

When the Islamic empire expanded into Spain in the 8th century, the vibrant learning centers established there became a refuge for persecuted communities and a hub for intellectual exchange—an environment where alchemy thrived. By the 12th century, the *Emerald Tablet* and other alchemical treatises had been translated into Latin, sparking a craze among European scholars for alchemical manuscripts. Latin translations of Arabic alchemical treatises began to appear, including works by Al-Razi, Jābir ibn Ḥayyān (Geber), Ibn Sīnā (Avicenna), and others. So much translation was happening that the archbishop of Toledo founded a new college entirely devoted to rendering Arabic texts in Latin.

By the 14th century, alchemical knowledge began to spread beyond Latin-speaking clergy and academics to a wider European audience. The Hermetica, a collection of ancient esoteric texts originating in Hellenistic Egypt and attributed to Hermes Trismegistus, were brought to Europe largely through the efforts of Renaissance scholars like Marsilio Ficino who translated these works from Greek and Arabic. During the Renaissance, alchemists continued their work with metallurgy and artistic materials while also advancing pharmacology and emerging fields of chemical science.

In the 18th century, mechanical philosophy was introduced, which was incompatible with the alchemist's spirit-based worldview. A new way of understanding the natural world emerged, based on the idea that the universe operates like a vast machine governed by fixed physical laws. This philosophy laid the intellectual foundation for the development of industrialization, emphasizing mechanistic thinking and the potential for mechanical devices to explain and control natural phenomena. To protect the developing science of modern chemistry from the negative associations that alchemy faced, Enlightenment-era academic writers had begun separating the "new" chemistry from the "old" practices of alchemy. This shift marked the beginning of the decline of practical laboratory alchemy. By the 1740s, alchemy had come to be primarily associated with the pursuit of gold-making, contributing to the popular belief that alchemists were charlatans and the entire tradition was a fraud.

The Industrial Revolution, spanning the end of the 18th century and the beginning of the 19th, ushered in profound social and economic changes, including rapid urbanization, technological progress, and a growing emphasis on materialism and rationalism. As these shifts took hold, many people longed to reconnect with the deeper mysteries of life, nature, and the cosmos—realms increasingly eclipsed by industrialization. This yearning sparked the occult revival, a cultural movement that reignited interest in astrology, divination, Hermeticism, and other esoteric traditions, leading to a renewed fascination with alchemy. Many esoteric schools interpreted the substances and operations described in alchemical texts as spiritual metaphors rather than practical or scientific practices, mainly because they did not understand the laboratory instructions encrypted there.

In the 20th century, Swiss psychologist Carl Gustav Jung reignited interest in alchemy by incorporating its symbols into his methods of spiritual psycho-analysis. This helped shape the modern understanding of alchemy as a practice centered on personal growth and self-improvement. However, this individualistic view contrasts with ancient alchemical texts, which emphasize growth through interdependence and collective responsibility. The alchemist not only transforms physical matter but also the spiritual and moral fabric of society, aligning their work with a cosmic imperative to support collective evolution.

To achieve this transformation, alchemists cultivated divine inspiration through various practices. These practices—such as visualization, meditation, singing, writing, and poetry—were designed to develop a contemplative mind attuned to the hidden laws of nature. This book explores these methods in depth, with each section ending in prompts and exercises to guide your own studies.

It's best to approach the exercises in order, allowing yourself time to fully absorb each concept before moving forward. Applying these lessons will revitalize your creative process, breaking through stagnation and self-doubt while strength-ening your vision. As you deepen your practice, alchemy will awaken within you, sparking unexpected shifts and revealing profound insights through surprising encounters. Alchemy will revolutionize your life—consider yourself warned!

BEFORE PROCEEDING, YOU WILL NEED

1. A beautiful new notebook.

2. Pens and pencils dedicated to this work specifically—savor selecting these tools.

3. To set aside time. Expect each chapter in part 2 and part 3 to give you at least an hour of work. Some exercises require that you attend to them for a month or longer. To grow as an alchemist is to apprentice yourself to time—working with commitment and duration and moving in rhythm with the slow, majestic cycles of the cosmos.

4. Dedication to incorporating prayer and contemplation into your cre-ative practices—these are key tools. One of the mottoes of alchemy is *Ora et Labora* (Pray and Work).

5. To be open to expanding your understanding of yourself and your creative process. You will undergo rapid changes.

6. To evolve this practice so that it works for you. Frater Albertus described alchemy as "consciously assisted evolution" (Bartlett 2009b, 14), and that includes the evolution of your own practice. If a task doesn't suit your body, materials, or present circumstances, adapt it. Skip what doesn't resonate. What matters most is the spirit of the work, not strict adherence to form. Alchemists are by nature people of faith, and the language of this discipline reflects that heritage. Some terms may not align with your own cosmology or spiritual framework. For instance, you may encounter the word *God*, which might not feel resonant; feel free to substitute any term that better fits your worldview. Other words may also benefit from adjustment to feel more authentic or inclusive. In my own practice, for example, I replace *purity* with *clarity* when describing alchemical refinement, as it better expresses my understanding of the process. Use language that aligns with your personal path, and don't hesitate to adapt it whenever necessary. Evolution—of practice, of language, of understanding—is itself part of the alchemical art.

Elixir Vitae
OUR LIFE IS OUR METHOD

I was born Eliza Swann on a freezing January night during a lunar eclipse. Some astrologers believe those born under the shadow of the dragon's tail are cursed—fated to walk the realms of the dead while still living. A lunar eclipse birthday is a classic zodiac placement for witches and those of unsound mind. Astrologically, an eclipse marks a reckoning between the rigid constraints of the self (the Sun) and the maddening boundlessness of mystery (the Moon); it is at this crossroads that we come undone. Among alchemists, the Latin phrase *Solve et Coagula*—meaning "dissolve and coagulate" or "destroy and create"— is a sacred directive symbolizing transformation through rupture and paradox, a process that unfolds through opposition. As Lao Tzu wrote in the *Tao Te Ching*, "The path into the light seems dark," and "the path forward seems to go back."

Raised by a single mom who worked full-time and attended night school, and with a brother seven years older—charming and socially active, unlike me—I spent most of my time alone. I'd go on long night rambles to escape our cramped apartment, but the streets were their own type of cage. Manhattan in the 1980s was electric and wild, nights pulsing with a heavy, menacing energy. The shadows cast by the towering buildings were thick with hidden eyes, and it was best to move quickly down the sidewalk; I was taught to trust no one. One of my few refuges was the public library just around the corner from our apartment: I had devoured every book in the children's section systematically—from science to fiction—by the time I was eight.

On weekends, my dad would take me to art museums. My dad went to art school and dreamed of becoming a painter. He loves to tell how, sometime in the 1970s, he showed up at Andy Warhol's Factory hoping to land a job. The gorgeous person at the front desk took one look at my dad, who was also gorgeous, and said, "You're hired!" When my dad asked about pay, they stared at him like he was from outer space and sneered, "We don't *pay* anyone." Dejected, he followed in my grandfather's footsteps working in shoes—first as a salesman, then as a designer.

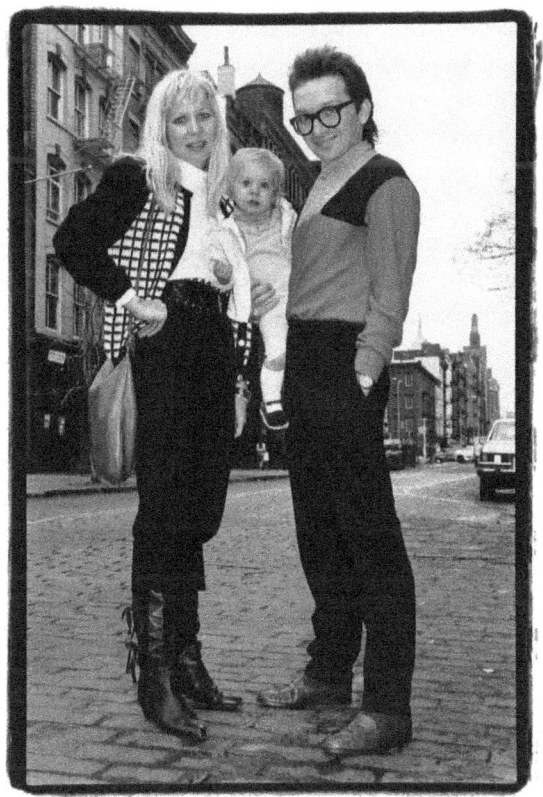

My parents and me; *Elvis Costello Glasses Family*, ©1982 Amy Arbus.

By the time I was two, my father had left my mom, my brother, and me for someone else. My mom used to call me a strangeling, a changeling, a fairy—and always added, "just like your father." Both of us are small and strange, attuned to a world just beyond this one, and painfully out of step with everyday life. Saturdays spent in his peculiar world watching *Pee-wee's Playhouse* and drawing were a safe haven for my eccentric spirit. He painted his walls electric green, silver, and neon orange as the mood struck him and wore pink backless shirts and silver shoes, each color signaling that if the outside world was drab, we could build our own in Technicolor, stepping into our version of reality like Dorothy emerging into Oz.

When I was seven, he brought me to an exhibition of Lucas Samaras's painted box sculptures at the Whitney Museum. Samaras's boxes, the same shapes and sizes as jewelry boxes, are layered and studded with glass and paper, creating violently vibrant rainbow swirls. Some boxes are propped open, revealing whirlpools of color and fragments of photographs inside—entire worlds pulse in there. I lingered at one for a long time, and my dad asked me what I liked about it.

"The colors, they're going into my heart," I answered, frustrated because I couldn't explain how the colors were so strong they hurt. Overcome, I burst into tears while my dad stood quietly by my side, nodding. I was overwhelmed by beauty on many of these museum trips, breaking down if I saw more than a few artworks at a time. My dad always took it in stride, stopping for ice cream afterward, excitedly discussing the pieces he loved most while I sat quietly, pulling myself together.

At the time, my mom worked in fashion, too. She was glamorous and popular, heading out to parties in a cloud of perfume, her wide mouth painted cherry red, bangles tinkling on her wrists. I kept to myself, staying in my room with my nose buried in a book most days. I ignored her when she advised me to be more social with the other kids, insisting that the few friends I had were "weird" and unsuitable for "a beautiful girl." In an effort to distance myself from whatever a "beautiful girl" was, I wore oversized clothes and dyed my hair turquoise at eleven. I loved queers and outcasts, and I embraced those qualities in myself. Besides, I had plenty of people to talk to—starting from age four, I spent hours conversing with angels in my room, beings who looked like staring into the sun for too long. Their communications trembled like light shifting in great feathery turnings.

My mom, who had passed her witch blood to me, believed in my angel companions and told her friends about my visitations. Before heading out for the night they'd often tap on my bedroom door to ask my angels about their money troubles and tangled love lives. I'd sit there, small and serious, answering their questions like a tiny oracle. It seemed some of my oddities were useful after all.

Throughout my childhood, I spent weeks at a time at my maternal aunt's house in Upstate New York, trailing behind her as she tended her herb gardens and taught me the healing magic of plants. After my parents divorced, we lived with her and her five children for a few years, and during that time, Aunt Chris— who I called Christmas—was my best friend. Leaving her wild, untamed house for the city was, to me, an utter tragedy. Each holiday season, when my mother asked what I wanted, I gave the same answer: "A tree! Growing in my room!" And every year I howled with disappointment when it failed to appear.

When I think back on Christmas's house, I see emerald green fields breathing life into fresh spring shoots, the wet whirls of grass beneath my feet, acorn caps filled with dew cracking underfoot, and the sun's fire glinting off impossibly yellow buttercups. There, I worshipped trees as gods and didn't put on shoes until early winter when the ground finally turned to ice.

Chris, an herbalist and energy healer, was deeply attuned to realms beyond the physical. She quickly noticed and nurtured my sensitivity to the unseen. I shared how blades of grass would reveal their songs when I stared at them closely, how the patterns in tree bark spoke to me. Her simple belief in my experiences allowed me to continue connecting with the nonhuman world long past the age when it was considered acceptable. The ability to converse with what others might dismiss as fantastical or lifeless would later play a crucial role in my understanding of alchemy.

My family was nonpracticing Catholics. While I enjoyed going to church when we did, our visits were infrequent, and I was raised with little formal mystical education. As I got older, I searched the library for others who spoke to angels, and I discovered a biography of St. Teresa of Avila. Her deeply personal conversations with God resonated with me. I became fascinated by her life and, much to my parents' dismay, started following some of the practices from her convent—vegetarianism and lesbianism among them. Being a queer kid in grade school was thorny: You risked being exiled by the other children if you were open about it. If you kept it secret, friends would often distance themselves quickly once rumors surfaced, as they inevitably did, afraid of being implicated.

At thirteen, I was accepted into a prestigious magnet school for academically gifted students known for its strict discipline and heavy workload. By fourteen, I was already meeting with a counselor to discuss which Ivy League school I would attend. My teachers encouraged me to give up writing poetry, which I loved more than anything, as a poor use of my talent. The pressure was overwhelming, and life at home was deteriorating.

After my beloved aunt was diagnosed with terminal cancer, everything began to unravel. My dad moved to Italy for his design work, and my mom eloped with a man whose alcoholism quickly shattered what little stability we had left. He pushed my older brother out of the apartment, claiming he was too old to be living at home. With my aunt dying, my dad overseas, and my brother gone, I was completely alone. I chopped off my hair, dyed the rest blood red, and started skipping school nearly every day. I'd retreat to the Metropolitan Museum of Art, losing myself in its endless rooms—especially the Egyptian wing, where I'd spend hours sketching artifacts. I smoked cigarettes on the front steps, waiting for my friends to get out of class. Eventually, the school held me back a grade—and then expelled me.

By the time I was fifteen, my aunt had lost her battle with cancer. In her final months, her mouth was so full of sores she couldn't speak, and her blue eyes glittered with pain. I was prevented from visiting her during her last weeks, my family afraid that seeing her ravaged by the disease would be too much for me. I collapsed internally without those final goodbyes and nowhere to channel my grief. Within a year of her death, I had been expelled from two schools for truancy. I was mute and withdrawn for nearly a year. I wouldn't see my friends, go to class, or answer any calls. I walked the streets for hours, circling the city like a dull asteroid, quietly crying.

Eventually, my grief changed from a thing that took me out of the world to something that catalyzed me to live on my own terms within it. At sixteen, I took a high school equivalency exam and moved out of my mom's house to escape my stepfather. I enrolled in a community college to take art classes, where I could write and draw without limits. I moved into an off-campus dorm with other young artists and landed a job at an art house movie theater. In my spare time, I devoured poetry at The Poetry Project on St. Mark's Place, absorbing Alice Notley's kaleidoscopic visions and Bernadette Mayer's droll observations like sacraments. Afterward, I'd duck into punk clubs down the street, drinking with my friends after shoving an older friend in front of me to order drinks.

My interest in mysticism found new intensity in the late nineties, as I explored New York's underground spiritual scene with my newfound freedom. The city offered a mix of goth covens, anarchist witch meetings, and dusty occult study groups mostly run by elders in their seventies. In one of the last, I met an old-school Greek Hermetic scholar who'd spent years digging through temples and libraries in Egypt and Greece. She became my mentor in Gnosticism and Hermetic philosophy. Through her and the web of esoteric scholars she knew, I started devouring the texts that would shape how I understood alchemy.

Hermeticism and Gnosticism uphold the belief in a singular, all-encompassing divine source known as the All, a unifying field of consciousness that gives rise to thought but remains beyond the grasp of the thinking mind. Both systems value personal spiritual experience—direct, intuitive knowing—over dependence on external authority. As a queer art punk, I resonated deeply with these ideas. Your world is shaped by what you know in your gut, not by what anyone tells you, and your imagination is the force that either builds or breaks your power within that world.

While I found these new spiritual practices liberating, many of the teachers who introduced me to Hermetic and Gnostic traditions interpreted them through a lens of rigid gender binaries, heterosexual supremacy, and 1950s morality codes. They never questioned how their biases contradicted the essence of these mysteries that prioritize liberation over dogma. This was particularly ironic given that Hermes, the deity after whom Hermeticism is named, embodies gender fluidity and was referred to using gender-neutral pronouns in antiquity. Similarly, Hellenistic astrology, a key component of Hermetic practice, depicts planets shifting through various gender expressions. When I pointed out these genderqueer aspects within the traditions, my interpretations were often dismissed as immature or irrelevant to the historical context of the scriptures—as if queer identities were a recent development, rather than an integral part of the communities that shaped these teachings.

The art worlds I was in had their own rigidities. Over a period of ten years, I studied art on and off at colleges where my queerness was accepted, but my interest in mysticism was often dismissed as naive confusion. My professors told me that mysticism belonged to outsider artists without ties to affluent academic institutions. While art and visual culture studies have evolved since the 1970s to include social, cultural, and political analysis, the religious roots of the modern art academy remain largely taboo. In art school, we were taught to frame our work as research, approaching our practice more like academics, creating polished, expensive pieces to illustrate a thesis, rather than artists with visions, communities, and connections that extend outside of intellectualism and into the weird and mysterious terrains of the unknown.

In contrast to the art academy's emphasis on individualism, which celebrates personal vision and unique self-expression, Hermetic and Gnostic traditions view artistic talent as a divine gift that belongs to no one. Creativity results from a relationship with a spiritual power that flows through us like wind through a flute. The word *inspiration* means "breath of God." In this liberatory view, art is a fluid exchange of continuous evolutionary imagining, passed from one plane to another. But my mystical teachers held fast to conventional ideas of what qualifies as "good" art—standards that, for me, felt disconnected from the radical, transgressive potential that arises when artistic expression is intertwined with spiritual exploration. In art and in spiritual communities, I was never entirely accepted, only certain parts of me fit in depending on the context.

In my twenties, I arranged lots of studio visits with art galleries in New York. During one visit, a curator casually mentioned he could see my nipples through my shirt. When I asked what he thought of my paintings, he distractedly mumbled that they "seemed like a good start." Another time, two gallerists from the Lower East Side stopped by. They were initially intrigued by my series of ink drawings of angels, but their interest faded within minutes of hearing that I actually spoke to these beings. Instead of engaging with my work, one gallerist pointed to a hurdy-gurdy in the corner and asked me to play it for her as if I were some sort of novelty act. I politely declined and asked what they thought of the art. They shrugged and told me I wouldn't fit in with the other artists on their roster.

Eventually, I stopped trying to show my paintings in galleries and instead toured with my witch-punk band, Our Lady of the Golden Dawn Pyramid, merging Gnostic ritual with performance art playing in venues that embraced whatever chaos we'd bring. In 2010, I opened a gallery in Brooklyn with my partner at the time and insisted we call it "Heliopolis." I had come across the name in an Isaac Jarnot poem and was drawn to its meaning—"City of the Sun." I didn't know then that it was the Egyptian city where, according to legend, the original Emerald Tablet of the alchemists was displayed for the world to see. When it was my turn to curate, I showcased mystical artists who had little access to the mainstream art world. I started giving tarot readings and leading talks on tarot and Hermeticism there.

Many of my spiritual teachers were uncomfortable when I began publicly lecturing on Gnosticism, Hermeticism, and magic. They took issue with my queer interpretations and believed these teachings should remain closed off from the general public. To me, restricting these teachings stifles their potential for growth and evolution and risks turning them into dogma. Without fresh perspectives and input from a broader audience, the interpretation of rituals and sacred texts becomes stagnant, undermining the traditions they are meant to preserve. To remain vibrant and relevant, they must be open to dialogue, reinterpretation, and critique. This difference in approach is where we parted ways.

In my early thirties, I left both New York and Heliopolis behind to pursue a master's degree in art in London. My goal was to teach art with an emphasis on mysticism within the framework of art school. I was fortunate to have gone to the San Francisco Art Institute for a couple of years, where I was taught by members of the Cockettes, Bill Berkson, and a handful of hippies who had us rendering tarot cards in class and using pendulums to draw out abstract forms with divinatory meaning. I had seen what was possible. I soon learned that the San Francisco Art Institute was a wild and incongruous presence in the arts educational landscape. Because of that school and the mystery schools I'd belonged to, I envisioned an art school for mystics—an environment where a community could yoke their artistic inspirations to the divine and to magic. I wildly underestimated how difficult it would be to bring mysticism into institutional art settings. In the same way that mechanical philosophy rendered alchemy obsolete by valuing only measurable outcomes, institutional art education attempts to impose standardized assessments on the unpredictable, wondrous process of creativity—ultimately stifling it.

In grad school in England, you're paired with one tutor for your entire first year, and they become your main point of contact for discussing your work and assessing your written thesis. My practice spans writing, performance, and painting, so they paired me with the one interdisciplinary tutor on staff. It was a disaster. I told her I wanted to create videos exploring the trance states achieved during certain Gnostic rituals. She coldly responded that I couldn't write a thesis on "that stuff." I assumed she meant the sacred, but she didn't clarify when I asked. I showed her my videos and writing, but month after month, she told me I was "not equipped to think critically" and said that my writing didn't meet academic standards.

For the thesis show, I created a video titled *Baba Yaga*, where I jumped on a trampoline wearing a demon mask, set to a soundtrack of spliced audio recordings of women describing their initiations into witchcraft. "I felt like I was falling into a great black hole" the witches chanted, while I bounced and bounced and bounced. It was largely a "fuck you" to my tutor, but my teachers loved it. Looking back, I can see that my anger carried a humor and vitality that fueled the new worlds that were to come. At the time, though, I was bereft; I had lost faith that the institutions of the art world could remember how to hold space for the divine.

I returned to New York and began seeking out artists who rooted their work in the sacred, driven by a need to understand how they continued to thrive in art spaces that so often dismissed these explorations. A friend eventually introduced me to Linda Mary Montano, a performance artist known for her intensely committed engagement with spirituality as a subject that she lives.

Linda Montano had founded the Art/Life Institute in the 1980s as a space to share her mystical art teachings with fellow artists, a gesture that deeply resonated with me. She hosted Summer Saint Camp for seven years, inviting artists to live with her for a week at the institute in Kingston, New York. The camp was rooted in simple living, the arte povera principle of minimalism, and the practice of creating healing art through reflections on lived experience. Drawing from her time as an novitiate, Montano structured the camp days like those in a convent, blending sacred living with creative practice. At the end of Summer Saint Camp, everyone received performance art/saint degrees.

Inspired by Linda, I began reaching out to more artists with an interest in mysticism. I was eager to learn how they balanced their spiritual practices with the structures of the art world. As my search expanded, so did my community. I wanted to create a space where artists felt safe presenting their magical artwork, and so in 2014, I founded the Golden Dome School. Drawing inspiration from my aunt, whose early acceptance of my creative and mystical path nurtured me, I built a community where artists' visions were trusted and valued, even—and perhaps especially—when these visions were difficult to categorize or define. Linda's faith in my work provided me with a profound sense of healing and the audacity to launch this school without fame or fortune to support me. I took on the role of director, collaborating with dozens and eventually hundreds of people eager to explore how art functions as a holy practice.

I was also deeply inspired by Diane di Prima, a mystic poet and teacher who, along with Audre Lorde—both of whom attended the prestigious high school I was expelled from—had formed a group called the Branded, where they skipped classes to hold séances for dead poets. Di Prima went on to teach Hermetic and esoteric traditions in poetry through a Masters in Poetics program at New College of California. She also cofounded the San Francisco Institute of Magical and Healing Arts (SIMHA), where she taught Western spiritual traditions from 1983 to 1992. Her fearless blending of mysticism and art profoundly shaped my vision for the Golden Dome School.

I started by organizing weeklong artist residencies, each inspired by a tarot card from the Major Arcana. Those early days were full of enthusiasm, rooted in the Greek meaning of the word, "filled with God." It was a time of play and experimentation, where creativity flowed freely, unbound by rigid dogma. At Golden Dome, we aimed to create an environment where artists could take bold leaps in their work, supported by a community that inspired and uplifted one another. Our classes focused on performance, sound, and movement, exploring how these practices intersect with ritual and initiation.

During the Magician-themed residency in 2015, artist Zeljko McMullen introduced us to alchemical breathwork techniques inspired by Dennis William Hauck's *The Emerald Tablet*, a book I have revisited many times since. This was my first experience of alchemy practiced in a contemporary arts setting, and it profoundly shifted my perspective. My earlier experiences had laid the groundwork for an interest in alchemical study, and in turn, alchemy took an interest in me. My dreams began to fill with alchemical symbols. During the early hours of the morning, I would wake up and immediately delve into alchemical texts and images, consumed by curiosity and a love for the Great Art.

In the spring of 2020, COVID-19 emerged in Los Angeles, where I had lived for a few years with my then-partner in a small cabin built into a cliff overlooking the city. As businesses closed, we both found ourselves unemployed, and the reports of hundreds of thousands of deaths from the little-understood virus brought the city to a standstill. Fear and confusion permeated our everyday lives. That summer, the Trump administration deployed the National Guard to suppress the Black Lives Matter demonstrations happening downtown, sending army tanks rolling through the streets and intensifying an already edgy atmosphere. By early September, a record-breaking heat wave combined with strong winds fueled explosive wildfires, creating the largest wildfire season in California's history and blanketing the city in thick, black smoke for months.

As the world seemed to spiral out of control, my partner's mental health began to unravel. His paranoia deepened, erupting into violent outbursts. He started hoarding trash and constructing walls of refuse around our yard to keep people out. He insisted my friends couldn't be trusted, accused me of lying about everything, and demanded I cut off all contact with our neighbors and loved ones. His rage exploded when I went to see a doctor for my worsening asthma, aggravated by the wildfires. He hurled accusations that I was faking illness, claiming I was only trying to get attention. Somehow, I had become the enemy in my own home—along with the rest of the world.

When he bought a gun for our "protection," I panicked. I called my mom, my voice trembling as I tried to explain. "Get out of there!" she hissed—and her ferocity snapped me out of the trance I'd been living in. I packed everything I could into my old Honda and drove toward the Mojave Desert, searching for solace in a solitude made absolute by quarantine.

Months earlier, when the pandemic forced the shutdown of in-person programming at Golden Dome, I'd created an online course called the Alchemical Imagination for artists. My aim was to teach the process of alchemical transformation, believing it would bring vision and unity to my community during such a turbulent time. By the time the course started, I was leaving Los Angeles in poor mental and physical health, but I felt strongly that I should hold the classes anyway. As the course unfolded, it became clear that exploring the stages of alchemical transformation alongside a group of artists was essential for my survival and growth. This experience kept my creativity alive and connected me with the networks of support—both human and nonhuman—there to nourish me through my trouble. Alchemy and the relationships created through it became my lifeline as I made my way back to New York and began rebuilding my life.

Fueled by my belief in the healing power of alchemical teachings, I proposed a fifteen-week course to Pratt Institute's interdisciplinary art department that same year. The proposal was enthusiastically received by students eager to explore magic. This success led to a series of research grants for studying alchemical manuscripts, which allowed me to share my love of alchemy by lecturing across the country.

In 2024, after a decade of running the Golden Dome without funding and managing countless unpaid administrative tasks, I found myself overwhelmed—juggling three jobs just to keep the organization afloat as living costs in the United States nearly doubled after the COVID-19 pandemic. By that point, Golden Dome was offering year-round classes, public performances, exhibitions, artist residencies, and a correspondence course, alongside unsuccessful attempts at grants and fundraising. In an effort to survive, I tried to professionalize the school and adopt a more corporate model, but this left me uninspired and disillusioned. I began thinking about the alchemical miracle of turning lead into gold—a process that unfolds across generations, cannot be hurried, and is rooted in nature, community, and love. I was reminded that magic does not move in straight lines or conform to institutional measures of success; it snakes through time and defines its own rhythms. Golden Dome was built to help a community of magicians carry artistic and societal burdens together. By returning to cycles of fallow time, rest, and dreaming, I allowed Golden Dome to slow down, trusting that patience, care, and shared responsibility are the conditions from which true miracles emerge.

In 2025, I founded the Emerald School of Alchemical Arts under the umbrella of Golden Dome, devoted to artists seeking alchemical wisdom—born from my own transformative encounters with this sacred technology. At Emerald School, I teach alchemy courses, curate exhibitions, and offer lectures that weave together esoteric practice, artistic inquiry, and lived transformation. While it's been rewarding to see elements of my pedagogy embraced by art institutions, I've found that alchemy thrives best outside those rigid frameworks—where mechanized assessments and schedules clash with the natural rhythms of the seasons and planetary cycles. Nowadays, I take joy in teaching alchemy when the timing is right, tending my garden, writing in the sunlight, and experimenting with alchemical painting techniques in my shed. It is from this rhythm of life that I write to you.

Alchemy hasn't led me down a neat, linear path toward "perfection." Instead, it has opened the door to facing life's ongoing challenges with deeper clarity and connection. Rooted in a queer, ecofeminist, Earth-loving, all-body-loving perspective, my approach to alchemy honors the natural cycles of growth, decay, and renewal as essential rhythms of transformation. Alchemy provides a path where cycles and connections are evident, urging us to confront challenges not as isolated individuals but as part of a vast, interconnected web of life. Throughout this text, I will share my own lived experiences with alchemy, revealing the struggles, self-doubt, and revelations that have shaped my transformation. I invite you to reflect on your own life as we proceed, noticing the alchemical processes within your lived experiences and viewing them as catalysts for your creative evolution as we go.

Alchemical Practice

I'm Nobody! Who are you?
Are you—Nobody—too?
Then there's a pair of us!
Don't tell! they'd advertise – you know!

—Emily Dickinson

Tell It to a Tree

Write a three-page autobiography. This writing is not meant to be a résumé or chronological list of events; it should be a personal narrative that captures the emotional essence of some of your life experiences. Write it as quickly as possible.

Once you've finished, go outside and find a tree that attracts your attention. Choose a spot where you can be relatively undisturbed and settle in. Take time to fully experience the tree—the texture of the bark, the shapes and shadows, the sway of their branches, the sounds they make, any inhabitants they may have, taking in their many fragrances and flavors.

When you feel that you and the tree are ready, read your autobiography aloud to them. As you read, you may begin to notice the world around you shifting—note any changes in your perception of the rustling of the leaves, the songs of the birds, and the moving light. Do any insects catch your eye? Do any new smells drift into your nose?

After you finish reading, sit in silence with the tree. Avoid trying to listen for a response. Let the tree hold your experiences. After some time, you may receive a sense of the tree's own life stories. A feeling of being held and in conversation may start to emerge. By engaging in this exercise, you could come to realize that your story and the Earth's story are interconnected.

Your Early Spiritual Life

This exercise is adapted from Linda Montano's *Art/Life Institute Handbook*, a collection of performance exercises based on the author's own work and observations.

Begin by examining any spiritual training or information you received as a child, which can include agnostic or atheist teachings. Examples of this could be having an experience with a religious relative or being told that God is not real by a childhood friend.

Create an artwork that speaks to this early impression. Examples of this could be writing a series of confessions in poem form, reenacting a scene where you tell your childhood best friend that you still believe in Santa, or making a giant crucifix out of candy wrappers. In the process, befriend your childhood self and observe their spiritual leanings and misgivings. How do these insights help you to think about your creativity and your sense of connectedness?

Build an Alchemist's Altar

Creating an alchemist's altar is both a physical and symbolic act that connects you with the transformative processes of alchemy. Start by choosing a space that feels sacred to you, where you can regularly engage with your spiritual and creative practices. This could be a small table, a shelf, or even a jewelry box if space and privacy are limited.

When I was in junior high, my altar lived in a cookie tin my grandmother had given me. She was a conservative Christian woman who would have been horrified to know what I was using it for—but she was also powerful and cunning and I loved her deeply. That tin, passed down from her, became the secret vessel for my earliest rituals.

Your altar, wherever it might be, will serve as a microcosm of your inner and outer transformation, amplifying the alchemical processes we'll explore together.

Begin by selecting a cloth or surface to serve as the foundation of your altar. Once the base is set, add one or two objects that resonate deeply with your artistic or spiritual practice. You might be drawn to images, texts, or items from figures who inspire you. As you progress through this book, you'll be encouraged to add new items to your altar that reflect particular teachings and concepts. Your alchemist's altar will not only serve as a space for reflection and meditation but will also evolve into a living entity that feeds your alchemical work.

PART II

Albedo

THE LUNAR DAWN

The Shape of Alchemical Thought

One Is All

In alchemical cosmology, all existence begins in the unfathomable Abyss—an infinity without form or differentiation. In a space before time, and for reasons unknown, the Abyss became aware of itself. This awareness is called the One Mind. Out of the tension between the boundless void and its dawning awareness arose the One Thing—the substance of creation, the Prima Materia, through which consciousness could take form. As the One Mind beheld itself reflected in the One Thing, vibration and sound were born—a holy resonance that ignited the first light. Through the encounter of the One Mind with the One Thing, the radiant fire of consciousness began to spread, expanding space and populating it with worlds, wormholes, and intricate webs of connection.

Alchemists perceive consciousness, the One Mind, as the driving force that animates existence and influences the evolution of forms. This consciousness can be cultivated, refined, and directed through alchemical practices to bring about changes in the material world. Therefore, contemplation, meditation, and prayer are essential aspects of laboratory work, as these inner disciplines create shifts in consciousness that resonate outward, ultimately guiding the evolution of matter. In the alchemical tradition, science is regarded as a physical form of prayer.

Alchemy is fundamentally the study and practice of transformation, grounded in the principles that govern change. One of the most significant of these principles is that of correspondence, famously paraphrased from the Emerald Tablet: "As Above, so Below." This idea highlights the reflective relationship between the microcosm (the individual) and the macrocosm (the universe). While Earth provides a grand stage for creation and evolution, the alchemist's flask serves as a smaller, personal arena where the same transformative processes unfold on a more easily observable human scale. Any transformation that occurs within the flask reverberates beyond it, shaping the alchemist's life, influencing their communities, and rippling outward to evolve the wider cosmos.

The flow of energy from the One Mind (consciousness) to the All (form) can be envisioned as a vertical axis that distinguishes the Above from the Below. Above is the radiant light of consciousness, while Below represents the primordial matter known as the Prima Materia. This continuous movement of energy between the One Mind and Prima Materia—rising and falling—generates the flow of material life.

The material world emerges from this vertical dynamic along a horizontal plane. Though the material world appears to have a beginning and an end, it in fact moves in a circular dance. Forms materialize along the tangible horizontal plane, only to melt back into the vertical spiritual realm, creating a continuous cycle of emergence and return. Prima Materia is the formless essence that underlies all things. It is the raw potential from which consciousness shapes reality and the substance that allows the alchemist to participate in the ongoing evolution of life, spirit, and cosmos. Lao Tzu, 6th-century BCE proto-alchemist and author of the Tao Te Ching, offers a poetic description of Prima Materia, calling it by its Chinese name Tao: "Something unformed and complete was born, Before heaven and Earth. Solitary and silent, It stands alone and unchanging, Pervading all things without limit. It is like the mother of all things under heaven, But I don't know its name—Better call it Tao. Better call it great."

European alchemists referred to Prima Materia as "The Root of Itself," believing that by uncovering its original essence, they could unlock the secrets of transformation and create the Philosopher's Stone—the ultimate catalyst for change.

We can look to dark matter in contemporary science to understand how a mysterious substance could control the universe without being directly knowable. Dark matter is an unknown substance that is theorized to make up 85 percent of the universe's total mass, or almost 30 percent of the universe's combined mass-energy. It neither emits, absorbs, nor reflects light, so instruments like telescopes cannot detect it. However, its existence is known due to its gravitational effects on visible matter. Dark matter influences how galaxies rotate, preventing stars on their outer edges from flying off into space. It also plays a critical role in forming galaxies and galaxy clusters. Although we don't know what dark matter is composed of, scientists believe it consists of particles that are very different from ordinary matter (Del Popolo 2021, np).

Robert Fludd
THE ROOT OF THE WATERS

Prima Materia can be challenging to understand from a logical perspective, which tends to cling to specificity and struggles with concepts like the void or abyss. In the alchemical tradition, subtler aspects of knowledge can be accessed through art-making and poetry, which can speak to nonlinear facets of consciousness.

Robert Fludd, a distinguished English physician and alchemist active in the 17th century, held a prominent position at the court of King James I. He was a prolific writer, producing vast multivolume encyclopedias that explored everything from mystical practices to bold theological ideas about the relationship between God, nature, and humanity.

In his most renowned work, *Utriusque Cosmi*, Fludd presents a cosmological theory in which God separates the original chaotic darkness, Prima Materia, into three divine elements: light, darkness, and spiritual waters. This vision of alchemical creation is illustrated through a series of detailed diagrams. The image shown on the next page is the first in that series, depicting Prima Materia at the dawn of the universe. Surrounding each side of Fludd's irregular, black-hatched square is the Latin phrase *Et sic in infinitum*, which translates to "And so on to infinity."

Grab a piece of paper and a mark-making tool, and prepare to create your own interpretation of *Et sic in infinitum*.

Begin by observing the blank page in front of you. Visualize a crown of starlight above you and feel your feet grounded in soft, mossy soil. Become aware of your breath and the flow of energy moving around your body from your head to your feet, sensing a circulation in your body that creates an axis between the Above and the Below. Your hands moving across the paper act as the horizontal axis, fixing ideas into a form in linear-seeming time.

Pick up your drawing implement, but before making any marks, take a moment to look at Fludd's *Et sic in infinitum*. Allow yourself to feel the lines moving through your body, letting Fludd's drawing guide some movements of your own. This may start with subtle wiggles in your fingers that gradually extend to your head, neck, torso, arms, and legs. Experiment with tracing shapes in the air using your feet and fingers, allowing yourself to create forms freely in space.

Once you've connected with Fludd's form through your body, return to your sheet of paper and begin to translate that experience by creating your own drawing of Prima Materia. Release any pressure to make it perfect; instead, focus on how each curve and angle you draw resonate with your inner understanding. Trust that you know, deep inside and beyond your thoughts, what Prima Materia truly is and how you might draw a picture of it.

When you feel your depiction of *Et sic in infinitum* is complete, step back and reflect on it. Ask yourself: *What is Prima Materia?* Jot down some notes.

The black square represents the nothingness and formless void that existed before the creation of the universe. From *Et Sic Infinitum. Utriusque cosmi maioris scilicet et minoris metaphysica, physica atqve technica historia in duo volumina secundum cosmi differentiam diuisa*, by Robert Fludd, 1621. Division of Rare and Manuscript Collections, Cornell University Library.

The Fourfold Structure
of Matter

In Western alchemy, matter is organized with four fundamental elements: fire, water, air, and earth. These elements embody essential qualities that shape the nature and composition of the material world. This concept of matter as a fourfold emanation is rooted in the teachings of Pythagoras, who believed that physical matter exists in a quaternity or tetrad. The first four numerical archetypes (1, 2, 3, 4) add up to 10, which Pythagoras regarded as a perfect number and the basis of the counting system. The alchemical Axiom of Maria, attributed to the 3rd-century Jewish alchemist Maria Prophetissa, describes the movement of the divine mind through the Tetractys: "One becomes Two, Two becomes Three, and out of the Third comes the One as the Fourth."

In modern science, matter is made up of chemical elements, which are organized in the periodic table according to their atomic structure and properties. When we reinterpret the alchemical elements of earth, water, air, and fire through the lens of contemporary science, we find they correspond to the physical states of matter: solid (earth), liquid (water), gas (air), and plasma (fire). The ancient concept of elements was based on the behavior of matter as it appeared in the natural world, rather than on its atomic composition.

In alchemical practice, the elements structure the material universe, balancing and harmonizing the interplay of various forces. The earth element represents the forces that create the illusion of solidity, such as gravity and magnetism, which help to hold solid matter together. The water element is associated with the laws of flux, such as wave dynamics, that govern the movement and behavior of fluids. The air element is connected to the invisible forces of momentum and velocity that dictate the motion of objects. The fire element pertains to the laws of energy that drive processes such as heat and light.

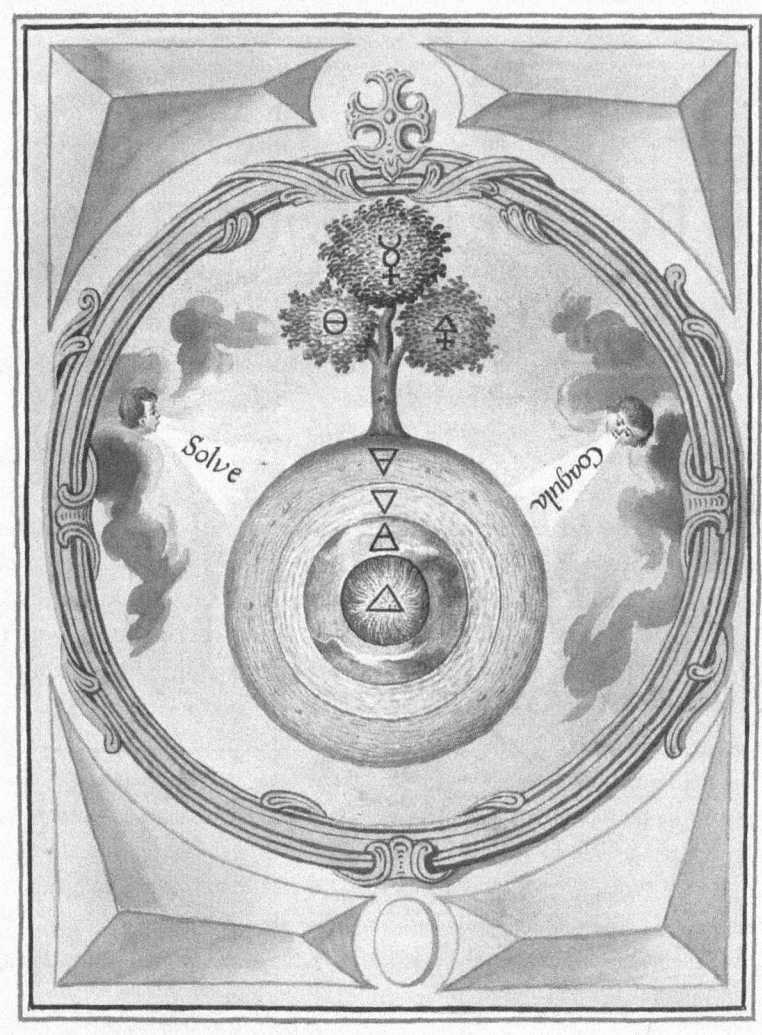

This three-branched tree represents the Philosopher's Tree. The branches correspond to the Tria Prima of alchemy, while the four elemental symbols surround the base. From *Sammlung Alchymistischer Schriften*, by Theobaldo Corsini and Johann Joseph Hubert, 18th c. Image provided by The John Rylands Research Institute and Library, The University of Manchester.

Empedocles, a 5th-century Greek philosopher and poet, proposed that these four fundamental elements are influenced by two opposing forces: love (or Eros) and strife (or Eris). Love attracts and unites, whereas strife divides and repels. Empedocles characterized fire and air as elements that expand outward and repel, while earth and water draw inward and attract. Hippocrates, a Greek physician and philosopher from the same era, applied the theory of the elements to psychology and medicine through the concept of humors.

Each humor corresponds to an element as it characterizes the body and temperament. Fire is associated with the choleric humor, linked to yellow bile, produced during digestion and energy transformation. The choleric temperament is hot and dry, and those with this temperament tend to be energetic, dynamic, and enthusiastic—"on fire" in their demeanor. Water corresponds to the phlegmatic humor, represented by phlegm, the clear bodily fluids carried by the lymphatic system and secreted by mucous membranes. The phlegmatic individual is cold and wet, often introspective, emotional, adaptable, and flowing. Air is linked to the sanguine humor; *sanguine* refers to a ruddy complexion, suggesting vitality. Sanguine individuals are hot and wet, typically changeable, flighty, and irritable, but fundamentally optimistic. Earth corresponds to the melancholic humor, represented by black bile, the waste left after digestion. Melancholic individuals are passive, stubborn, sluggish, yet practical and grounded. Ancient thinkers believed poets and visionaries were often melancholic, as their tendency to delve into the darker, "waste" aspects of life would grant them visionary insight.

Through these theories, alchemists explored how the elements shape the physical world and influence temperament, psychology, and spiritual life. The elements are keys to understanding both the human experience and the greater mysteries.

Aether, the Fifth Element

Aether, also known as quintessence, is a mysterious fifth element that exists beyond the familiar four of earth, water, air, and fire. This elusive substance fills the heavens and binds the cosmos. In the Hermetic tradition, the cosmos is imagined as a series of concentric spheres, with Earth at the center and the planets and stars radiating outward. The sublunary world, which encompasses all matter beneath the orbit of the Moon, is composed of the four classical elements. In this realm, all things are subject to change, decay, and renewal. In contrast, the region beyond the Moon is composed of aether. Unlike the earthly elements, aether is believed to be incorruptible and eternal.

Apollonius of Tyana was a 1st-century Greek philosopher and mystic known for his teachings on spirituality and ethics, as well as for the miraculous healing powers attributed to him. In his philosophical dialogues, he explored the nature of the four elements and the esoteric concept of a fifth element. His life and teachings were documented by the philosopher Philostratus in *The Life of Apollonius of Tyana*. In the following passage, Apollonius engages in a dialogue with his teacher Iarchas posing the question: What is the cosmos made of?

> *"Of elements," came the reply.*
>
> *"Are there then four?" Apollonius asked.*
>
> *"Not four," answered Iarchas, "but five."*
>
> *"And how can there be a fifth alongside water, air, earth, and fire?" Apollonius questioned.*
>
> *"There is the aether," Iarchas replied, "which we must consider as the substance of the gods; just as all mortal beings breathe air, the divine inhale aether."*
>
> *Apollonius further asked which of the elements was first. Iarchas replied:*
>
> *"All are simultaneous, for a living creature is not born piece by piece."*

"Should I then see the universe as a living creature?" Apollonius asked.

"Yes," said Iarchas, "if you understand it well, for it gives rise to all living things."

"Should I call the universe female or both male and female?" Apollonius inquired.

"Both genders," Iarchas answered. "It nurtures itself, acting as both mother and father in the creation of living beings. Its love for itself is deeper than any individual's love for another, binding it in harmony. Just as an animal moves through its limbs, the Universe adapts its parts to nurture all creatures that are conceived."

In this text, the fifth element is understood as the breath within the Creator's lungs—an animating atmosphere that fills existence with life and love. It emerges from the cosmos's deep affection for its creations, nurturing life with the care of both a mother and a father. In many spiritual traditions, *holy spirit* is synonymous with *breath* or *air*. The words for the divine are the same as those for respiration in Hebrew, Arabic, and Ancient Greek.

Early Vedic scriptures describe a void that longs for light, creating a wind born of this yearning that stirs the primal waters of creation. Islamic texts describe a holy wind that supports the first waters, carrying the throne of God, propelled by countless invisible wings. Ancient Syrian writings depict a dark wind that mated with itself to give birth to the universe. Across these various cultures, wind or breath is recognized as the first movement of life, connecting the beginnings and endings of all things. In a continuous cycle of inhaling and exhaling, our breath links us to the births and deaths of great cosmic epochs.

The understanding of breath as a cosmic life force is present in alchemical traditions across various cultures as well. In Indian alchemy, practitioners use pranayama—a combination of *prana* (life force or breath) and *ayama* (to extend or control)—to circulate vital energy throughout the body, facilitating mental, physical, and spiritual transformation. Similarly, Chinese alchemists incorporate breath and movement to guide qi, their concept of life force, in the pursuit of bodily alchemy and physical transmutation.

Egyptian and Greek alchemists also integrated breathwork into their laboratory and mystical practices. The different breathing patterns we experience during various emotional states—such as anxiety, arousal, anger, calmness, or joy—each have unique qualities. By mimicking these patterns, we can encourage desired emotional states. Alchemists utilize both emotional states and breathing techniques to influence the outcomes of their experiments and to connect themselves with the aether, the breath of the immortals.

Quintessence is the Latin term that refers to the fifth element, which, when transformed into an elixir, is known as the Elixir of Life, said to grant immortality. Paracelsus believed that quintessence represents the spiritual substance of the stars, suggesting that every living being contains a hidden star within them that embodies their quintessence. The star itself is a common symbol for quintessence, while another notable symbol is the pentagram enclosed within a circle, which divides the circle into five equal sections.

The creative process depends on the balance and interplay of the five elements. The forces that govern nature likewise shape artistic success. Understanding how to transform the balance of elements is essential to realizing any creative vision. In alchemy, we are encouraged to interact with the natural world and its elements not just on an intellectual level, but also through emotion and deep connection. Just as a lover devotes their full attention to their beloved, the alchemical imagination calls for heightened sensitivity to the unfolding of life, recognizing the flow of energy and transformation in every living form.

Pause here and add a representation of each of the five elements to your alchemist's altar. For instance, you might include a stone for earth, a candle for fire, wine for water, fragrance to perfume the air, or a bell to fill the aether with sound. Let your selections arise from your own experience—things offered by friends or found in places that shaped you.

Return to the Maternal Source
ANA MENDIETA'S ELEMENTAL ARTWORKS

My art is grounded in the belief of one universal energy which runs through everything: from insect to man, from man to specter, from specter to plant, from plant to galaxy. My works are the irrigation veins of this universal fluid. Through them ascend the ancestral sap, the original beliefs, the primordial accumulations, the unconscious thoughts that animate the world.

—Ana Mendieta, 1981, unpublished statement

Ana Mendieta was a Cuban American artist recognized for her diverse body of work that includes performance art, sculpture, painting, and video. Her artistic career spanned from the 1970s until her tragic death in 1985; she was only thirty-six.

In 1973, she began a series called *Siluetas*, which she continued exploring until her death. The *Siluetas* examine the relationship between the body, natural elements, mortality, and cycles of rebirth. In these works, Mendieta used her own body as her template, carving and shaping it into various natural forms.

In one *Silueta*, she incised her figure into mud with her arms raised; in another, her form was etched into ice with her arms lowered. She created bodily imprints using materials such as flowers, tree branches, moss, gunpowder, fire, and animal hearts, sometimes leaving her handprints directly branded into the earth. Of her process, Mendieta said, "My art is the way I re-establish the bonds that unite me to the universe. It is a return to the maternal source" (*Ana Mendieta* 1987, 10).

Mendieta's elemental works connect us to the natural cycles of birth and decay, embodying the alchemical principle of Solve et Coagula—dissolution and reconstitution. Often ephemeral, the *Siluetas* exist only as long as nature permits, now living on through photographs and film.

Ana Mendieta Exercises

Begin by exploring images of Mendieta's *Siluetas* series either online or through a book such as *Ana Mendieta: Earth Body, Sculpture and Performance, 1972–1985*. Analyze the ways that different elemental forces evoke particular feelings in her work. How do Mendieta's shapes feel distinctly different when formed from ice as opposed to mud? What are the different qualities and poetic inferences in each of the different elements in her practice?

Next, reflect on a creative work you have made in any medium. Consider how you might use the theory of the five elements to push your work in a new direction. For instance, if you've created a drawing, imagine the impact of adding dirt—would it alter the spirit of the piece? If you've written a story, consider how the introduction of a fire might change it. You can use the following questions to push the boundaries of your creative practice by consciously invoking a full spectrum of elemental forces.

Earth: How does the physicality of earth—its solidity, weight, and grounding force—inform your work? Where does gravity come into play? Is there a way to make your work heavier? What would happen if you introduced materials like dirt, stone, or clay?

Air: How does the element of air—movement, thought, and breath—affect the flow of your work? Could introducing elements of lightness, space, or breath transform the atmosphere of your piece? In what ways does the invisible presence of air hold your practice together?

Fire: How does the presence of light, heat, or energy show up in your work? Can you make the work brighter or hotter? How would the introduction of fire reshape your work's meaning? How does fire's transformative force challenge, refine, or consume your creation? How might you represent combustion?

Water: How does water's fluidity, adaptability, weight, and wetness show up in your work? Does your work need rain, a sea, or a flood? How might you use the reflective or cleansing qualities of water to deepen emotional resonances in your work?

Aether: Aether represents the unseen, the spiritual, and the unifying force between the elements—how can you evaluate its presence in your work? Can you define aether for yourself? Is it divine breath, the motion of light, or something else? What would happen if you allowed the invisible, connective energy of aether to guide the flow of your work, uniting all the other elements? How might you approach this—through prayer, meditation, or another method?

Wake Butterfly—It's Late
THE ELEMENTAL POEMS OF MATSUO BASHŌ

No matter what we may be doing at a given moment, we must not forget that it has a bearing upon our everlasting self, which is poetry.

—Bashō

Matsuo Bashō, a poet active in the mid- to late 17th century, is widely recognized as one of the leading innovators of the haiku form in Japanese literature. Born Matsuo Kinsaku into a samurai family, he adopted the name Bashō in 1680 after receiving a banana plant (bashō) from a student. Bashō's work is marked by a reflective, often wry voice that shares his observations of the natural world.

During his adolescence, Bashō faced uncertainty about fully committing to a life of poetry. He later reflected that "the alternatives battled in my mind and made my life restless." Despite this, Bashō continued to publish. In 1672, he compiled *The Seashell Game*, an anthology that included his own works and those of fellow poets. Around this time, he moved to Edo (now known as Tokyo) to deepen his engagement with poetic composition and theory.

A significant turning point occurred during the winter of 1682 when a fire destroyed Bashō's home, followed by the death of his mother in early 1683. These personal tragedies marked a new phase during which he embarked on a series of extended journeys on foot, dressed in the simple robes of a Zen monk. On these travels, he developed haibun, a literary form that combines prose and haiku to express both the external landscape and the poet's internal reflections.

Bashō's most famous haibun, *Oku no Hosomichi* (*The Narrow Road to Oku*), recounts a 1,200-mile journey he undertook in 1689 with his disciple Sora. Over the course of five months, they traversed the Japanese countryside meeting fellow poets and composing verses along the way. Bashō's itinerant lifestyle, although austere—traveling with minimal provisions and relying on the hospitality of Buddhist monks and fellow writers—allowed him to fully dedicate himself to both artistic expression and spiritual pursuits. Bashō's verses are vibrant with life, and his remarkable ability to capture the world's movements comes from his being fully present with them.

In *Oku no Hosomichi*, he explains:

> *Go to the pine if you want to learn about the pine, or to the bamboo if you want to learn about the bamboo. But in doing so, you must leave behind your own subjective preoccupations. Otherwise, you impose yourself on the object and fail to truly learn from it. Your poetry flows naturally when you and the object become one—when you've immersed yourself deeply enough to see something hidden within it. No matter how well phrased your poetry may be, if it isn't born from a natural feeling—if the object and yourself remain separate—then your poetry isn't true poetry, but merely a subjective imitation.* (Bashō 1997, 143)

Elemental Exercise with Bashō

Elemental theory provides a valuable methodology for reimagining and transforming artworks. When applied poetically, each shift in elemental composition brings a distinctly new energy or atmosphere. We'll practice adjusting the elemental essence of a haiku, with Bashō as our guide.

Haiku is a traditional Japanese poetic form structured in three lines, typically adhering to a 5-7-5 syllable count. It is celebrated for its brevity, clarity, and close relationship with nature and the seasons. Haiku often includes a kigo (seasonal reference) and a kireji (cutting word or pause), which together create a moment of reflection or illuminating juxtaposition.

In order to write closely with the elements of nature, Bashō says, "One must first concentrate one's thoughts on an object. Once the mind achieves a state of concentration and the space between oneself and the object has disappeared, the essential nature of the object can be perceived. Then express it immediately. If one ponders it, it will vanish from the mind" (Bashō 1997, 143).

MATERIALS NEEDED

- Fresh melon (e.g., cantaloupe or honeydew)—substitute any round fruit if melons are unavailable

- A sunlit outdoor space or candles

- Writing materials

Read the following Bashō poem:

Coolness of the melons
flecked with mud
in the morning dew.

In this poem, we can recognize the elements of cool water and stable earth. Water, characterized by its fluidity and adaptability, represents qualities such as wetness and cold, while earth embodies solidity and stability, signifying heaviness, dryness, and coolness. Together, these elements create a serene, refreshing atmosphere. What words might transform this poem into something hotter and drier? Here is my example:

Sunlit melons, hot,
speckled with gold unraveled
from cracked earth yawning.

Now, let's try pushing Bashō's original poem toward a warmer, drier feel using his methodology of engaging with a melon and merging your consciousness with it. Obtain a melon or any other easily accessible fruit or vegetable, and sit with it for about ten minutes. You might enhance the hot and dry element by placing it in the sun or observing the fruit by candlelight.

Once you have the fruit before you, allow your eyes to rest on its surface. Take a moment to breathe deeply, feeling the air fill your lungs, and then exhale slowly, grounding yourself in the present. Observe the interplay of light and shadow across the melon's skin. With your fingers, explore its texture. Expand your awareness, tuning in to its weight and how it feels resting in your hands. Bring the skin to your nose and inhale deeply. Close your eyes and envision traveling across its surface, sensing each bump and groove. Hold your ear up to the melon—what do you hear? As you explore its exterior, feel the pulse of energy within it.

Now, visualize moving inside the melon. Picture yourself crossing a threshold, leaving the outer skin behind and entering a space filled with the sweet, fragrant aroma of the fruit's flesh. Let the vibrant colors wash over you, each hue pulsing with vitality. Sit within this interior, absorbing its richness, and notice how light refracts and dances in this hidden sanctuary. Turn your attention to the seeds nestled here, each one a tiny blueprint mapping out patterns of growth.

When you're ready, gradually bring your awareness back to the surface of the fruit, then to your own body, and finally to the space where you began. Open your eyes, carrying this sense of connection and presence with you as you reenter your surroundings. Compose a haiku about the world of the melon you just experienced. Now, rewrite Bashō's poem using hot and dry imagery.

Explore more of Bashō's poems to see how he employs elemental imagery, and continue practicing pushing and pulling the five elements in your poetry.

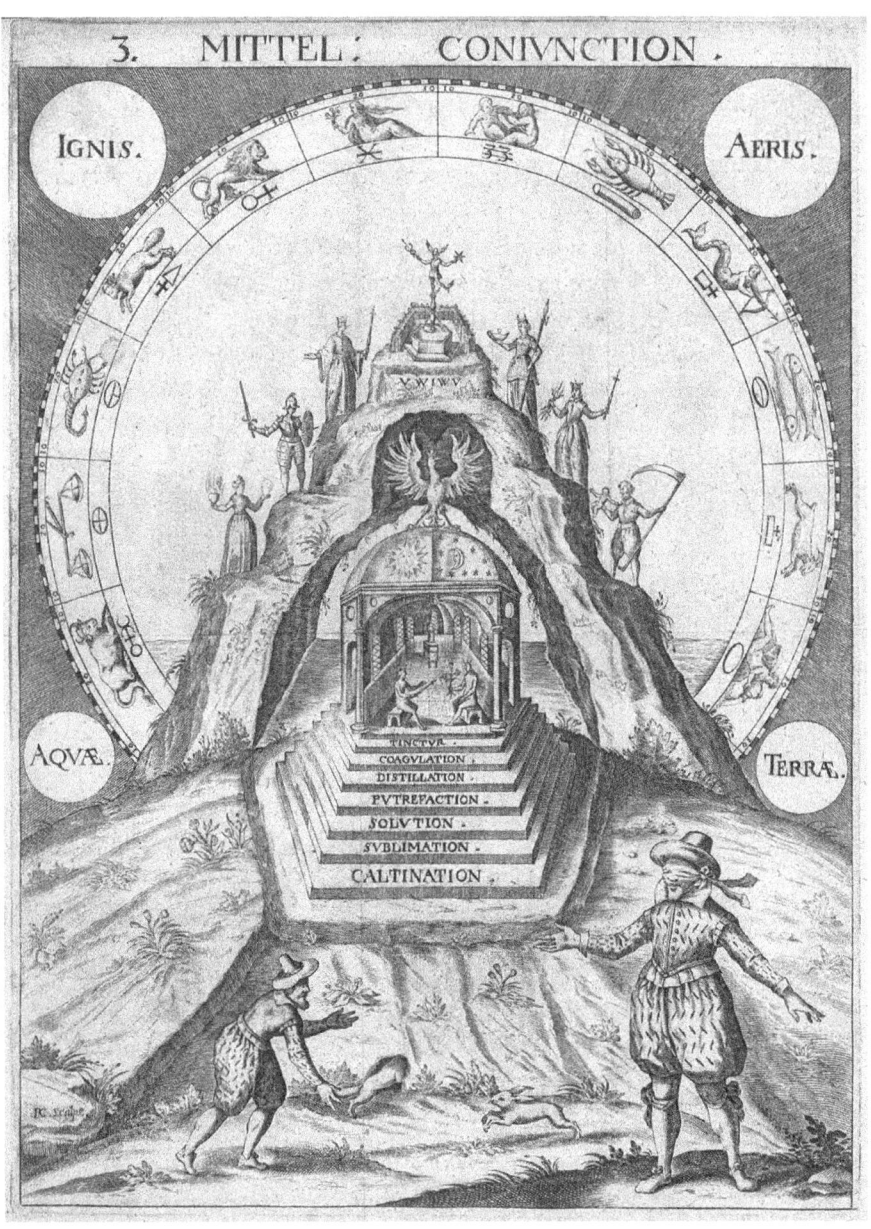

The steps to the building in the foreground feature seven stages for creating the Philosopher's Stone; the people on the mountain in the background represent the seven classical planets. Plate 3 from *Cabala, Spiegel der Kunst und Natur*, by Steffan Michelspacher, 1616. Getty Research Institute, Los Angeles (1380-833).

The Seven Celestial Spheres

You're all instruments. Everyone's supposed to be playing their part in this vast orchestra of the cosmos.

—Sun Ra, *Space Is the Place*

Early alchemists identified any visible nonfixed object in the sky as a planet. The word *planet* comes from the Greek word *planētēs*, meaning "wanderer." These ancient wanderers are the seven classical planets: Saturn, Jupiter, Mars, the Sun, Venus, Mercury, the Moon. In this system, planets are arranged by their apparent speed when moving across the sky, from Saturn as the slowest to the Moon as the fastest. Alchemists linked these seven planets to specific attributes collectively known as the seven planetary aspects. Astrology and alchemy are considered sister sciences, deeply connected through their shared goal of understanding the relationship between the larger universe (macrocosm) and the individual (microcosm).

The origins of Western astrology can be traced back to Mesopotamia during the first and second millennia BCE, where a complex system of planetary omens developed. This system later spread to Egypt, Greece, and India. In the Hellenistic world, astrology began to merge with philosophical schools established by influential figures like Plato, Aristotle, and the Stoics, who all viewed the cosmos as a unified, living entity. Hellenistic astrology adopted both the Mesopotamian zodiac, which includes planetary exaltations, triplicities, and the significance of eclipses, and the Egyptian division of the zodiac into thirty-six decans, each spanning ten degrees. Additionally, Hellenistic astrology integrated Greek concepts of planetary gods, sign rulership, and the four classical elements.

Eventually, astrology faced challenges when Christianity became the official religion of the Roman Empire, but went on to thrive in the Islamic world, where significant advancements were made in astronomy, astrology, and mathematics. One of the most influential Islamic astrologers, Abu Ma'shar, authored the *Introductorium in Astronomiam* in the 9th century which was crucial in reviving astrology and astronomy in medieval Europe. Additionally, Islamic scholars continued the tradition of integrating medicine and astrology by associating the healing properties of herbs with specific zodiac signs and planets. For instance, Mars was linked to hot and dry qualities, ruling over plants with strong or pungent flavors like hellebore, tobacco, and mustard. European herbalists later adopted these practices.

In the Hermetic tradition, the cosmos is envisioned as a series of concentric planetary spheres radiating outward with Earth at the center. A specific planetary deity governs each sphere, and the seven spheres are surrounded by an eighth containing the fixed stars. When a soul is conceived, they descend into physical existence by passing through the seven spheres, absorbing qualities from each one. Along the way, a person might inherit temporal limitation from Saturn, executive power from Jupiter, courage from Mars, and intellectual capacities from the Sun. Once the soul passes the Moon, they begin to grow a body. Upon death, the soul ascends in reverse order, shedding its earthly body first and then its astral coverings, gradually rising through the spheres back toward the divine.

Alchemists believe that by understanding and applying astrological correspondences, they can align their work with the immense powers of the cosmos. They negotiate with these celestial forces, seeking to amplify beneficial influences while mitigating harmful ones. Each planetary sphere is associated with unique qualities, including specific metals, deities, colors, musical tones, days of the week, organs, body parts, diseases, medical effects, and plants. By studying these planetary archetypes, alchemists uncover the biochemical, energetic, and psycho-spiritual forces that shape and influence the material world.

In alchemical tradition, the seven planets are said to have planted seven metal seeds on Earth, each carrying the unique signature of its celestial origin. These metals then grow like plants, nurtured by the Earth's moisture and fueled by the Sun's vital energy. These correspondences guide alchemical practice. For instance, Mars is traditionally associated with iron due to its reddish hue, which resembles the color of rust. Although ancient alchemists lacked the tools to empirically confirm this, Mars appears red because of iron oxide on its surface. Mythologically associated with war, Mars rules over the nettle plant, whose combative sting mirrors his fierce nature and whose leaves are rich in iron like the planet.

The planet Jupiter, ruled by the god Jupiter (the Roman counterpart to Zeus), governs lightning and thunder. Interestingly, Jupiter is the only planet, besides Earth, known to experience violent lightning storms, but it wasn't until the Voyager 1 spacecraft flew by Jupiter in 1979 that scientists recorded the first evidence of lightning on the planet. This example highlights how alchemists' observations and symbolic connections predated modern scientific discoveries yet still offered a resonant and meaningful way of understanding cosmic relationships.

In addition to looking for physical signatures linking the planets to earthly manifestations, alchemists tap into a telepathic communion with planetary forces. By immersing themselves in the planet's "mind," they experience it as an extension of their own consciousness and record their impressions. This deep, intuitive engagement allows them to understand the nature and influence of the planets beyond the reach of their physical limits. Grasping the qualities associated with each planetary sphere is essential to harnessing alchemical principles effectively.

In our planetary exploration together, we will begin with an introduction to each planet itself, along with the key metals and plants traditionally associated with it. Next, we will delve into the mythology surrounding each planet, uncovering the stories that have shaped its cultural significance. I will also introduce a contemporary artist whose work embodies the planet's energy, offering a modern perspective on its influence. Afterward, I will provide a creative arts or worship prompt to help you connect with the planet and build a personal bond.

A powerful way to strengthen this connection is by incorporating specific symbols, elements, or items on your alchemist's altar corresponding to each planet as we progress. These serve as physical anchors, enhancing your alignment with the planetary sphere and deepening your practice of creative planetary work.

♄

Saturn

Saturn, as viewed from Earth, is the slowest-moving planet, appearing shadowy and sluggish in the night sky. Its dusky light creates a foreboding presence, leading ancient astrologers to associate this planet with feelings of melancholy, solitude, and a stern form of power. In ancient Mesopotamia, Saturn was called Kajamānu, which means "the constant" or "the steady." The Mesopotamians called Saturn a "nighttime sun" because its synodic period of 378 days is close to the solar year's 365 days. Due to its seeming heaviness, Saturn symbolizes boundaries, limits, discipline, authority, rules, judgment, and traditions. The qualities of restriction and limitation associated with Saturn are crucial in the processes of growth and transformation. Saturn governs Capricorn by night and Aquarius by day—two zodiac signs that emerge during the darkest time of year in the Northern Hemisphere. Capricorn derives discipline and wisdom from looking inward, while Aquarius gains insight by reaching outward to seek new structures, systems, and inventions.

In the alchemical tradition, Saturn planted the seed of lead, one of Earth's heaviest and darkest metals. Lead tends to form inert and insoluble compounds and is highly resistant to tarnish and decay. Its nearly unalterable and impermeable nature makes it an ideal material for containing radioactive substances. Also, lead has poor heat conductivity, allowing it to melt easily; this property is essential for soldering, a process that holds structures together. Mixing lead with ores lowers the melting point, facilitating the efficient extraction of valuable metals such as gold and silver. Alchemists revered lead as a metal that sacrifices itself for the extraction of noble metals and held a deep respect for the planet Saturn.

The major organ system traditionally associated with Saturn is the bone structure. This includes not only the skeleton but also tough, dense, structural body parts such as teeth, hair, nails, connective tissue, and the firmness of our skin. Additionally, Saturn is connected to the spleen, which serves as the primary filter of our blood and helps build red blood cells to strengthen our immunity. Herbs linked to Saturn tend to dry and mineralize, supporting the body's bone structures. Saturnian plants are typically robust, stiff, and slow-growing, often reaching significant sizes and featuring thick, hairy leaves. Reflecting Saturn's solitary nature, many of them grow alone and take time to reach full maturity. Culinary plants associated with Saturn include grounding and nourishing roots like parsnip, burdock, angelica, and mineral-rich greens such as spinach that promote bone health. Aromatic herbs like sage are tied to the wisdom of Saturn and can be burned ritually to invite a mature perspective.

Saturn is the Roman name for the Greek god Kronos, associated with time and the harvest. In Greek mythology, Kronos was the leader of the Titans during the Golden Age, a period marked by peace and prosperity among the older generation of gods. During his reign, Kronos received a prophecy that one of his children would overthrow him, just as he had overthrown his own father Uranus. To prevent this, he swallowed each of his offspring at birth, fulfilling his role as the agent of time that devours all things. His wife Rhea was devastated by the loss of their children—Hestia, Demeter, Hera, Hades, and Poseidon. When she was pregnant with their youngest child Zeus, Rhea devised a plan to save him.

After Zeus was born, Rhea hid him in a cave on Crete and gave Kronos a stone wrapped in swaddling clothes to swallow instead of the baby. Unaware of the deception, Kronos consumed the stone. As Zeus grew up, he devised a plan to rescue his siblings. He eventually tricked Kronos into drinking a potion that caused him to regurgitate the swallowed children. With his siblings freed, Zeus led a rebellion against Kronos and the Titans, ultimately overthrowing them and becoming the leader of the new gods, the Olympians. This myth symbolizes the futility of resisting change, the cyclical nature of power, and the inevitable rise of new generations over the old.

The glyph of Saturn preserves the sickle of Kronos, symbolizing Kronos's connections to harvest, sadness, old age, death, and the father figure archetype. In astrology, Saturn is called the Greater Malefic, representing challenges, restrictions, death, discipline, consequences, and the seemingly unfeeling nature of fate. Saturn was commonly associated with the melancholic temperament during the medieval and Renaissance periods. As a planet, Saturn is characterized by coldness, slowness, and darkness, ruling individuals noted for their feelings of loneliness, miserliness, and emphasis on tradition. The melancholic humor was also seen as a temperament that mines deep wisdom, and those influenced by Saturn are naturally drawn to divination and poetry.

Saturn grants the gifts of discipline and steadfastness, valuable traits for artists who need a relentless quality to persist in their work despite obstacles.

Saturn's Child Sun Ra

In the 1930s, while enrolled in a teacher training course at a college in Huntsville, Alabama, jazz musician and philosopher Herman Poole Blount (1914–1993) had an extraordinary encounter with extraterrestrials from Saturn. These beings, who had small antennas above their eyes and ears, recognized Blount as a kindred spirit. They told him he had been chosen for his "perfect discipline," noting that, unlike many humans, he possessed the mental and physical control necessary for space travel. The beings then transported him to Saturn, revealing that a more meaningful path awaited him beyond being a schoolteacher. The Saturnians encouraged him to pursue music full-time to spread the spiritual teachings he was receiving.

After this encounter, Blount changed his name to Sun Ra and claimed the planet Saturn as his birthplace. Thereafter, his music carried strong cosmic overtones, and he took as his motto "Space Is the Place." He also began to turn to ancient Egypt for his spiritual outlook and sartorial style. In 1953, he formed a big band called the Arkestra, and over the next forty years, the group pioneered modern collective improvisation and exemplified the mystical spirit of free jazz.

Sun Ra was a pioneer in the use of electric instruments, playing the electric piano as early as 1956. In the late 1950s, he started Saturn Records, which released dozens of his albums during the next few decades. In the early 1960s, the Arkestra set up communal living quarters in New York and eventually Philadelphia. Sun Ra directed spectacular concerts with dancers and dazzling costumes, space-age prophecy, tales of intergalactic travel, and chants of "next stop Mars!"

In 1973, Sun Ra released the film *Space Is the Place*, which captures his distinctive blend of music, mythology, and Afrofuturism. In it, Sun Ra and his Arkestra embark on a journey to another planet, advocating for spiritual awakening and liberation, reflecting Ra's philosophy that art should transcend the ordinary and explore higher realms of existence.

The Call of Saturn

Connecting with the energy of Saturn, as demonstrated by Sun Ra, invites us to engage with our artistic purpose and legacy, ultimately helping us to establish long-lasting creative practices. Saturn also supports us when we may feel too intimidated to pursue new directions in our work. Consider Sun Ra's decision to become a mystical leader and artist rather than a schoolteacher after his experiences related to Saturn; this unorthodox choice ultimately led to greater stability and a more enduring legacy. Saturn's influence challenges us to abandon false roles and embrace a more authentic path, emboldening us to take visionary risks that possess genuine power.

On a Saturday, to begin aligning with Saturn's energy, choose one of the planet's traditional herbs—comfrey, mullein, or Solomon's seal are good choices—and prepare a cold infusion by placing the dried herb in a jar of water and covering it. Draw Saturn's glyph onto a piece of cloth or paper—a symbol with its scythe evoking time, death, and rebirth. Put this on your altar, and place the glass jar of steeping herbs directly over the glyph, allowing the symbol to subtly imprint its energy onto the infusion over a week.

The following Saturday, put on Sun Ra's "Saturn's Rings" and strain the herbs out from your infusion. Use some of the Saturn potion to wipe down your altar and its objects, baptizing them all with the essence of Saturn's steadiness and focus.

When you are finished with this, take a sip of the infusion to connect with the grounding energy of the planet. Sit quietly, and as you taste your Saturn elixir, meditate on Saturn's magnificent rings and this distant giant's slow, steady motion. Allow yourself to feel the weight of Saturn's presence as a teacher of discipline, responsibility, and the lessons that time imparts.

Working with Saturn can usher in a time of engaging with the limitations of your family of origin. What dreams did they leave unrealized? What words were they unable to say? What talents lived in them unrecognized? If you don't know the answers to these questions, intuitively seek them out in your bones.

Write a story about an ancestor's unrealized dream, real or imagined, where you give them what they did not have—true love, freedom, a place for public artistic expression, a sense of belonging, a voice . . . Whatever they lacked, hand it to them.

Recognize that Saturn can do this for you—awaken and bring the resources to realize a dream that was unimaginable before.

♃
Jupiter

When observed with the naked eye, Jupiter appears as a bright silver light in the night sky. Jupiter is so large that it could hold approximately 1,300 Earths inside its volume, and therefore symbolizes expansion, growth, abundance, and plenty. Hellenistic astrologers referred to Jupiter as the Greater Benefic and associated the planet with good fortune. Jupiter also governs higher learning and guides us in moral and ethical choices. Jupiter rules over two zodiac signs: Sagittarius by day and Pisces at night. These signs express their connection to higher knowledge in different ways: Sagittarius seeks understanding through outward exploration and adventure, while Pisces discovers wisdom through inner spiritual cultivation.

This planet is connected to tin in alchemy. Tin is a shining, white-silver metal that resists weathering and does not oxidize. It has a highly crystalline structure sensitive to temperature. Tin is used mainly in metal alloys, where it strengthens other metals and prevents corrosion.

In alchemical medicine, the liver is the primary organ associated with Jupiter. As our largest internal organ, the liver reflects Jupiter's immense size in our solar system. It is known for its ability to purify our blood, metabolize fats, and continuously regenerate and detoxify. In ancient Egyptian medicine, the liver was the center of emotions and life-force energy. A healthy liver was believed to contribute to a happy, courageous, and kindhearted disposition.

Jupiter's plants are characterized by abundance; they flourish rapidly, often becoming large, bushy, and tall with broad, thick leaves. Many of Jupiter's plants emit delightful fragrances and have sweet flavors. They can also possess bitterness, which aids in bile production and digestive processes that support liver and blood health. Numerous culinary herbs and foods, such as oregano, marjoram, rhubarb, basil, licorice, and mint, fall under Jupiter's domain. Jupiter's plants frequently showcase flowers that begin as yellow, highlighting their liver-supportive benefits, and later transition to red, indicating their role in blood cleansing.

Jupiter the planet was named after the ancient Roman god of thunder and lightning, known as Zeus in the Greek pantheon. As the ruler of Mount Olympus, Zeus presided over the Olympian gods and was often invoked for protection, justice, and order. As the god of the sky and heavens, Jupiter controlled the weather. He was called the "Light-Bringer," and places struck by lightning were considered his property. Because of this, the Greeks and Romans built temples where lightning had struck, viewing them as places of power. Zeus embodies growth, expansion, and luck, while his father Kronos—known as Saturn in Roman mythology—represents limitations, discipline, and time. The dynamic between these figures highlights the balance between freedom and responsibility, as well as growth and restraint, essential for creative success. Gardeners understand that to cultivate healthy plants, the time for growth and flourishing holds equal importance to the time for pruning and dormancy.

The animal symbol for Jupiter is the eagle. The eagle's sharp vision represents Zeus's watchful gaze from his vantage point on Mount Olympus. The eagle also carries his thunderbolts, aiding him in enforcing his authority and power. This command is tempered by Zeus's good humor. The term *jovial*, derived from the Latin name for Jupiter, Jovis, describes individuals born under the influence of this planet. Jupiter's children are cheerful, optimistic, and naturally buoyant in temperament. The lively combination of authority and affability that Jupiter can bring benefits artists in being persuasive, pitching ideas, speaking in public, or performing. Additionally, Jupiter can strengthen the intellectual and philosophical aspects of creative endeavors and help artists curry favor with institutions of higher learning.

Lightning with a Stag in Its Glare
JUPITER AND JOSEPH BEUYS

Joseph Beuys (1921–1986) was a sculptor, teacher, political activist, pioneering environmentalist, alleged charlatan, and proven liar—an enigmatic figure who resists easy definition. Efforts to trace his biography are quickly muddled by contradictions, with many details either disputed or reshaped by his own self-mythologizing. Born to devoutly Catholic, middle-class parents, Beuys was an only child. He was twelve when the Nazis rose to power, and his adolescence unfolded in the shadow of their brutal regime. In later years, Beuys became an outspoken critic of Nazism and the political systems that enabled it. Some interpretations of his work suggest that Beuys used his own past experiences as a member of the Hitler Youth to inform his artistic and political activism, aiming to promote social and environmental healing as a means of personal atonement.

As a child, Beuys dreamed of becoming a doctor. Though he ultimately chose the path of art, the impulse to heal remained central to his life and work. In a 1974 interview with *Art Papier*, he reflected, "Yes, perhaps I have a mission ... to change the social order" (Beuys 1982, 4–5). Beuys became widely known for his "expanded definition of art," grounded in the belief that creativity could serve as a catalyst for political and social transformation. He frequently organized open forums and public discussions, inviting active engagement with urgent political, ecological, and cultural issues.

His vision for art as reshaping society echoes the symbolic role of Jupiter, the Roman god of justice, law, and moral order. Beuys often invoked Jupiter in both title and imagery, aligning his practice with the mythological figure's ethical authority and commitment to societal balance. His work frequently features symbols linked to Jupiter—lightning, eagles, the planet itself, and oak trees. Oaks, the trees most commonly struck by lightning, were regarded in antiquity as sacred and manifestations of Jupiter's favor and divine power. Oak groves were seen as earthly sites of spiritual governance and cosmic law. Beuys harnessed this powerful connection in one of his most ambitious and influential projects titled *7000 Oaks*. Launched at Documenta 7 in Kassel, Germany, in 1982, the project involved planting 7,000 oak trees, each paired with a basalt stone, throughout the city. This massive, participatory artwork was not only an environmental gesture but also a statement about long-term ecological healing, social transformation, and the role of art in reshaping urban space. By planting oaks, Beuys aimed to do more than simply green the city; he sought to invoke the tree's ancient symbolism to bring strength, stability, and regeneration to the fabric of modern life.

In the 1970s, Beuys created a series of works on paper titled *Hauptstrom Jupiter*—Mainstream Jupiter—further signaling his alignment of art with natural forces, mythic symbolism, and a reimagined form of ethical leadership. One of his most theatrical installations, *Lightning with Stag in Its Glare* (1958–85) reflects Beuys's deep fascination with the forces of nature, the transmission of energy, and states of transformation. The arrangement of this enigmatic piece suggests a natural setting similar to a forest clearing. In this work, a stag—represented by an ironing board resting on wooden "legs"—is illuminated by a powerful lightning bolt, which takes the form of a heavy triangular structure suspended precariously from a beam. Through this installation, Beuys invokes the creative energy of nature as a lightning strike. The stag, highlighted by the lightning, holds a special significance in Beuys's work; he often referred to it as a conductor of the soul. The stag's annual shedding and regrowth of antlers symbolize resurrection and the potential for redemption.

The Call of Jupiter

My favorite way to connect with Jupiter is through the vibrant resonance of its metal, tin. You can find sheets of tin at most hardware stores, and, by shaking them, you can mimic the thunderous sounds of Jupiter's powerful lightning storms.

On a Thursday, Jupiter's day, set aside time for a moving meditation. Place an offering to Jupiter on your alchemist's altar. Traditional offerings include oak bark, cinnamon, fruit, or cakes. Use your intuitive senses to determine what Jupiter would appreciate receiving from you.

Next, grab your tin sheet and let the metal wobble and shake, creating a dynamic sound connection to the planet's energy. You can also play thunderstorm sounds on your stereo and let the power of the sound inspire you to dance for this bountiful planet.

If you can't participate in a noisy or physically demanding exercise, you can still connect with Jupiter through your mind. Start by focusing on the symbol of Jupiter. In many tarot decks, the Emperor card depicts a king sitting with his legs crossed in a shape resembling the number 4, which forms the glyph of Jupiter. The Emperor also carries an eagle on his shield, another symbol of Jupiter. You can use this card as a focal point to channel Jupiter's expansive energy.

Begin by praising the virtues of Jupiter: the brilliance of his lightning, the depth of his sense of justice, and the strength of his oak trees. Next, visualize an endeavor or project you wish to bless with luck. See it clearly, imagining its success as it attracts the resources and connections it needs to thrive.

Rub your palms together above your head to generate warmth, and feel the energy of lightning forming between your hands. When the sensation of heat and light feels just right, direct that energy outward by imagining throwing your lightning bolt at your project. This will imbue it with divine favor and protection.

Thank Jupiter and keep track of your project's progress, energizing it with lightning bolts as necessary.

Jupiter is particularly adept at currying favor with higher education institutions, as well as with philosophy, religion, and law. What creative project of yours needs resources connected to Jupiter? How can this planet assist? Make an offering to Jupiter and thank his en-lightening bolts for bringing you flashes of insight that will connect you to the resources you require.

♂

Mars

Mars is quite striking when viewed with the naked eye, appearing as a bright, reddish-orange point of light, strong and red as a bull's-eye. Mars's reddish hue comes from iron oxide, or rust, on its surface. In the alchemical tradition, Mars is associated with iron, the metal that gives both the planet and our blood their red color. In antiquity, iron was the metal used to forge swords and other instruments of battle. In more recent times, iron forged the instruments of the Industrial Revolution that have so far wiped out 70 percent of all wildlife. Iron can survive the blistering heat in stars where it lives comfortably—iron-rich meteorites fall to the Earth hot enough to turn sand to glass. This connection to iron reflects Mars being the god of war, violence, bloodshed, heat, and destruction. In astrology, Mars rules Aries by day and Scorpio by night, two signs embodying raw energy and how we express it, including fighting, sports, and sex. Aries showcases power through vigor, determination, and an unstoppable drive to take action. Scorpio channels raw power through sexuality and fearlessness in exploring the shadowy aspects of human nature.

Mars is associated with the gallbladder, which is responsible for storing, concentrating, and secreting bile, an intensely bitter fluid that helps break down fats and aids digestion. Mars also governs the immune system, the blood, and our libido—key forces that help us fight for life. Mars-associated plants typically thrive in harsh, desertlike environments: hot, dry, sandy, and rocky. The plants of Mars, like soldiers, often sport protective features like thorns or spikes. His plants are also identified by their red color, as in chilies and peppers, and can have sharp, pungent, or bitter flavors, such as ginger, garlic, peppers, leeks, onions, and radishes. These plants warm the stomach, stimulate bile production, aid digestion, and can increase metabolism, libido, and blood circulation.

For the Babylonians, the deity of planet Mars was Nurgal, whose name means "to scorch." He was an underworld god who ruled over war, plague, and disease. In

Greek mythology, Mars is ruled by Ares, the god of war known for his bloodlust, violence, anger, destruction, and severing relationships. He was reviled by most of the other gods, except Eris, whose predilection for sowing discord served his purposes of enmity, and Hades, who appreciated that Ares would populate his realm with the dead by waging war. The Romans, as an intensely warlike society, were much fonder of their chief martial deity, whom they called Mars. In Roman mythology, Mars was conceived when Flora, goddess of flowers and love, touched a flower to Juno's belly and made the goddess pregnant. The Romans associated Mars with *virtus*, a virtue of courage, manliness, and excellence. One of Mars's sacred animals, the wolf, is also a symbol of Rome.

While Martian energy may seem negative, Mars holds the force of life, and wherever you see it in an astrological chart, it gives vigor to the whole sphere. Think of the strength required to be born and how much bloodshed attends birth. Think of the cut umbilical cord that gives us the beginnings of our independence. Mars represents the energy that moves us to act, rise, conquer, and push beyond our limitations. Call upon Mars when you feel depleted, conflict-avoidant, or in a place of stasis, and the planet will rally you. If you need to exit a relationship, Mars can lend you the strength to leave; if you are up against a formidable enemy, Mars can help you fight. Mars gives artists the strength to bring challenging artworks into being and to defend their worthiness.

Marble Stained with Rust

DOVE BRADSHAW

Dove Bradshaw (b. 1949) is an American artist known for channeling natural forces such as time, weather, and erosion into dynamic, evolving forms made with elemental materials. In her *Indeterminacy* series, Bradshaw places pyrite stones on marble slabs, leaving them to oxidize outdoors. As the iron in the pyrite transforms into limonite, the marble becomes streaked with iron stains that resemble bloodstains, representing a slow, organic hemorrhaging that echoes the inherent violence within birth and death. This act of elemental bleeding evokes the warlike symbolism of Mars, where beauty and brutality intertwine.

For her *Unintended Consequences* series, Bradshaw collected spent bullets— warped and shattered from impact—then enlarged them thirtyfold through 3D scanning and printing. Patinated in rubber or metal and placed on pedestals, these gleaming forms turn instruments of death into objects of veneration. They are not abstract shapes, but the physical residue of violence reframed as poetic otherworldly artifacts: bullet wounds frozen in time, fragments of destruction placed in space for contemplation.

In some of her paintings, Bradshaw applies liver of sulfur to silver leaf on linen, creating unpredictable chemical reactions that leave black streaks and burn-like marks. The result is less painting than alchemy—a slow corrosion that transforms polished surfaces into volatile, entropic landscapes. John Cage remarked, "The things that happen in [Dove Bradshaw's] work are full of not her determination but its determination, such as chemical change or gravity"(McEvilley 2003, 83).

Unlike the expressive and self-referential gestures of Abstract Expressionism, Bradshaw's marks are not personal emotional outbursts but the results of unseen forces at work. These canvases evoke Mars's scorched, volcanic terrain: distant and brutal. In all her mediums, Bradshaw reveals destruction not through spectacle but through quiet, gleaming remnants, where bullets become fossils and every surface suggests a planet shaped by violence.

The Call of Mars

On a Tuesday, begin a ritual to connect with Mars by placing an iron object on your altar. Mars is associated with strength, courage, and protective, fiery energy. Historically, alchemists intentionally rusted iron by exposing it to heat and air. This process, known as creating a calx, was believed to break down the metal, preparing it for further transformation. Rust was also used to produce pigments and dyes.

In this ritual, you will use iron to channel the protective essence of Mars, creating a rust-water mixture that can be sprinkled around your home for energetic defense. First, gather a small handful of iron items, such as nails or bolts, and place them in a glass container. Fill the container partway with distilled white vinegar, ensuring the iron is at least partially exposed to the air, as exposure to oxygen accelerates the rusting process. Allow the iron to sit in the solution for several days, watching as rust forms and the liquid becomes charged with Mars energy. Keep the container in a safe, well-ventilated space, away from children and animals, and ensure it's stored where the rust won't spread to other rust-prone objects. If it isn't possible to do this safely, you can instead procure some iron shavings and use them in the ritual. As you work with Mars energy, ask yourself what you need protection from, where your boundaries may need strengthening, and how the power of Mars can support you in asserting your needs and defending your work.

Once the rust-water has formed, sprinkle it around the perimeter of your home in a clockwise direction when in the Northern hemisphere, and counter-clockwise when in the Southern, using all of the concoction. As you do this, visualize Mars's protective energy enveloping and safeguarding your space. If you wish to amplify its protective properties, add black salt to the mixture before sprinkling it. After you've sprinkled the rust-water, thank Mars for its protection and strength.

Working with Mars can help us with our relationship to anger. I grew up in an angry household where yelling, impatience, and sharp words flew easily, at least for other household members. I was encouraged, as the youngest and the girl, to hold my tongue, not to get angry, and to duck out of the way when anger was directed at me. In my twenties, with the guidance of several teachers, I was finally able to look at anger and recognize that my suppression of its forces was one of the primary impediments to my creative practice. Without its energizing fires, I was shy and withdrawn, unable to fight for the life of my work. Anger can drain our creative energy when suppressed, keeping us stuck and disconnected from the flow of life, and can consume us when not allowed a healthy outlet for expression and transformation.

Anger has evolved as a response to our need to prevent intrusions, right wrongs, or obtain what is lacking. As artists and alchemists, anger provides valuable insights and energy. In your creative practice do you experience frustrations? Where does this frustrated energy lead you? What is hindering your progress? Can you harness the energy of Mars to advocate for yourself and your work?

The Sun

The brilliant Sun radiates vitality; its fiery light is a zenith of power and electrical energy, animating all life on our planet. The Sun is an active, radiant force that pulses at the heart of our sky, circulating life energy like our hearts do within our bodies. Its symbol—a circle with a dot in the center—represents the divine spark, the seed of the soul that radiates outward. In alchemy, consciousness is described as light, and as the brightest planet, the Sun is closely associated with intellect and clear perception. Its essence encompasses life, illumination, reason, and understanding. In Hellenistic astrology, the Sun's position in a natal chart is crucial, revealing an individual's core personality. Leo, the zodiac sign ruled by the Sun, embodies creativity, confidence, intelligence, and a drive for recognition.

The Sun is the king of alchemy, embodying the soul and the essential nature of things. For alchemists, gold is the earthly manifestation of the Sun, with both representing illumination, clarity, and perfection. Gold does not react with oxygen or moisture in the air, unlike most metals, so it does not oxidize or corrode. It is also nonreactive with most acids, remaining unaffected by environmental factors, earning it the title of "immortal metal." *Aurum potabile*, or "drinkable gold," was a theoretical alchemical substance believed to be a cure for all ailments. Medieval alchemists used colloidal gold, ground so finely that it could be suspended in aqueous solvents, as a remedy for various conditions.

In astrological herbalism, the Sun governs charisma and vitality, as well as ruling the heart and arteries. Plants linked to the Sun often display golden yellow or orange hues, reflecting the warmth and radiance of sunlight, like Saint-John's-wort. Many of these plants feature round, disklike flowers or petals, resembling the Sun, such as calendula. Solar plants typically thrive in warm, dry climates and light-drenched spaces. When used in herbal remedies, they tend to have warming and drying effects on the body or offer balancing properties to counteract excessive heat. Solar herbs, such as rhodiola, turmeric, and chamomile, are commonly used to soothe, relax, and alleviate pain and emotional discomfort.

Sun gods hold a prominent position in the sky, which enables them to observe everything that occurs on Earth and connects them to the powers of divination. Their light symbolizes clarity, wisdom, and the ability to uncover hidden truths. In Greek mythology, Apollo, the god of the Sun, is closely associated with prophecy and healing. His Oracle at Delphi is one of the ancient world's most revered sites for divination.

In ancient Egyptian mythology, the sun god Ra descends into the underworld each night and rises again at dawn, with his journey representing themes of death, rebirth, and spiritual resurrection. The Sun is also embodied in Jesus Christ, often called the "Light of the World," with his life, death, and resurrection reflecting solar themes of illumination, salvation, and rebirth. From dawn to dusk, the Sun's daily cycle is a metaphor for the soul's journey from ignorance (night) to understanding (day).

Connecting with the Sun can help us step into our power, embrace visibility, and confidently take our place in the spotlight as artists. Ask yourself if you feel comfortable being seen, sharing your work, or presenting your creations to others, especially those in positions of authority. Explore the reasons behind these feelings and try to shed some light on them. The Sun can also strengthen our connection to the heart-centered aspects of our creativity, especially when we've become overly intellectual or formulaic in our practice.

Infinite Suns

GIORDANO BRUNO

Giordano Bruno (1548–1600) was an Italian philosopher, poet, alchemist, astrologer, and cosmological theorist. He was known for being one of the most outspoken and controversial figures of his time, openly expressing his ideas without fear.

At seventeen, Bruno joined the Dominican Order at the monastery of San Domenico Maggiore in Naples. He quickly gained recognition for his intellectual brilliance and open-mindedness, even being invited to present his memorization techniques to the pope. However, Bruno's groundbreaking ideas often placed him in conflict with the Catholic Church. His controversial claims, such as the assertion that Mary was not a virgin, that the Holy Ghost was female, and that reincarnation was real, deeply unsettled church leaders. Among his most powerful and contentious insights was his profound understanding of the Sun and its movements.

Bruno delivered public lectures on the alchemical Emerald Tablet, interpreting its reference to the "Operation of the Sun" as supporting the idea that the Earth revolves around the Sun. This perspective directly challenged the Catholic Church's belief that the Earth was the center of the universe. In his 1584 book *On the Infinite, the Universe, and the Worlds: Five Cosmological Dialogues*, he proposed that all stars are distant suns, each surrounded by their own planets, and asserted that these planets could support their own forms of intelligent life. Additionally, Bruno insisted that the universe is infinite and lacks a central point, further angering the church.

In 1576, the Inquisition attempted to arrest Bruno on charges of heresy, but he escaped and continued to publish his works across Europe. Over the next fifteen years in exile, he refined his innovative memory techniques, wrote provocative literature, and engaged in public debates with some of the greatest thinkers of his time.

In 1592, Bruno made an ill-advised journey back home to Italy, where he was captured by the Inquisitors. Throughout a seven-year trial, Bruno was compelled to defend each heretical statement he had made. When he refused to renounce his beliefs, he was tortured. Despite his suffering, Bruno remained unwilling to retract his views on the Sun and the existence of multiple worlds.

Unable to break his resolve, the Inquisition ultimately condemned him to death for heresy. Legend has it that he made a rude gesture toward his judges and replied, "Perhaps you pronounce this sentence against me with greater fear than I receive it." In 1600, Bruno was publicly executed—gagged to silence his voice and burned alive at the stake.

His conversant relationship with the Sun put him in touch with its truth: that it shines at the center of our solar system. And he stood by this truth no matter the cost. It took the Catholic Church another 200 years to officially accept the idea of the Sun as the center of the solar system. In 1822, the church finally lifted the ban on publishing works advocating for the Earth's motion and the Sun's stability, effectively accepting the Copernican theory.

A monument to Giordano Bruno was erected in 1889 in the Campo de' Fiori in Rome, Italy, to honor the philosopher burned there in 1600. This thirty-foot-tall bronze was funded through private donations, primarily from a subscription initiated by students at the University of Rome. The national councils of state miraculously did not oppose its construction. The inscription on the base of the statue reads: "A BRUNO - IL SECOLO DA LUI DIVINATO - QUI DOVE IL ROGO ARSE," which translates to: "To Bruno – dedicated to him by the Age he predicted – here where the fire burned."

The Call of the Sun

Meditating with the Sun can be a profoundly joyful practice. Each moment of gratitude for its light, strength, and life-giving energy becomes a silent prayer to our central star. To deepen this connection intentionally, try dedicating time on a Sunday to making a cyanotype, a print produced in collaboration with sunlight.

A cyanotype is a photographic printing process that involves a photosensitive solution made from ferric ammonium citrate and potassium ferricyanide, which turns blue when exposed to ultraviolet light. This process results in distinctive blue-and-white prints. The cyanotype process was developed in the 1840s by Sir John Herschel and Alfred Smee. Anna Atkins, a friend of the Herschel family, used the method to hand-print botanical and textile specimens, creating the world's first photographically illustrated books.

To make your own cyanotype, buy photosensitive solutions that can be applied to fabric or paper and allowed to dry in a dark place or purchase pretreated cyanotype paper. Wear gold and yellow colors on a sunny Sunday, and begin your cyanotype project. To start, place a gold or gold-colored object on your altar to invite and honor the Sun's radiant influence. Then close your eyes, focus on the Sun's symbol, and envision the dot at the circle's center as a vibrant energy core. See this core of light in your heart, imagining it as a glowing Sun, radiating warmth and vitality.

Next, thoughtfully place objects, photographic negatives, or printed transparencies onto the sensitized material. Choose items that resonate with what you most want to draw from the Sun—its radiance, electricity, visibility, power, or heart-centeredness. Then, expose the material to sunlight for ten to twenty minutes, depending on the intensity of the light. The uncovered areas will darken to a rich blue, while the shapes of your objects will remain white, capturing their silhouettes. Once exposure is complete, rinse the paper or fabric thoroughly in water to halt the chemical reaction. This will wash away the unexposed chemicals, revealing your image in vivid blue and white contrast, a collaborative imprint between you and the Sun.

The Sun represents boldness, radiance, and resilience. If you struggle to be visible and recognized in your creative pursuits, consider inviting the Sun into your practice. You can do this by regularly making offerings to this star and acknowledging that its presence serves as a reminder that we are meant to shine.

♀

Venus

Venus is the brightest object in the sky after the Sun and the Moon, shining with a brilliant bluish-white hue. Similar to Mercury, Venus orbits the Sun within the Earth's path. This positioning gives Venus both a Morning Star and an Evening Star phase, visible either just before sunrise or after sunset. In various mythological traditions, these phases of Venus's visibility are linked to shifts in gender expression. In ancient Egyptian astronomy, Venus was regarded as two distinct celestial bodies: the morning star Tioumoutiri and the evening star Ouaiti. Ancient Greeks referred to Venus's two aspects as Phosphoros during the day and Hesperos at night.

Venus, with its 13:8 orbital ratio to Earth, traces a pentagram in the sky over eight years, creating a curved shape that resembles a five-petaled rose. Perhaps because of this rose or its double-bodied mythologies, Venus is associated with love and lovers. The origin of the astrological glyph for Venus is the Egyptian ankh, symbol of life, and Venus loves all that is beautiful. This planet is associated with comfort, luxury, pleasure, touch, connection, and nourishment. Venus rules the zodiac signs Taurus by day and Libra by night. Both signs are deeply connected to art, beauty, and sensual pleasures. Taurus is passionate about external pleasures, such as food, fragrance, and beautiful clothing, while Libra finds fulfillment in the more introspective aspects of pleasure, like balance, harmony, and the beauty found in art.

In alchemy, Venus is connected with the metal copper, which, like the planet, has a twofold nature. Usually bright orange, copper is a sea green when molten, tarnishes to a green-blue color, and burns with a blue-green flame with flashes of red. Foods containing copper are ruled by Venus, including dark leafy greens and dark chocolate. Venus-ruled plants often have a five-pointed star shape in their cores, like apples and oranges, or the ability to attract with beautiful fragrances, like rose and geranium. We can identify Venus's plants in nature by their beautiful flowers, often appearing in soft colors like pink, violet, or white. These blooms have sweet fragrances and delicate petals. Organs traditionally attributed to Venus are in the genitourinary system, which includes the bladder and kidneys. Venus, with its associations to desire, love, affection, and sexual connection, is also connected to genitals and reproductive function.

Aphrodite, the Greek counterpart of Roman Venus, is the goddess of love and beauty. She was worshipped in various androgynous and gender-transcending forms across her many cults. One manifestation is Aphroditos, a bearded, male-presenting version of the goddess, depicted with both masculine and feminine attributes. Roman Venus is the goddess of love, birth, death, and sex. Temples dedicated to Venus in Rome included schools for instruction in sexual techniques, led by priestesses known as the venerii. These teachings imparted a spiritual grace known as venia, and the term *veneration* originates from the practice of paying homage to Venus. In this tradition, Venus also governs death, which was seen as another form of sexual climax. In Ovid's *Metamorphoses*, the character Iphis expresses a longing for death by stating, "Let me go in the act of coming to Venus; in more senses than one, let my last dying be done!" (Ovid 1986, 258).

Venus governs art and relationships of all kinds, making the planet a supportive ally for artists. This planet can light the way if you need to meet people in your field or generate an audience. This planet also offers support when your creative work feels stagnant, mechanical, or dull. Venus can infuse your efforts with fresh energy with the same force that causes a rosebud to unfurl its petals into a grand spiral.

Burn Galleries Not Calories

PIPPA VENUS GARNER

Pippa Venus Garner (1942–2024) was an American artist, illustrator, industrial designer, and writer, recognized for her satirical reinterpretations of consumer products. She was known for her *Immaculate Misconceptions* series, which includes hundreds of inventions that transform everyday household items into humorous or absurd devices designed to mock the perversity of American consumer culture. An example is the "Hurl-A-Burger" machine, which is intended to "promote cultural exchange" by launching fast food over international borders with a catapult. For much of her career, Garner worked outside art institutions, often using her body as a medium and a billboard for T-shirts she made with slogans like "Power to the Peephole" and "Burn Galleries Not Calories."

In the 1980s, Garner began to transition, framing the experience as part of what she described as an "art project to create disorientation in my position in society, and sort of balk any possibility of ever falling into a stereotype again" (Watlington 2023, 1). Reflecting on this in a 2021 conversation with artist Hayden Dunham for *Interview Magazine*, she explained, "There was something that always seemed odd about being saddled with a gender, or being isolated by your gender. Because the advertising, consumerism, in the background in my life, was very much gender-oriented. There were things for women and things for men. It was all-out masculinity or all-out femininity, macho or made up. And if you didn't feel that yourself, you felt uncomfortable" (Dunham 2021, np).

Later, she added Venus to her name—a reference to the Roman goddess of love and beauty, whose Greek counterpart Aphrodite was worshipped in various gender-transcending forms. These mythological layers—along with Aphrodite's long-standing associations with desire, transformation, and the creative life force—resonate with Garner's lifelong exploration of embodiment and the subversive power of art.

Although Garner was highly productive, her professional art career was virtually nonexistent between 1986 and 2014. This was largely due to gender discrimination, transphobia, and the art world's resistance to her experimentation across diverse mediums. However, in the final decade of her life, Garner finally received widespread acclaim. By then, cultural attitudes had shifted, embracing a queer consciousness that blurred traditional gender binaries as well as the boundaries between mediums and disciplines. A new generation emerged, eager to celebrate the full range of Garner's eclectic, insightful, and transdisciplinary work.

The Call of Venus

The planet Venus, the embodiment of art and beauty, has long influenced the visual arts on a material level through the use of copper. The renowned Egyptian blue, recognized as the first synthetic pigment, was created more than 5,000 years ago from a combination of silica, lime, copper, and alkali. Copper is the component that gives Egyptian blue its vibrant color and is used in the manufacture of other green-blue pigments such as verdigris and azurite.

In the early 16th century, European artists began experimenting with painting on small sheets of copper. The stunning color of the metal shines through in the thinner layers of the painting, giving the artwork a sparkling, gemlike quality. Artists who created works on copper include Leonardo da Vinci, Jan Brueghel, El

Greco, and Rembrandt. Inspired by this rich artistic tradition, we will make our own copper painting as a tribute to Venus.

To begin, procure a piece of copper sheeting or a copper object, such as a penny or a copper bracelet. Use steel wool or sandpaper to roughen the copper's surface. Next, rub a garlic clove onto the copper to improve adhesion. If you're using oil paint, you can apply it directly to the prepared copper surface. If you're using acrylic paints, it can be helpful to use a primer. You can also experiment by using nail polish or markers.

Fingerprints will show on the copper, and exposure to water will cause the metal to patina, which can lead to the peeling or chipping of water-based paints over time. I enjoy embracing the natural changes copper undergoes, but if you prefer to keep your painting pristine, consider wearing gloves and using oil paints.

Once your materials are prepared, choose a Friday to begin this art ritual. You may want to wear Venus's colors, which are white or green, and offer Venus an apple on your alchemist's altar. Before you begin painting, hold your copper object in your hands and close your eyes. Feel a warm resonance building between yourself, the metal, and the radiant energy of this planet. Allow yourself to sense the metal's unique energy—a living correspondence with Venus—and let that energy flow through you. What you choose to paint is entirely up to you, but for this exercise, consider that the piece is a tribute to Venus when choosing a subject. Once finished, place your painted copper offering on your alchemist's altar and invite Venus to connect with your creativity.

Venus can bring jewellike beauty to our artistic endeavors and help us attract like-minded artistic or alchemical counterparts. Relationships are just as essential to our art as the work itself, and Venus can guide us in attracting creative unions and social connections. Who supports and surrounds your work? What is your level of attachment and responsibility to your artistic community? How might you cultivate a community if you don't yet have one? Think of a living artist you admire. Send them a message, either virtually or mentally, expressing what their work means to you without inviting or expecting a reply. Freely giving praise and admiration is part of building a healthy Venusian artistic network.

☿

Mercury

Mercury is challenging to see with the naked eye because of its small size, rapid movement, and close proximity to the Sun. Due to the planet's fast orbit, its position in the sky changes quickly, which can cause it to disappear from view for long periods. Additionally, Mercury experiences a phenomenon known as retrograde motion several times a year, where it appears to move backward in the sky. Because of its swift, erratic shifts, Mercury is associated with the mind, particularly learning, thinking, and communication. The planet is governed by a nonbinary entity traditionally referred to using gender-neutral pronouns. Its glyph combines symbols for the Sun, representing masculine energy, and the Moon, representing feminine energy. In astrology, Mercury governs two signs: Gemini during the day and Virgo at night. Both signs are characterized by adaptability, energetic natures, and sharp intellectual abilities. Gemini expresses these traits outwardly through a love of performance, gregariousness, and quick wit, while Virgo demonstrates them inwardly, leading to thoughtful and methodical communication and artistic expression.

Mercury's bright silvery appearance and fluid movement led alchemists to associate the planet with the metal mercury, which has similar characteristics. This striking, silver, gelatinous metal is unique because it is the only metal that remains liquid at room temperature, making it the heaviest naturally occurring fluid on Earth. Alchemists often referred to the element as "quicksilver" due to its characteristics. Its chemical symbol, Hg, is derived from the Latin term *hydrargyrum*, meaning "watery silver." In the alchemical tradition, it was believed that all metals began as liquids deep within the Earth, but only mercury retained its primal purity and life force, never fully solidifying. For this reason, the ancients referred to it as *mercurius vivens*, or "living mercury."

The bodily systems traditionally ruled by Mercury include the lungs (breath), tongue (speech), and brain (thought). Plants that contain mercury, like cassia and dulse, are connected with the planet, as are plants that affect thought and the nervous system. Mercury's plants counteract excess moisture, relieve anxiety, calm overactive thoughts, and restore digestive balance. These plants can often be identified by their finely branched foliage, which reflects the intricate pathways of the nervous system and the lungs' bronchioles. Mercury's plants, such as lavender, typically have a subtle fragrance and thrive in dry, sandy environments. Their seeds are often enclosed in pods or husks, such as those of fennel and celery.

In Greek mythology, Hermes, known as Mercury in Roman tradition, is a complex and multifaceted god. Hermes is swift and clever, serving as the messenger of the gods and acting as a bridge for communication between the divine and mortal realms, as well as between the living and the dead. Hermes guides souls to the afterlife and governs transformation, adaptability, and the pursuit of magical knowledge. Hermes is also the patron of merchants, thieves, artists, and those living outside societal norms. Hermes is also gender nonconforming and was traditionally referred to using gender-neutral pronouns. Celebrated as a trickster and thief, Hermes disrupts binary concepts of right and wrong. As the deity of transformation, Hermes plays a central role in alchemy, where they are believed to initiate alchemists into the divine arts of transmutation—knowledge once reserved for the gods.

As a baby, Hermes snuck out of their crib at night and stole fifty cows from Apollo's pasture. They cleverly tied brooms to the cows' tails to erase their tracks. After hiding the cows, Hermes sacrificed two of them and used their remains to create the first lyre. Then Hermes returned to their crib and fell asleep. An oracle revealed to Apollo that Hermes was the thief, and Apollo angrily took the baby god to Zeus. Zeus made Hermes confess, and the trickster led Apollo to where the cows were. However, Apollo discovered that two were missing.

Unfazed, Hermes played an enchanting tune on the lyre they had made from the cows' intestines. Captivated by the music, Apollo offered his entire herd in exchange for the instrument. Hermes agreed, but only if Apollo would teach them magic, which Apollo did. Impressed by Hermes's cleverness, Zeus rewarded them with winged sandals, a golden hat, and a magical cape. With these gifts, Hermes could travel between the worlds of the divine, the dead, and the mortal.

Mercury, the planet of communication and transformation, supports artists in discovering their unique voice and expressing their vision clearly. This planet helps build meaningful connections with our creative lineages, erecting bridges with artists who came before us and speaking to our future audiences. This planet can be a valuable ally when you feel unsure of how to talk about your work. Mercury helps clear mental blocks, offers fresh perspectives, and guides you toward more powerful forms of expression. For artists working across multiple disciplines, Mercury can support the enjoyment and expression of their creative multiplicity, helping them navigate and integrate diverse modes of making.

Hermes of the Ways

H.D.

H.D. (1886–1961) was an American modernist poet, novelist, and memoirist known for her deep engagement with Greek mythology, mysticism, and the occult. Openly pansexual, she entered into a lifelong partnership with the English novelist Bryher in 1918. Together, they embraced a nontraditional and expansive approach to romance and life, sharing homes in England, Switzerland, and Greece throughout their relationship. Both adopted nonbinary names that reflected their fluid orientations and rejection of conventional gender roles.

H.D.'s creative and spiritual life was profoundly influenced by her fascination with ancient Greek literature, which she studied and translated. The figure of Hermes served as a significant source of inspiration in her work. Known for moving freely between genders, worlds, and identities, Hermes is honored as a guide for poets, queer people, and practitioners of magic—supporting those who navigate various realms and assume multiple identities. In her poem "Tribute to the Angels"—one of many she dedicated to the deity—H.D. expresses her kinship with the boundary-crossing god, drawing on their liminal and transformative energy to reclaim her own experiences of spirituality and artistic expression:

Hermes Trismegistus
is patron of alchemists;

his province is thought,
inventive, artful, and curious;

his metal is quicksilver,
his clients, orators, thieves, and poets;

steal then, O orator,
plunder, O poet,

take what the old-church
found in Mithra's tomb,

candle and script and bell,
take what the new-church spat upon

and broke and shattered;
collect the fragments of the splintered glass

and of your fire and breath,
melt down and integrate,

re-invoke, re-create . . . (H.D. 1973, 1)

Born in Bethlehem, Pennsylvania, within a Moravian community outside Philadelphia, H.D. formed an early romantic and creative relationship with poet Ezra Pound, who recognized her talent and helped introduce her work to the literary world. Initially associated with the Imagist movement, H.D. eventually transcended its constraints to explore forms that reflected her diverse spiritual interests, including Christianity, Greek and Egyptian religions, Spiritualism, Hermeticism, alchemy, tarot, and astrology. She perceived her later work not as the precise verse praised by early critics but as something more elemental and visionary, writing, "This is not the 'crystalline' poetry that my early critics would insist on. It is no pillar of salt nor yet of hewn rock-crystal. It is the pillar of fire by night, the pillar of cloud by day" (Malone 2022).

The Call of Mercury

The Orphic Hymns are a collection of ancient Greek religious texts dedicated to the gods and attributed to Orpheus, a bard, poet, and prophet in Greek mythology. These hymns were used in rituals to invoke divine powers and establish connections with the gods. They are rich in symbolic language and contain prayers, praises, and offerings to the deities aimed at gaining their favor. When working with the Orphic Hymns to connect with Mercury (Hermes in Greek tradition), we align ourselves with divine qualities of communication, intellect, and swift movement.

On a Wednesday—Mercury's sacred day—begin by lighting a yellow candle to symbolize their energy. Prepare an incense blend using dried herbs traditionally linked to Hermes/Mercury, such as mastic, frankincense, clove, or marjoram. Sit quietly, placing an image of the glyph of Mercury before you—a circle crowned with a crescent and grounded by a small cross. This symbol weaves together the energies of the Sun (the circle) and the Moon (the crescent), representing a harmonious balance of masculinity and femininity, intellect and intuition. As you focus on these energies, allow the ritual to open a channel for a more profound connection with Mercury's influence. When you feel centered and attuned to the symbol for Mercury, recite the following invocation:

> Hermes, draw near, and to my pray'r incline,
> Angel of Jove, and Maia's son divine;
> Prefect of contest, ruler of mankind,
> With heart almighty, and a prudent mind.
> Celestial messenger of various skill,
> Whose pow'rful arts could watchful Argus kill.
> With winged feet 'tis thine thro' air to course,

O friend of man, and prophet of discourse;
Great life-supporter, to rejoice is thine
In arts gymnastic, and in fraud divine.
With pow'r endu'd all language to explain,
Of care the loos'ner, and the source of gain.
Whose hand contains of blameless peace the rod,
Corucian, blessed, profitable God.
Of various speech, whose aid in works we find,
And in necessities to mortals kind.
Dire weapon of the tongue, which men revere,
Be present, Hermes, and thy suppliant hear;
Assist my works, conclude my life with peace,
Give graceful speech, and memory's increase.

Light your incense now and recite a line or two describing how Hermes can assist you specifically in this moment of your creative life. Sit in silence for a while, allowing the energy of Hermes/Mercury to envelop you. When you feel ready, close your practice with gratitude and blow out the candle.

You can build on this practice by working with Mercury, who can travel to the realms of the dead, to connect you to artists in your creative lineage. Last year, I began writing a series of poems as part of my daily practice to develop my writing skills, with no intention of ever publishing them. I have a habit of placing photographs of deceased artists I love and admire on my desk and leaving them offerings. One morning, as I sat down to write a poem, I placed a photograph of H.D. on my desk and decided to put a statue of Mercury next to her for inspiration. I lit a candle and began to write. Later that day, I couldn't shake the sense that I should publish these poems, but I dismissed the thought, feeling too shy to self-publish or to approach a publisher myself.

The next day, the inspiration to publish came again, and I said aloud, "I will not self-publish these poems." On the third day, after lighting a candle next to the photograph and statue on my desk, I finished writing and checked my email. A publisher I loved wrote to ask if I had any work that I wanted to publish. I sent them the poetry book, and they loved it, asking me to formally publish and distribute this work. Not only did Mercury arrive to give me inspiration, but they brought H.D. to me, who insisted on publication, and these energies brought external forces together to make this a reality.

I recommend getting a statue of Mercury/Hermes and acquiring an image of a deceased artist you admire. Place them both in your workspace and ask them to support and assist you while also remembering to offer them incense and candles. The results can be miraculous.

The Moon

The Moon reflects the Sun's life-giving light, casting a protective glow into the darkness. Its silvery radiance awakens the senses needed to "see in the dark"—shedding light on our inner world when external light fades away. These senses include intuition, dreams, instinct, telepathy, and psychic ability. While the Sun represents our outward energy, vitality, and action, the Moon aligns with our regenerative capacity and receptive functions. Through its waxing and waning cycles, the Moon embodies death, renewal, and regeneration. The Greek word *meno*, meaning "month," connects the Moon to menstruation and menopause, highlighting its link to cycles of time, birth, and death and the waxing and waning of life force. In many agricultural traditions, the thirteen lunar cycles of a year determine the best times for planting and harvesting, as the Moon's phases guide rhythms of growth and decay. The Moon rules the zodiac sign Cancer, symbolized by the Crab constellation. Cancer is associated with loyalty, protection, emotional depth, heightened intuition, and maternal instinct.

Alchemists revered silver as the metal of the Moon, admiring its brilliant white luster, which tarnishes black when exposed to air or sulfur. Silver is the most conductive of metals, allowing heat and electricity to flow freely. Silver has long been used for its healing properties, as biological silver possesses astringent and antibacterial qualities. Ancient Egyptians wrapped wounds in silver to prevent infection, and many cultures have lined drinking vessels with silver to harness its antibacterial benefits.

In astrological herbalism, plants associated with the Moon affect menstruation, emotions, hormonal balances, digestive secretions, and intuition. The organ systems traditionally governed by the Moon include the stomach, bowels, bladder, uterus, and ovaries. Lunar plants are identifiable by their soft, thick, juicy leaves and may have a sweet, watery taste, as seen in melons, watercress, and lettuce. These plants tend to grow quickly, mirroring the rapid movement of the Moon through the sky, and thrive in damp, boggy environments. Many lunar plants are pale or bear white flowers, reflecting the color of the Moon and the stars in the night sky. Some may have silver-toned undersides to their leaves—another celestial signature—indicating they are particularly beneficial for addressing lunar-related health imbalances. Mugwort, or *Artemisia vulgaris*, named after the Greek goddess of the Moon, has a silvery underside to its leaves as well as mild emmenagogue properties, meaning it can stimulate menstrual flow. Mugwort is also used to enhance dream recall and intuitive abilities.

The Mesopotamian Moon god Sin is often depicted riding in a crescent-shaped boat that glides across the night sky. Sin is portrayed as an ancient, wise man with a lapis lazuli beard and accompanied by seven demons that consume the Moon. He is the keeper of time and governs fertility and pregnancy. In Greek mythology, the Moon is ruled by a trio of goddesses. Artemis, the goddess of the early waxing crescent Moon, symbolizes new beginnings, growth, and youthful energy. Artemis is frequently associated with fertility and the wild instincts of femininity. She is a fierce hunter and an independent figure, embodying the assertive and active energy of the crescent moon as it begins to grow. Selene, the Full Moon goddess, radiates a calm and illuminating presence representing completion, clarity, and fulfillment. She embodies the peak of intuitive and empathetic lunar energy when the Moon is at its fullest and most potent. Hecate, the goddess of the waning and Dark Moon, symbolizes endings, transformation, and the unknown. She is linked with the mysterious, liminal spaces between life and death, offering protection and wisdom to those navigating these thresholds. Hecate governs magic, intuition, and the shadows, and her energy is one of introspection and deep spiritual understanding.

The Moon's associations with dreams and emotional depth make it an essential guide for artists in their explorations of nonlinear thought and intuitive expression. The Moon enhances emotional resonance and encourages the creation of visionary, dreamlike artworks that transcend rational logic. By utilizing the Moon's divinatory energy, artists can also bring artworks from the future into the present, leading to startling innovations in form and concept.

Digital Moonscapes

WENDY CARLOS

Wendy Carlos (b. 1939) is an American musician, composer, and electronic music pioneer. As a child, Carlos constructed a high-fidelity audio system for her parents using wood and soldering wire, and at just fourteen, she won a science contest for building a computer. Her passion for music led her to create her first tape machine, which would become a pivotal tool in her exploration of electronic music. After pursuing a hybrid major in music and physics at Brown University, she earned an M.A. in music composition at Columbia University, studying with pioneers Otto Luening and Vladimir Ussachevsky at the first electronic music center in the United States. This set the stage for her groundbreaking album *Switched-On Bach* in 1968, a transformative release that not only made the Moog synthesizer a household name but also made Carlos the first artist to bring classical music into the world of synthesizers. The album became the second classical album in history to achieve platinum status in the United States.

Carlos's influence continued to grow with her iconic soundtracks for *A Clockwork Orange, The Shining,* and *Tron,* pushing the boundaries of what electronic music could achieve in cinema. Before Brian Eno's ambient works gained recognition, Carlos had already released the pioneering *Sonic Seasonings,* anticipating a genre that would later define much of modern electronic music.

In 1984, Carlos released *Digital Moonscapes,* another groundbreaking album that significantly evolved her musical exploration. It showcases her mastery of digital synthesizers and sound design, featuring compositions inspired by various moons, including our own Moon and those of Mars, Jupiter, and Saturn. The analog-to-digital technology shift gave *Digital Moonscapes* its cold, lunar sound. Unlike the warm, fuzzy tones produced by analog synthesizers, which employ oscillators to generate basic waveforms, digital synthesizers generate complex, precise effects, perfectly capturing the cool, silvery light of the Moon with digital signal processing (DSP) to break sound into samples, offering greater flexibility and control.

Wendy Carlos is a visionary in music and technology. Much like the Moon's ability to reveal the unseen, Carlos has an uncanny knack for predicting the future of sound and digital innovation. She instinctively understands how new technologies can push the boundaries of music, crafting soundscapes that feel timeless while anticipating the sonic evolutions for the years to come.

The Call of the Moon

On a Monday, place a silver object on your alchemist's altar as an offering to the Moon. On a Full Moon, go for a walk (or head up to your roof) with a jar of water and an empty dish. Find a space where the Full Moon is clearly visible. When you arrive, gently pour the water from the jar into the dish, allowing it to catch the Moon's silvery light. You can add a piece of silver to the water to strengthen the potion. If you wish, you can burn lunar herbs such as mugwort or jasmine as an offering. Position yourself comfortably before the water dish, and take a few deep breaths to center yourself. Allow the moonlight to call to you, feeling points of attraction in your body rising and stirring. Notice how the moonlight alters your perceptions. Pay attention to any changes in your eyesight; be aware of the tastes in your mouth; and listen closely to the sounds around you, noticing shifts in resonance. Take inventory of what the Moon is bringing to your attention in your environment, in your body, in your mind, and in your emotions.

You may feel called to ask the Moon a question—something you've been holding quietly within. Begin by bringing the question into your awareness. Then, silently form the words in your mouth and gently blow the question into the water. Imagine the water receiving it fully. Like the Moon, water is receptive and flowing, capable of carrying your question into the unseen realms. Now wait and watch for an answer to come floating to the dish's surface. It could arrive as an image, a sound, a set of words, a shift in temperature, or an inner movement that isn't connected to any external sense. Breathe with the Moon and thank this celestial being for any wisdom you receive. When you're ready, pour the water from the dish into your jar for safekeeping and return home.

Notice any changes in your sleep or dreams afterward. We all know that when our external life changes, our inner life reflects that in dreams. We can also affect our external world by altering our dreams. Try adding your Moon-charged water to bathwater. You can also put it in a spray bottle and spritz yourself and your bedding before you retire. Think of three words expressing changes you want to see in your creative life. Repeat these words to yourself as you fall asleep, pairing them with a clear and simple image. For example, if you made a blue painting and you'd like to see it hanging in a museum, you could say "blue, shining, museum" and see the painting in the Metropolitan Museum. Try working with your exact phrase and image for a few weeks, and see if your dreams shift. More importantly, notice how your external world adjusts to make this creative breakthrough a reality.

The Moon encourages us to explore the mysteries within that are essential for creating impactful art. Although initially unsettling, lunar insight challenges the carefully crafted personas we present to others and initiates a process that compels us to seek liberation. The freedom of authenticity awaits us on the other side of calling to the Moon. When the Moon's light enters your creative process, it may guide you to create unfamiliar or frightening work. This is because the work is being shaped by a future version of yourself—one who has learned to express with greater authenticity and depth than you can today. The Moon helps illuminate the hidden depth, beauty, and potential of your creativity, revealing what you're capable of—even if you haven't fully stepped into it yet.

The Philosopher's Stone

The Philosopher's Stone is the Holy Grail of alchemy—a legendary substance believed to hold the key to transforming base metals into gold, a precious metal that resists rust, tarnish, and corrosion. Beyond its material power, the Stone is also thought to confer this same enduring quality upon the body and spirit. Alchemists often refer to it as the *alkahest*, a universal solvent capable of dissolving any substance to extract its essence or life force. This purified essence could then be used to create powerful elixirs, such as the Elixir of Life or *aurum potabile* (drinkable gold), believed to restore vitality, promote immortality, and remove the burdens of time. The Stone was said to cure illness, slow aging, and heal the fragmentation—or tarnishing—of the soul. It was even thought to possess the power of palingenesis: the ability to bring the dead back to life.

The Philosopher's Stone is both a symbolic concept and a tangible object that can be created through the practice of alchemy. However, this creation is possible only when the alchemist has attained a level of inner knowing that supports its formation. The term *philosopher* means "lover of wisdom." The Philosopher's Stone, which symbolizes ultimate transformation, is so named because it can only be discovered through the cultivation of wisdom. According to the Book of Proverbs, wisdom existed before the earth, mountains, or springs were formed and played a crucial role in the creative emergence of the world. In this text, wisdom is personified as a feminine presence, though she is left unnamed; later, alchemists would identify this feminine principle of wisdom as Sophia.

> *I was set up from everlasting, from the beginning, Before the earth was.*
> *When there were no depths, I was brought forth,*
> *When there were no fountains abounding with water.*
> *Before the mountains were settled, Before the hills was I brought forth;*
> *While as yet he had not made the earth, nor the fields,*

Nor the beginning of the dust of the world.
When he established the heavens, I was there:
When he set a circle upon the face of the deep,
When he made firm the skies above,
When the fountains of the deep became strong,
When he gave to the sea its bound,
That the waters should not transgress his commandment,
When he marked out the foundations of the earth;
Then I was by him. (Proverbs 8:23–30, American Standard Version)

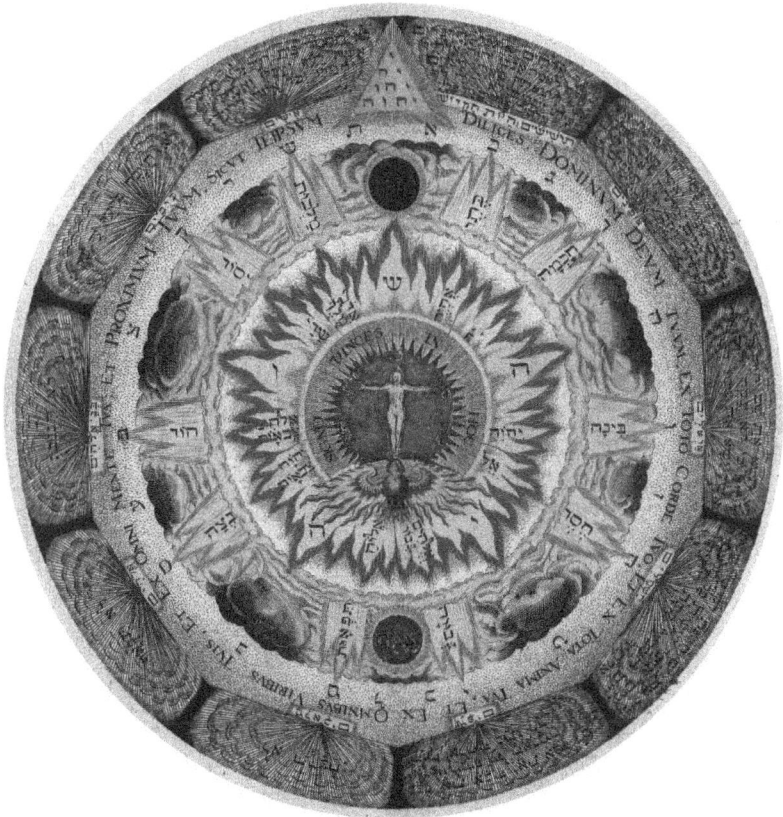

A circular engraving depicting a phoenix at the center. Plate 4 from *Amphitheatrum Sapientiae Aeternae Solius Verae*, by Heinrich Khunrath, 1609. Courtesy of the Department of Special Collections, Memorial Library, University of Wisconsin-Madison.

The wisdom essential to the alchemist's work involves deep, intuitive understanding—an inner awareness that transcends logic and analytical thinking. This type of wisdom emerges from direct, lived insights into the hidden patterns of the universe. This is what the ancient Greeks referred to as *gnosis*, a feminine noun meaning "knowledge" or "awareness." Gnosis is not about theoretical knowledge, but rather, it encompasses personal and spiritual insight. Through gnosis, the seeker awakens the divine spark within, beginning the quest for liberation from the illusions and limitations of the material world.

The power of the Philosopher's Stone lies in its ability to bridge different levels of existence—spirit and matter, light and darkness, the Above and Below. It exists in a liminal space, suspended between what is and is not, between energy and matter. Zosimos of Panopolis described it as "not a stone," something precious yet without value, a shapeless entity of many forms, known universally yet unknowable.

The Philosopher's Stone is called by many names, including Milk of Virgin, Spittle of the Moon, Urine of Boys, Menstruum, and the Toad, each representing different materials used to create this elusive object. The oldest known cipher for the Philosopher's Stone is the sign for cinnabar, a naturally occurring mineral that unites sulfur and mercury. Cinnabar typically forms in a bright red trigonal crystal structure, and is often found in volcanic or hot spring regions. When cinnabar is heated in an open flame, pure mercury weeps from cracks in the crystal.

In 1564, English magician John Dee created the Hieroglyphic Monad, a symbol that served both as a philosophical emblem and a tool for alchemical transmutation. Dee designed this symbol as a key to unlocking the secrets of the cosmos and gaining spiritual insight. He shared with fellow alchemists that his symbol represented the precise interrelationship of planetary energies that form the Philosopher's Stone, and he believed that his symbol was, in fact, the Stone itself. As a painter and writer, I find Dee's interpretation of the Philosopher's Stone as a science of forms particularly compelling, as it suggests that the Stone is, essentially, a work of art.

The creation of the Philosopher's Stone is often referred to as the Great Work or Magnum Opus. This process unfolds in stages, each involving laboratory procedures, chemical color changes, spiritual practices, physical exercises, and artistic creation. Alchemists have developed various systems to describe these stages, with a notable contributor being George Ripley. Ripley was an English canon at the Priory of St. Augustine in Bridlington, Yorkshire, who dedicated much of his life to studying alchemy and the physical sciences. He is best known for his book *The Compound of Alchymy*, which outlines the "right and perfectest meanes" to produce the Philosopher's

Stone. We will use his stages in this text as a guide to unlock our own artistic Great Work. Let's engage in some exercises to prepare ourselves for these phases.

A Holy Experiment
CALL YOURSELF

To start cultivating the Philosopher's Stone, you must first gather yourself together. Find a quiet place—such as a park, a rooftop, the banks of a river, or the edge of a lake—and arrive in the present, switching off your phone and taking time to appreciate your environment with all of your senses. Start by calling your own name aloud (whichever name you most identify with), over and over, as if calling to a lost pet. Say it with intention and focus, letting the sound of your name fill the air. If you can't call your name loudly, perhaps due to your surroundings, you can call softly or even silently, and the exercise will work just as well.

Repeat this until you feel a response, as if a lost part of yourself is acknowledging the call and coming home. When you sense that response, pause and wait for that part of you to fully return, hearing or feeling anything that needs to be understood. Repeat this several times until you feel a sense of resolution.

Once this initial call-and-response phase seems complete, shift the sound of your name. Instead of repeating it as usual, allow it to transform. You might elongate it, drop vowels, add a growl, or turn it into a hum. Let your body and voice guide you to a sound that feels right in the moment. When you find a sound that resonates, place both hands gently over your heart and continue making the sound, focusing on the vibration in your chest. These altered sounds may draw aspects of yourself that respond to other names, including those not yet known to you. As you continue, new or hidden names may emerge organically through the practice. When the sounding feels complete, allow yourself to rest in stillness, giving space for insights, images, or sensations to arise.

This exercise helps gather parts of yourself that may have been left behind or scattered in past moments, bringing them into the present. It prepares you to approach the work of the Philosopher's Stone with clarity and a more total presence.

Failure Is God
HENNIG BRAND

Hennig Brand was a German alchemist active in the 17th century. Originally a merchant, Brand turned to alchemy in search of the Philosopher's Stone. In his experiments to create a substance that could transform materials into gold, he concentrated on urine, which he regarded as a "liquid gold" naturally produced by the body.

According to legend, Brand visited various pubs to collect urine from beer drinkers, as he needed a substantial amount for his experiments. Over several weeks, he boiled down over one thousand gallons of urine, which he reduced to a tar-like substance. Brand then mixed this substance with sand and charcoal, heating it to the highest temperature his furnace could reach. A white vapor began to form after he maintained the mixture at this extreme heat, which eventually condensed into thick drops that were highly flammable and emitted an eerie, greenish glow in the dark.

The substance discovered by Brand, which he later named phosphorus, derived from the Greek word *phosphoros*, meaning "light-bearer," captivated him immediately. The glowing light it emitted seemed supernatural, as if it were not just a physical phenomenon but a divine manifestation, a sign of God at work in nature. Brand believed he had found the very material at the heart of the Philosopher's Stone! As was common for alchemists of his time, Brand kept his discovery a secret and continued experimenting with phosphorus, hoping to use it to create gold. Despite his efforts, he was unsuccessful. Though Brand didn't fully understand the significance of what he had discovered, his work laid some of the foundation for the early development of modern chemistry.

Within fifty years, phosphorus began to be produced and sold to apothecaries, natural philosophers, and showmen, who highlighted its glowing properties in demonstrations at princely courts and scientific societies. By one hundred years after its discovery, phosphorus was included in chemistry textbooks. Another fifty years later, it had found practical household applications as mineral phosphates gradually replaced urine as the primary source material.

Hennig Brand did not profit from his discovery, but from an alchemist's perspective, "failure" is a crucial part of the process. Although his work did not yield the material gold he sought, it deepened his understanding of alchemy. The path toward creating the Philosopher's Stone is filled with challenges, setbacks, and failures, all of which are necessary stages in its development.

As we progress through the twelve stages of creating the Philosopher's Stone, there will be moments when things need to decay, break down, and rot in order to make way for new growth. Unexpected and strange things will arise, and goals may not always be met in the ways we anticipate. It is essential for an alchemist to approach these challenges with clarity of mind, humor, and the ability to confront limitations honestly and with flexibility.

For example, this past week, I received several rejection letters from artist residencies, which felt humiliating and disappointing. But then I thought of Hennig Brand and his glowing urine. Often, it's hard to tell whether something is a setback or part of a larger process. The key is practicing nonattachment. A scientist too focused on a specific outcome can unintentionally sabotage an experiment. Artistic experimentation, like scientific inquiry, is about embracing uncertainty and discovery as essential aspects of the process. Through trial and error, artists uncover new techniques, materials, and perspectives that would never have come about otherwise.

After reading the rejection letters, I printed out a picture of Hennig Brand and wrote "FAILURE IS GOD" beneath it, taping it above my work table. In *The Queer Art of Failure*, Jack Halberstam argues that failure prompts us to challenge capitalism, individualism, and conformity—things many people fail at. He writes, "The queer art of failure turns on the impossible, the improbable, the unlikely, and the unremarkable. It quietly loses, and in losing, it imagines other goals for life, for love, for art, and for being" (Halberstam 2011, 16). Are our failures actually jubilant reimaginations of the world? What a beautiful thought. Alchemists are masters of this kind of failure.

Scientific and artistic inquiry is riddled with unintended breakthroughs. Acts of creation occur as much by accident, limitation, and surprise as by deliberate technique. As we move through the stages of creating the Philosopher's Stone, we are called to honor this unpredictability. Transformation demands that we embrace every part of this undertaking: expansion and contraction, growth and loss, death and rebirth. The path is not straight but spiraling.

PART III

Rubedo

THE ROSY DAWN

The Twelve Keys to Create
the Philosopher's Stone

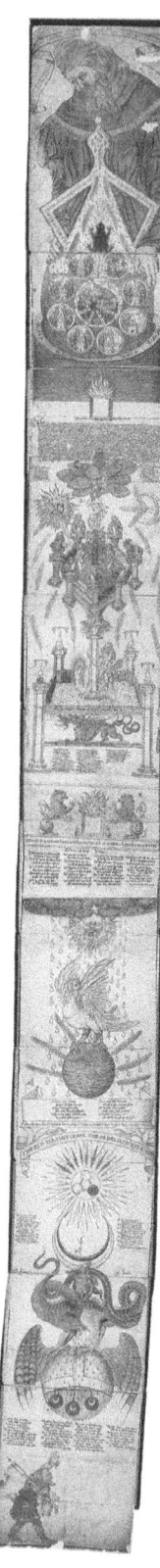

The full Ripley Scroll (1570) illustrating how to make the Philosopher's Stone. Beinecke Rare Book and Manuscript Library, Yale University.

The secret processes by which alchemists sought to create the Philosopher's Stone were structured into conceptual frameworks known as ladders, typically consisting of seven, twelve, or fifteen rungs. In George Ripley's *The Compound of Alchymy*, also known as *The Twelve Gates*, he outlines twelve distinct stages in the production of a Philosopher's Stone: calcination, solution, separation, conjunction, putrefaction, congelation, cibation, sublimation, fermentation, exaltation, multiplication, and finally, projection—the culminating act. The *Twelve Gates* references the Gospel of Matthew, where it says:

> *Enter through the narrow gate. For wide is the gate and broad is the road that leads to destruction, and many enter through it. But small is the gate and narrow the road that leads to life, and only a few find it. (Matthew 7:13–14, New International Version)*

The number twelve holds significant spiritual meaning across various cultures, symbolizing cosmic order, completeness, and divine harmony in ancient Egyptian and Greek thought. Twelve is linked to time cycles, as most solar calendars consist of twelve months in a year, and there are twelve hours in both day and night. In astrology, the twelve zodiac signs represent the soul's journey through different stages of life, with each sign offering unique spiritual lessons. The number twelve recurs in sacred mythologies and symbolic traditions, appearing in the twelve Olympian gods of Greek mythology, the twelve Apostles of Christianity, the twelve knights of King Arthur's Round Table, and the twelve animals of the Chinese zodiac.

In this guide, we will examine Ripley's twelve stages through three interconnected perspectives: their historical and laboratory applications, the symbolic and literary imagery associated with each stage, and their significance within both traditional alchemy and contemporary art practices. Additionally, you will find creative and contemplative exercises intended to promote personal insight. Ideally, you should dedicate about one month to each of the stages of this process, allowing a year for deep immersion into this transformative work. As you progress, you'll begin to integrate alchemical principles into your creative practice, gradually shaping your own Great Work.

I.

Calcination

THROUGH THE MEDITATIONS
OF THE ONE MIND

Zodiac: Aries ——————— **Planet:** Mars

Images: Flames, fire, cremation, phoenixes, dragons, salamanders, furnaces, funeral pyres, birds rising from flames, lions, hell, skulls, devils and imps

Material Applications: Burning, cremating, firing, scorching, spinning, friction, generating heat, emotions that generate heat (e.g., anger and enthusiasm)

> *Calcination is the purgation of our stone,*
> *And restoration also of its natural heat.*
> *Of radical humidity it looseth none,*
> *Inducing solution into our stone most mete.*
> *Seek after philosophy I you advise*
> *But not after the common guise,*
> *With sulphur and salts prepared in diverse ways.*
>
> —George Ripley, *The Compound of Alchymy*

The first step in climbing the "Mountain of the Wise" is calcination. *Calcination* is derived from the Latin root *calx*, meaning "lime" or "bone." To calcine a substance is to subject it to intense heat until it turns white or is reduced to ash. Alchemists, often called the "Philosophers of Fire," believed fire to be the primary agent of transformation. As the 20th-century alchemist Fulcanelli states, "All our purifications are done in fire, by fire, and with fire" (Fulcanelli 1984, 8). Calcination represents both the moment we ignite the Bunsen burner in our laboratory and the moment we spark our inner desire for transformation.

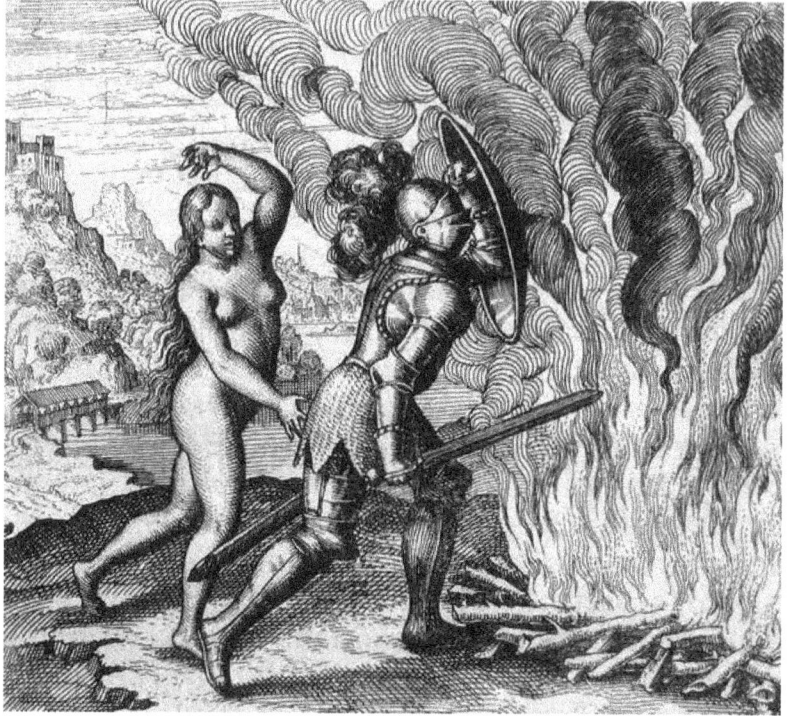

Sophia pushing the alchemist into the fires. Emblem 20 from *Atalanta Fugiens*,
by Michael Maier, illustrated by Matthäus Merian. Oppenheim, Germany, 1618.
Science History Institute Digital Collections, Science History Institute, Philadelphia.

During laboratory calcination, a substance is heated over an open flame or in a crucible until it turns to ash. Alchemists also viewed corrosive acids as a form of fire initiating the calcination process synthetically. One of the most famous goals of alchemy is to transform base metals into gold. Alchemists believed that to achieve this, base metals, which are more abundant and reactive than precious metals, needed to be "unmade" or dissolved as part of the process. To accomplish this, they employed mineral acids, known as vitriol, to dissolve the metals. Sulfuric acid, for example, is highly reactive and can dissolve most metals and cause charring on their surfaces. It reacts violently with alcohol and water, generating heat and behaving like a liquid fire.

Calcination also applies to our lived experiences and is connected to the "trials by fire" that test our commitment, resolve, and strength. During this stage of alchemy, our lives get "unmade" like base metals. When calcination arrives as an initiation, it can often feel as though we are trapped in the fires of hell. Surprisingly, it is not until these fires are burning that true transformation begins. As poet T. S. Eliot put it, "We are redeemed from fire by fire."

Calcination refers to those moments when we feel as though we have lost everything. These experiences prompt us to discover what is truly indestructible within us, teaching us humility and encouraging us to let go and allow for change. Calcination can ignite the courage needed to confront and dismantle the rigid structures we hold on to internally. Those who bravely face their own inner rigidity can become catalysts for collective change, sparking a transformative fire that challenges societal structures that have become tyrannical and intolerant.

After my first marriage ended explosively, I spent the better part of a year driving back and forth across the country in my old Toyota, fueled by anger and a desperate desire for revenge, unable to cede even an inch of rage. On a scorching 110-degree day in Arizona, with the air-conditioning in my car long broken, I was reduced to wearing only my underwear—my skin lobster red and drenched in sweat—as I drove without aim. After what felt like an eternity of roasting inside the magnifying glass of my car, I turned a corner and suddenly found myself overlooking Bell Rock, a vibrant, rippling red mountain glowing like an ember against the bright blue sky. I silently repeated lines from Sylvia Plath's poem "Lady Lazarus":

> *Out of the ash*
> *I rise with my red hair*
> *And I eat men like air (Plath 2004, 70)*

I pulled over, jumped onto the hood of the car, and shouted that last line into the scorching horizon—"I eat men like air!" I laughed so hard that the rage I had been trapped in began to shake loose. The calcified anger eventually melted enough that I could park my car back in New York and begin to slowly rebuild my life. The first stage of alchemy teaches us that when we avoid suffering, we create even more suffering. By accepting our suffering, we open ourselves to the courage necessary to make changes and seek support where we need it.

Pause here and remember a time when your carefully laid plans crumbled before your eyes. The identity you had built, the goals you believed defined you, and the way you thought others perceived you seemed to dissolve. It's sometimes true that what appears to be destruction in our lives may also be a form of grace. Eleventh-century Tibetan Buddhist nun Machig Labdrön, also known as the "Singular Mother Torch," reminds us:

You may think that Gods are the ones who give you benefits, and Demons cause damage; but it may be the other way round. Those who cause pain teach you to be patient, and those who give you presents may keep you from practising the Dharma. So it depends on their effect on you if they are Gods or Demons. (Edou 1996, 81)

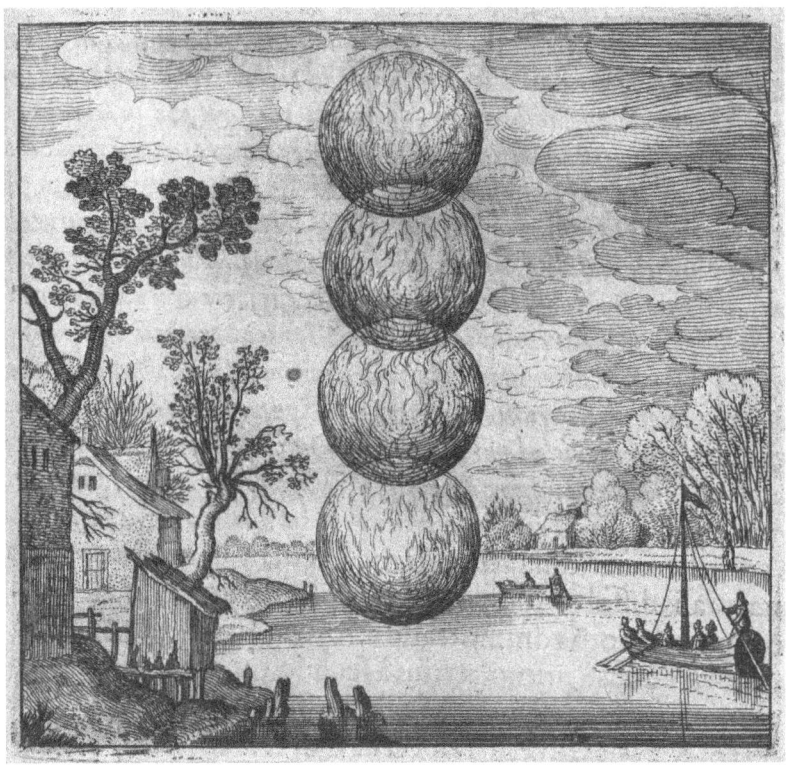

Four orbs of fire floating above a river. Emblem 17 from *Atalanta Fugiens*, by Michael Maier, illustrated by Matthäus Merian. Oppenheim, Germany, 1618. Science History Institute Digital Collections, Science History Institute, Philadelphia.

In the Beginning, There Was One Mind

European alchemists classified fire into four distinct categories: elementary fire, secret fire, central fire, and celestial fire. Elementary fire refers to the tangible fire we encounter in our daily lives, such as flames from a lighter, stove, or a vial of vitriol. These fires are physical and induce changes on a material level. Secret fire symbolizes the inner fire within an alchemist's consciousness. It represents awareness, thought, and cognitive power. Central fire denotes creativity itself—the catalyzing energy that brings things into existence. It serves as the driving force of life and growth throughout the cosmos. Lastly, celestial fire embodies the cosmic consciousness that pervades the entire universe.

Ultimately, fire serves as a metaphor for the force of creativity. In the alchemical tradition, the One Mind ignites our existence through a flash of light, and this spark continues to operate through the individual fires that burn within our minds. Consciousness becomes cosmos, and every creative principle that flows from this origin is known as natural law. Alchemists believed that all things—both material and immaterial—possess a form of awareness, an inner fire passed from the creator like a torch.

To understand their own creativity and the process of creation, alchemists often look to the origins of the universe itself. The Emerald Tablet is a short text regarded by Arabic and European alchemists as the foundation of their art. Attributed to the legendary Hermes Trismegistus, the Emerald Tablet first appears in several early medieval Arabic sources, the oldest of which dates to the late 8th or early 9th century. Numerous interpretations and commentaries followed. Dr. Edward Edinger calls the Emerald Tablet "the cryptic epitome of the alchemical opus, a recipe for the second creation of the world" (Edinger 1985, 18).

We'll be working with Dennis William Hauck's modern translation of the Emerald Tablet, from his book *The Emerald Tablet: Alchemy for Personal Transformation* (2003, 45). This text is designed to be contemplated over one's entire practice as an alchemist, allowing its meaning to evolve over time. For now, we'll concentrate on the second and third rubrics.

In truth, without deceit, certain and most veritable.

That which is Below corresponds to that which is Above,
and that which is Above corresponds to that which is Below
to accomplish the miracle of the One Thing.

And just as all things have come from this One Thing
through the meditation of One Mind, so do all created
things originate from this One Thing, through Transformation.

Its father is the Sun; Its mother the Moon.
The Wind carries it in its belly; its nurse is the Earth.
It is the origin of All, the consecration of the Universe;
Its inherent Strength is perfected, if it is turned into Earth.

Separate the Earth from Fire, the Subtle from the Gross,
gently and with great Ingenuity. It rises from Earth to Heaven
and descends again to Earth, thereby combining within Itself
the powers of both the Above and the Below.

Thus will you obtain the Glory of the Whole Universe.
All Obscurity will be clear to you. This is the greatest
force of all powers, because it overcomes every Subtle thing
and penetrates every Solid thing.

In this way was the Universe created.
From this will come many wondrous Applications,
because this is the Pattern.

Therefore am I called Thrice Greatest Hermes,
having all three parts of the wisdom of the Whole Universe.
Herein have I completely explained the Operation of the Sun.

The first rubric urges us to take the Emerald Tablet seriously and remain open to deeper truths. The second rubric introduces the Doctrine of Correspondences, which describes the connection between the spiritual realm (Above) and the material realm (Below). The second paragraph of this rubric explains how alchemists viewed creation: they believed the One Mind, or divine consciousness, gave rise to the One Thing, the primal substance. This dynamic created a flash of light from which all creation emerged.

Contemporary science explains creation through the Big Bang theory, which suggests that the universe began as an infinitely hot and dense point that expanded over 13.7 billion years into the cosmos we know today. According to the Emerald Tablet, this dense point is seen as a mind expanding its consciousness.

The term *Monad*, derived from the Ancient Greek *monas* meaning "unity" or *monos* meaning "alone," is sometimes used interchangeably with One Mind. In Pythagorean cosmology, the Monad represents the Supreme Being, divinity, or totality of all existence. According to this system, the Monad was the first entity to come into existence, from which the Dyad (the two) emerged, eventually giving rise to all other numbers. The Monad is depicted as a dot that leads to a line, that leads to more lines, surrounded by the chaotic abyss from which it emerges.

Practice Calcination

THE MIND AS A DOT

Place a pen or a pencil on a piece of paper and make a single dot. Allow the pen or pencil to radiate outward from this dot, making marks freely. When you are finished, set a timer for three minutes. Freewrite about what a mind is. Then freewrite about what *your* mind is. When the timer goes off, contemplate the dot and what emanates from it.

Intuitively feel the movement of a dot making lines. What is this movement? Is it a thought? Is it knowledge? Is it awareness?

Next, write a list of seven things you know about yourself with certainty. Then, list seven things you absolutely don't know about yourself. As you write the second list, does the first one start to feel less certain? Does creating these lists expand your understanding of what it means to *know* and to know yourself?

In the construct of the cosmos presented in the Emerald Tablet, our concept of self derives from our concept of the creation of this world. Alchemical texts encourage us to widen our concept of self so we can expand our creative process as well. In one particularly beautiful section of the *Corpus Hermeticum*, the student Tat asks the teacher Hermes Trismegistus how he can come to know God. Hermes answers:

> *If then you do not make yourself equal to God, you cannot apprehend God; for like is known by like. Leap clear of all that is corporeal, and make yourself grown to a like expanse with that greatness which is beyond all measure; rise above all time and become eternal; then you will apprehend God. Think that for you too nothing is impossible; deem that you too are immortal, and that you are able to grasp all things in your thought, to know every craft and science; find your home in the haunts of every living creature; make yourself higher than all heights and lower than all depths; bring together in yourself all opposites of quality, heat and cold, dryness and fluidity; think that you are everywhere at once, on land, at sea, in heaven; think that you are not yet begotten, that you are in the womb, that you are young, that you are old, that you have died, that you are in the world beyond the grave; grasp in your thought all of this at once, all times and places, all substances and qualities and magnitudes together; then you can apprehend God.*

But if you shut up your soul in your body, and abase yourself, and say "I know nothing, I can do nothing; I am afraid of earth and sea, I cannot mount to heaven; I know not what I was, nor what I shall be," then what have you to do with God? (Copenhaver 1995, 22)

Alchemy encourages us to recognize the extraordinary nature of our creative abilities, inspiring us to achieve what may seem impossible. Imagine the cosmic energy that created the universe as a reflection of your own consciousness, and understand that your consciousness holds the same creative power. This is the essence of alchemy.

John Baldessari

THE CREMATION PROJECT

John Baldessari (1931–2020), an influential American conceptual artist, used the fires of calcination to dismantle the fixed and rigid ideas he held about himself as an artist.

Initially an abstract painter in the 1950s, Baldessari eventually grew disillusioned with both his own work and painting as an art form. In 1970, he symbolically destroyed his past by gathering a collection of paintings from his early career—created between 1953 and 1966—and taking them to a funeral home in San Diego to be cremated.

This ritual, known as the *Cremation Project*, involved photographing the paintings before burning them. The ashes of the paintings were then collected and placed in numbered, signed boxes. A memorial plaque was created to commemorate the dates of the destroyed works, like an epitaph for his earlier artistic life. A catalog for an exhibition of this work featured photographs of Baldessari tearing up canvases with his hands alongside the words "a life's work goes up in flames."

Through this act of destruction, Baldessari freed himself from the constraints of traditional painting and embraced a diverse range of media, including video, photography, text-based art, and hybrid forms like text paintings. Art historian Lynne Cooke described the act as "a liberation," viewing it as a shift toward a broader creative realm that has no limits, which is precisely the way the *Corpus Hermeticum* encourages us to operate (Cooke 1990, 512).

Practice Calcination

AN ARTIST'S FUNERAL PYRE

John Baldessari's *Cremation Project* serves as a powerful exercise in breaking free from rigid artistic identities and exploring the potential for creative reinvention. For this exercise, you will symbolically destroy one aspect of your artistic practice that feels limiting or outdated—something that has become fixed in your approach, whether that's a medium, style, habit, or belief about your work. An example in my own practice is a hardened habit of scatteredness that prevents me from finishing anything.

Begin by examining your past work, focusing on a particular piece you feel represents an outmoded phase in your creative evolution. It could be a painting, a sculpture, a photograph, or even a specific technique that you've clung to. Acknowledge why you feel this part of your creative life has completed its purpose for now. For myself, I chose an unfinished painting for this exercise.

Like Baldessari, take photographs of the work. Then, physically alter it in a way that symbolizes its destruction. This could involve cutting the piece, tearing it up, painting over it, or digitally altering an image. The key is not to destroy the work for the sake of destruction, but to signify the end of one creative phase and the opening of something new.

Create a symbolic memorial for the work you've let go of. This could be a small written piece, a plaque, or a digital file that includes the name of the work, the date it was destroyed, and a brief description of its significance in your creative development.

Finally, take the energy of this release and use it as a springboard for creating something new. Try a medium or approach that you've never explored before, whether it's text-based art, video, hybrid forms, or something else entirely. Embrace the freedom that comes from letting go of old conventions and allow yourself to experiment.

II.

Solution
LETTING IT GO IS
WHAT MAKES IT STAY

Zodiac: Pisces ——————— **Planet:** Jupiter

Images: Water, pools, oceans, lakes, rivers, floods, underground streams, whales, two fish, mermaids squirting breast milk, figures swimming out to sea, tears, bodily secretions, menstruation, melting, overflowing vessels, tubs

Material Applications: Bathing, baptism, submerging, dissolving, erosion, crying, secreting, softening, acceptance

> *One in gender they be, and in number two,*
> *Whose father is the Sun, the Moon the mother,*
> *Mercury moves between,*
> *These and no more be our Magnesia, our Adrop,*
> *And no other things be here, but only sister and brother,*
> *That is to mean, agent and patient,*
> *Sulphur and Mercury, co-essential to our intent.*
>
> —George Ripley, *The Compound of Alchymy*

Solution, also known as solutio or dissolution, is an alchemical process in which solid matter is transformed into a liquid state, typically by immersing solids in a solvent, such as water. This process follows calcination to further loosen rigidity and hardness. Solution softens the boundaries between self and other, blurring the lines that separate them. This union and release can feel like an ecstatic flooding of the soul, a deep emotional surrender that often results in tears. Indian saint Anandamayi Ma describes this state by saying, "When the flood of your tears causes the inner and outer worlds to merge as one, you will discover Her, whom you have sought with such anguish, closer than anything else—like the very breath of life and the core of every heart" (Ma 2002, 61). For the alchemist, dissolving solid matter symbolizes liberation—a removal of superficial separateness and hardness that limit evolutionary potential and cause isolation and dangerous othering.

In her book *The Interior Castle*, St. Teresa of Avila compares prayer to flowing water, describing her experience of union with God as "water in water." She writes:

> *Here it is like rain falling from the heavens into a river or a spring; there*
> *is nothing but water, and it is impossible to divide or separate the water*
> *belonging to the river from that which fell from the heavens. Or it is as if a tiny*
> *streamlet enters the sea, from which it will find no way of separating itself...*
> *(Teresa of Avila 1961, 64)*

Water is known as the universal solvent because it can dissolve more substances than any other liquid. The process of solution encourages us to let go of the rigid parts of our psyche that prevent us from experiencing the true intimacy needed for alchemical work. A genuine connection with our ideas, a bond with our materials, and a deep affection for the Soul of the World, which is inseparable from our own, are crucial for the success of our creative endeavors.

As Lao Tzu says in the *Tao Te Ching*: "Water is fluid, soft, and yielding. Yet water can wear away rock, which is rigid and unyielding. Generally, what is fluid, soft, and yielding will ultimately overcome what is rigid and hard. This presents another paradox: what is soft is strong" (Lao Tzu 1988, 78). It is through this process of softening and the willingness to flow that true strength is revealed.

Personal experiences of solution can often be found in communal activities such as dancing, falling in love, participating in group rituals, or choral singing—anything that connects you to a greater sense of wholeness and blurs the boundaries between self and not self. However, my most profound experiences of solution have occurred in moments of solitude away from other humans when I felt completely at ease and able to let go.

One humid afternoon when I was around ten years old, the air was thick with the smell of impending rain and the sounds of buzzing insects. I found myself alone in the forest behind my aunt's house. A wave of inspiration compelled me to run down the trails through the trees as fast as I could, shedding my clothes along the way. After racing through the forest until it became a green blur, I eventually stopped to catch my breath. My heart was pounding, and I felt a surge of explosive joy. In that moment, I was one with the forest: naked, alive, and exhilarated by our union. The sensation of my sweating skin against the scaly bark of the trees, the cool, slick moss underfoot, the shimmering emerald shells of beetles, the rhythmic pounding of my blood, and the melodies of the birds combined to create a singular being.

Medieval alchemists believed that the salt in tears was the residue of crystallized thoughts and prescribed crying for a wide range of psychic ailments. A few years ago, I was dealing with trying and failing to conceive. Month after month, pregnancy tests came back negative, and I felt helpless. One afternoon, after receiving another negative test result, I clenched my jaw and decided to run errands, trying to steel myself against my sorrow and pretend that nothing was wrong. I spent a miserable afternoon walking the city streets, weighed down by shopping bags and a sense of disappointment I didn't want to face. I walked by St. Thomas Church in Manhattan and decided to step inside to rest for a while. As I walked in, I nodded ruefully toward a wooden statue of the Virgin Mary with a plaque beneath it that read, "Our Lady of Fifth Avenue."

Then I caught her gaze. In her eyes, I saw the grief of all beings who experience loss. There she sat, cradling her baby, who would soon be crucified. Images of Mary cradling Christ's lifeless body flooded my memory. Overcome, I sat down in front of her, lowered my head, and began to sob. I cried until my grief expanded beyond my own losses and flowed into the grief of other beings experiencing despair. The pain of my own loss brought me closer to the sea of sorrow that has the power to break a heart wide open. I sat there weeping for the rest of the afternoon, not just for myself but for people suffering everywhere. When I finally left the church, I felt as light as the wind and as tender as an infant. I was full of love.

In early childhood, we start to distinguish between the self and the other, as well as between what is "mine" and what is not. Over time, our understanding of identity deepens, evolving into a more defined sense of me and mine. This concept of self—with its unique traits, preferences, and roles—is essential to our well-being. It supports our mental and physical stability, provides a sense of continuity across time, and helps us measure personal growth. Through it, we come to recognize our strengths and acknowledge our limitations.

As we mature and develop a broader awareness, we can begin to question these fixed ideas of self and other. Take some time to reflect on how solution has presented itself in your life. What are some of the most potent experiences that have allowed you to feel connected to something beyond your individual identity? How might embracing a sense of interconnectedness enrich your relationships and deepen your compassion? In what ways does solution emerge in your creative practice?

Practice Solution

THE ART OF BAPTISM

The term *baptism* derives from the Greek word *baptizo*, meaning "to immerse" or "to dip." Ritual washing and purification were common in ancient Greece, Egypt, and the broader Hellenistic context, often associated with cleansing impurities or sin. In Judaism, for instance, the mikvah was used for spiritual cleansing, particularly before major religious observances. Similarly, in certain Hellenistic mystery religions—such as those honoring Dionysus—water immersion symbolized death and rebirth, marking a transformative passage or initiation. Early Christians drew from these traditions, reinterpreting them in light of Jesus's resurrection and infusing the practice with their own theological meaning.

In alchemy, it is essential to incorporate the concept of baptism into both personal and creative practices, using acts of immersion and cleansing in physical and symbolic ways. Ritualized bathing can serve as a practice of personal rebirth, preparing you for new beginnings or transformations. This can be achieved by submerging the body in sacred waters outdoors or by preparing pitchers of water indoors that are infused with elements such as moonlight, sunlight, plants, metals, and minerals, each chosen to evoke a specific transformation. You can then pour these charged waters over yourself in a shower or bath or use them to wash your hands and feet before practicing alchemy or use magical waters to cleanse your tools and workspace.

Ritual washing before beginning an experiment or creative practice helps attune you to the sacred rhythms of nature. It clears both inner and outer obstacles, creating space for focus and openness. To begin this practice, choose an object from your alchemist's altar that you feel called to baptize. Select a fluid based on the emotions it stirs and its connection to personal or planetary energies—such as ocean water, rain, tears, or perfumes. Then align the ritual with a meaningful moment in the cosmic or natural cycle. This might be a New Moon, symbolizing fresh starts; a Jupiter cazimi, when Jupiter is conjoined with the Sun and amplifies expansion; or the brightest hour of the summer solstice, when solar energy reaches its zenith. For example, I have a statue of Jupiter that I regularly bathe with thunderstorm water I've collected—always on Thursdays, the day ruled by Jupiter. Over time, these acts of devotion create a sense of rhythm, deepening your relationship with both the object and the energies it embodies.

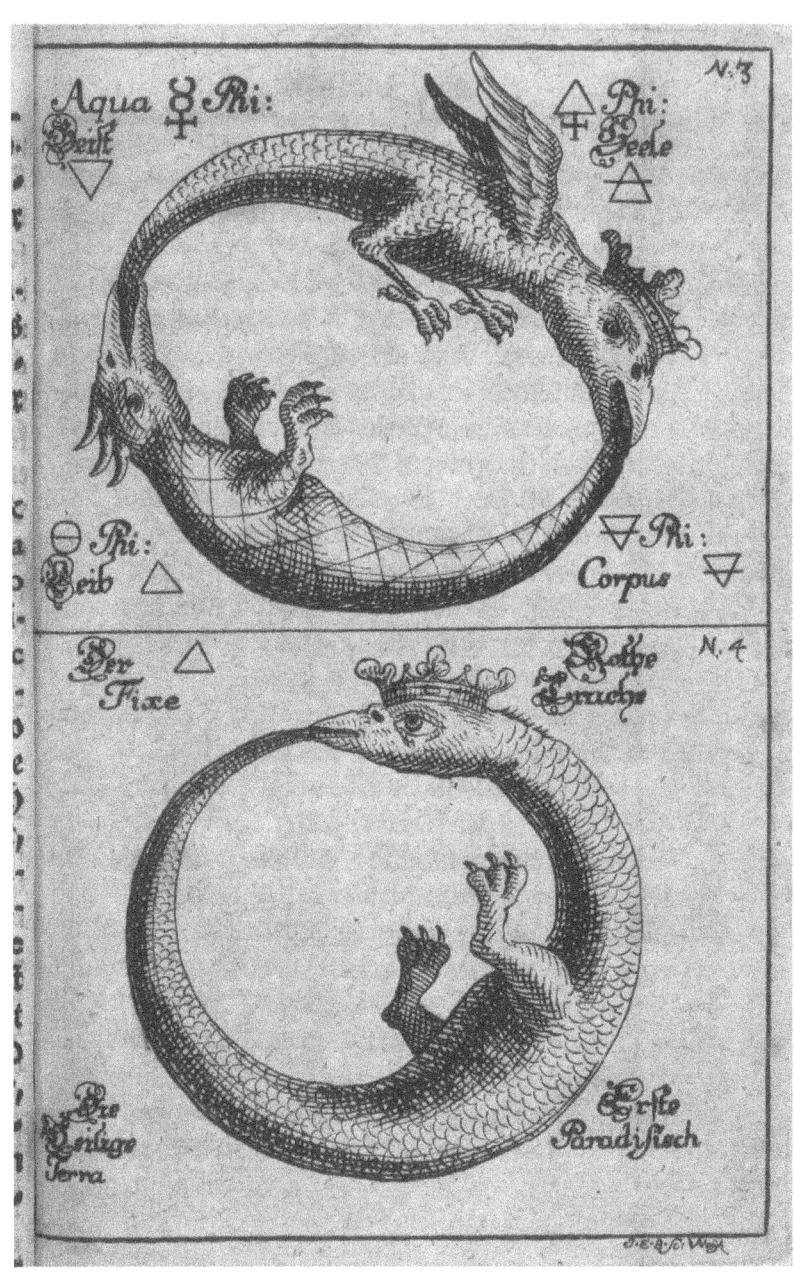

From *Uraltes chymisches Werck*, by Abraham Eleazar. Erfurt, 1735.
Embassy of the Free Mind | Bibliotheca Philosophica Hermetica Collection.

Repeat these baptisms weekly, and observe how the object's energy evolves with your own. Notice how it begins to hold a charge—reflecting your intentions, deepening your relationship with it, and becoming a living part of your creative and spiritual practice.

Being and Nonbeing Arise Together

This image of two dragons forming a circle, with a third dragon completing its own circular motion, is taken from an 18th-century alchemical manuscript, *Uraltes chymisches Werck*. The image symbolizes the unity of opposites—a core principle in understanding the alchemical concept of solution. When we examine one idea, its opposite naturally arises alongside it—for example, we can only understand *up* in contrast to *down*. In alchemy, these opposites are not seen as conflicting forces but as interdependent aspects of a greater whole.

In the alchemical tradition, dualism is regarded as an illusion—one that can be transcended by "those who have eyes to see." This phrase points to the deeper vision required to perceive the hidden unity behind apparent divisions. Consider how red-and-blue 3D glasses create the illusion of depth: each eye sees a slightly different image, but together they reveal a unified, three-dimensional form. In alchemy, you develop a "solar" eye to perceive the material world and a "lunar" eye to recognize the immaterial aspects of existence. When combined, the solar perspective (which views things as separate) and the lunar perspective (which sees things as a whole) create a more accurate picture of reality. The alchemist learns to hold opposing truths simultaneously, recognizing that all dualities ultimately arise from—and return to—the One Mind.

The *Tao Te Ching* is a foundational text of Taoism, attributed to the Chinese philosopher Lao Tzu and written in the 6th century BCE. It consists of eighty-one short chapters that combine poetry and philosophy, exploring themes such as the nature of flow, the relativity of opposites, and the interconnectedness of all things.

From chapter II of the *Tao Te Ching* as translated by Ursula K. Le Guin (1998, 16):

> *Everybody on earth knowing*
> *that beauty is beautiful*
> *makes ugliness.*
> *Everybody knowing*
> *that goodness is good*
> *makes wickedness.*

For being and nonbeing
arise together;
hard and easy
complete each other;
high and low
depend on each other;
note and voice
make the music together;
before and after
follow each other.
That's why the wise soul
does without doing,
teaches without talking.
The things of this world
exist, they are;
you can't refuse them.
To bear and not to own;
to act and not lay claim;
to do the work and let it go:
for just letting it go
is what makes it stay.

This passage emphasizes that nothing exists in isolation; everything is interconnected. We must be careful not to judge the natural flow of the world based on our limited perceptions and experiences. Instead, we should approach our preferences for one thing over another with openness and flexibility, resisting the urge to pit opposites against each other.

For example, the dominant American culture values youth over old age, even though both are natural stages of life. By prioritizing youth, we create an environment where aging is feared and disrespected, leading to feelings of loss, alienation, and suffering as time progresses. This fear of aging often translates into a fear of death, hindering our ability to prepare for this inevitability. For older individuals, ageism can result in feelings of invisibility, isolation, and diminished self-worth associated with the perception of being irrelevant or burdensome. This bias fosters a divide between the young and the old, obstructing the natural flow of life.

It's essential to reflect on the binaries and biases inherent in our perspectives. Do we prefer beauty over ugliness? Who defines these concepts of beauty and why? What forms of suffering do these distinctions create?

Lao Tzu introduces the concept of *wu wei* in the passage we read. This central idea in Taoism is often translated as "nonaction" or "effortless action." It does not imply passivity; instead, it refers to the art of aligning with the flow of life, allowing things to unfold without unnecessary force or resistance. It represents a state of acting in harmony with the Tao, or the natural order, where movement is spontaneous, fluid, and in tune with the world's rhythms.

In this state, there is a profound sense of ease, akin to a river flowing effortlessly around obstacles. Wu wei encourages individuals to act with clarity, simplicity, and grace, free from attachment to specific outcomes or excessive control. This illuminates the practice of achieving more by doing less—recognizing that true wisdom and effectiveness come from being present and allowing events to unfold in their own time and manner rather than striving forcefully to shape them. It embodies the paradox that we often achieve the best results by letting go.

Sophia

THE VOICE OF THE THUNDER HERSELF

The Thunder, Perfect Mind is a Coptic text believed to be part of the Gnostic canon. It follows the style of aretalogy, which was used to praise goddesses like Isis, who was often identified with Sophia in the Hellenistic world. In the poem, Sophia describes herself paradoxically—both honored and cursed, masculine and feminine, life and death, the cause of peace and war. The text focuses on the interconnection of opposing forces as a source of strength without denying any aspects of the polarities she embodies:

Do not be ignorant of me.
For I am the first and the last.
I am the honored one and the scorned one.
I am the whore and the holy one.
I am the solace of my labor pains.
I am the bride and the bridegroom,
and it is my husband who begot me.
I am the wife and the virgin.
I am the mother and the daughter.
I am the members of my mother.
I am the barren one,
and many are her sons.

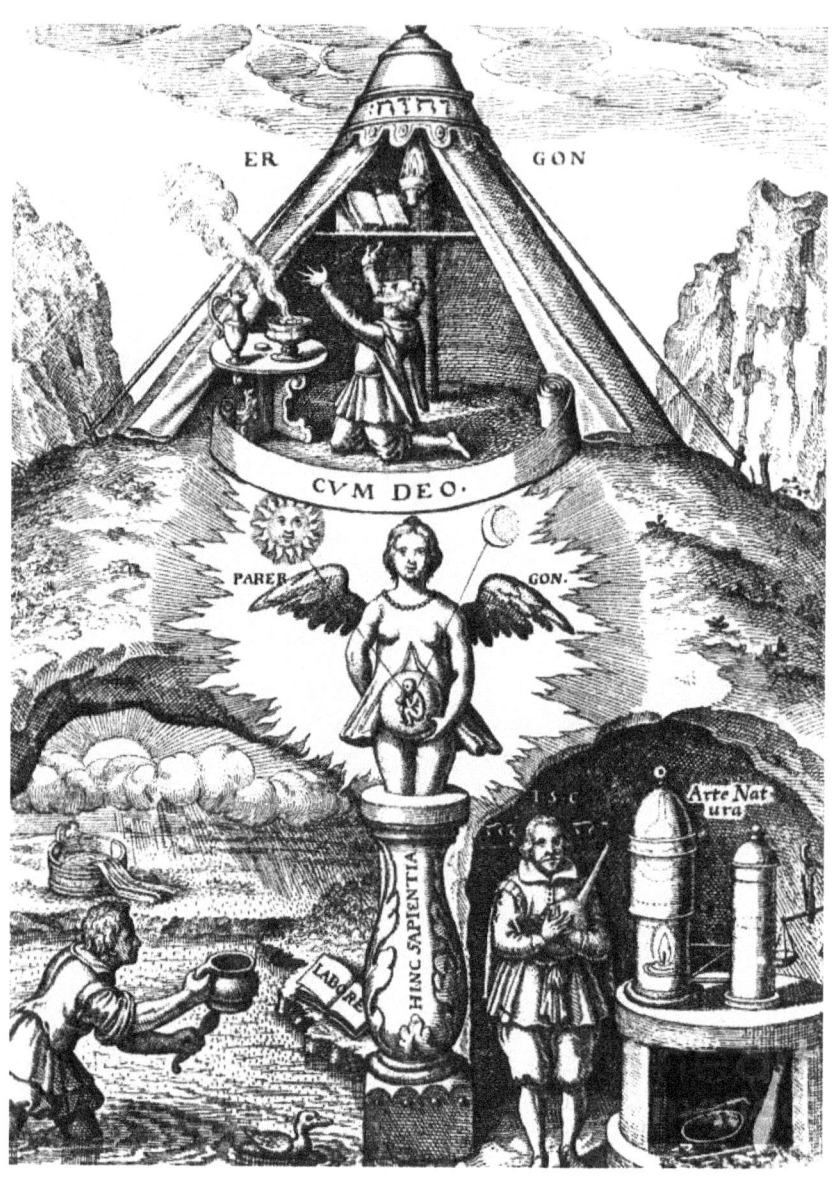

Ilustration of Sophia, surrounded by seekers. From *Speculum sophicum Rhodo-Stauroticum*, by Theophilus Schweighardt, 1618. 17th Century Prints, Saxon State and University Library Dresden, Germany.

I am she whose wedding is great,
and I have not taken a husband.
I am the midwife, and she who does not bear.

. . . .

You who tell the truth about me, lie about me,
and you who have lied about me, tell the truth about me.
You who know me, be ignorant of me,
and those who have not known me, let them know me.
For I am knowledge and ignorance.
I am shame and boldness.
I am shameless; I am ashamed.
I am strength and I am fear.
I am war and peace.
Give heed to me. (Robinson 1988, 295)

This text is powerful precisely because it is filled with contradictions. The speech gains strength as it highlights the polarities that have defined the goddess, transcending and dismantling them in the process.

Within a European context that deeply repressed the divine feminine, Renaissance-era alchemists revered Sophia. They referred to themselves as the Sons of Sophia and called her the Anima Mundi, Sapientia, or Lady Alchymeia. They viewed Sophia as the creator of the Soul of the World, believing that she could initiate them into the mysteries of nature and the natural sciences. Sophia crowns the alchemist after they have achieved the Great Work of creating the Philosopher's Stone.

Just Let It Go

SOPHIA STUNS THOMAS AQUINAS INTO SILENCE

Thomas Aquinas (1225–1274) was a towering figure in medieval philosophy, Catholic theology, and alchemy, whose writings have profoundly influenced Western thought. His most famous work, the unfinished *Summa Theologica*, addresses a wide range of theological and ethical questions, and his ideas on ethics, metaphysics, and the nature of God have shaped Christian doctrine for centuries. In his writings, Aquinas subscribed to the prevailing medieval view that women were inferior to men. In *Summa Theologica*, he argued that women were "imperfect" men, created as a "secondary" form of humanity. He contends that women's intellectual and moral capacities are lesser than men's and maintains a fixed view that women are more susceptible to sin.

In 1273, Aquinas had a profound mystical vision that changed the course of his life and work. This event, sometimes referred to as his "vision of Sophia," occurred during an afternoon of deep prayer and contemplation in the solitude of his study. For Aquinas, who had dedicated much of his life to writing and teaching about God, reason, and the relationship between faith and knowledge from a patriarchal rationalist perspective, this experience was transformative.

Sophia appeared in his study and revealed to him that reality was far greater than anything he could truly know, helping him recognize that the depths of divine truth surpassed all human understanding and intellectual pursuits. He famously declared afterward, "All that I have written seems like straw to me."

After this encounter, he withdrew from his scholarly work, believing that his vision had revealed a more profound, unutterable truth beyond human reason or the written word. Several of his most famous works end abruptly in the middle of a paragraph, never to be finished. He told his fellow monks that he had found the Philosopher's Stone in the silent wisdom of Sophia.

An alchemist must be willing to let go, ultimately, of every single idea they have and soften into a wisdom beyond words. This is the gift of solution.

Divine Tears

BAS JAN ADER

Bas Jan Ader (1942–1975?) was a Dutch conceptual artist known for his emotionally charged and poetic performance works that explored themes of vulnerability, failure, and the sublime. His use of fluids—particularly water and tears—played a central role in his exploration of fragility and the human condition.

Ader's works frequently explore themes of risk and uncertainty, with water serving as both a literal and metaphorical medium for the artist's struggle against forces beyond his control. In one of his most iconic pieces, *I'm Too Sad to Tell You* (1971), Ader filmed himself in close-up, weeping passionately. The film engulfs the viewer in his tears and connects to them in a grief too overwhelming to describe.

Water also figures prominently in his works involving canals, such as *Fall* (1970). The short, black-and-white film shows Ader riding a bicycle along the edge of an Amsterdam canal. After a brief, calm moment of balance, he suddenly veers off and plunges—bike and all—into the water. His final performance took place in July 1975. Ader set sail from Chatham, Massachusetts, in his tiny boat

Ocean Wave, bound for Falmouth, England, as part of his artwork *In Search of the Miraculous*. Planned to last two to three months and conclude with an exhibition at the Groninger Museum, the voyage would have made *Ocean Wave* the smallest vessel ever to cross the Atlantic, but the boat never arrived. The vessel was found floating at a strange angle some months later, with no trace of Ader on board. His disappearance and presumed death marked the tragic conclusion of work grappling with the fleeting nature of life, the search for meaning, and the mysterious forces that govern our existence.

Practice Solution

POEMS FROM THE DEEP—INK GAZING

Water gazing, also known as hydromancy, is a method of divination that involves gazing into a body of water—typically a calm, reflective surface, such as a bowl or crystal clear glass of water—to receive visions, insights, or guidance. As the still water becomes a mirror, it is said to open a doorway to the other realms where images, symbols, or intuitive impressions may arise. The practice encourages a meditative, receptive state of mind. I like to do this with sumi ink to tap into the depths of my psyche and allow for creative turns of line and shape in painting that would not otherwise occur to me.

To try this yourself, set up a small, shallow dish of sumi ink, a brush, and a piece of paper. Place the dish of ink at an angle where there are as few reflections in the surface as possible in your line of sight. Surround the container with a ring of salt, creating a protective boundary that shields you from inviting in any energies not aligned with your intentions.

Take a deep, steadying breath, and then gaze into the ink's surface, letting your mind soften. The gaze should be gentle: allow yourself to blink lightly and your breath to loosen and become calm. Find the deepest spot in the ink, the one with a type of magnetism that feels like it's pulling your eyes, and fix your gaze there. Spend ten to twenty minutes softening and softening into this deep, mysterious space.

When you're ready, dip your brush into the ink and allow yourself to intuitively pull shapes and words out of the ink onto paper. Allow this to continue flowing, and do not look too closely at what you're creating. When you're ready to close the session, carefully dispose of the salt, clearing away any lingering energies. Finally, return the ink to its bottle using a small funnel. This is now an ink that has been consecrated with your gaze; treat it as precious. Look back at the sheet of paper with your intuitive marks—what's there?

III.

Separation
FINDING THE INNER STAR

Zodiac: Aquarius ——————— **Planet:** Saturn

Images: Swords, knives, hatchets, axes, dismemberment, decapitation, divorce, crows, heaven and earth splitting, the parting of the seas

Material Applications: Cutting, cleaving, extracting, editing, dissecting, chopping, decluttering, disagreement, refusal, hermitude, silence

> *Separation does each part from the other divide,*
> *The subtle from the gross, the thick from the thin,*
> *But look you set aside manual Separation,*
> *For that pertains to fools that little good do win,*
> *But in our Separation Nature does not cease,*
> *Making division of qualities elemental,*
> *Into a fifth degree till they be turned all.*

> —George Ripley, *The Compound of Alchymy*

Alchemical preparations traditionally unfold in three main stages: separation, purification, and recombination—the final stage often called the Chymical Wedding. In the separation stage, specific components are extracted from the alchemist's materials. For example, alchemists developed methods for effectively removing lavender essential oil from the plant using steam distillation, which involves passing steam through cut-up plant material, causing the essential oils to evaporate and collect in a concentrated form. Alchemical laboratory work is not just a series of mechanical processes, however; the alchemist's soul is intricately connected to their experiment, and the extent of the alchemist's emotional and spiritual wakefulness influences the success of the transformation. Separation is understood as a profoundly sacred and emotional event, where materials experience suffering before they yield to transformation—as people often do. Before yielding essential oil, a lavender plant undergoes the painful processes of being cut, dried, boiled, and cooled.

In the book *Visions of Zosimos*, which discusses the transmutation of metals, copper speaks to Zosimos in a dream, describing the agony they endure during chemical transformation. "I undergo an intolerable violence," copper says, "Someone came hastily in the morning, and he assaulted me, stabbing me with a sword, and dismembered me, according to the rules of the combination. He removed all the skin from my head, with the sword he held in hand" (Zosimos of Panopolis 1937, 89). Zosimos feels the pain of his copper as keenly as if it were his own—because it is.

Alchemists do not shy away from representing the pain involved in separation; instead, they emphasize it, understanding its role as a challenging teacher. In alchemical thought, the process of separation prepares us for the ultimate task: the separation of our soul from the body at the time of death.

Our lessons in separation start at the moment of our birth; as infants, we leave our mother's womb, take a big gulp of air, and have our umbilical cord severed as we scream in our terror and discomfort. A baby's first cry is crucial in transitioning from fetal circulation to life outside. It clears excess fluid from their airways, nose, and mouth and helps the baby's lungs adapt to breathing independently. As we navigate through life, separation continues. Separation from groups of belonging, schools, systems of thought, lovers, jobs, and family members continues to mark our stages of development.

Those who walk the mystic's path often experience a sense of separation from their communities, whether by choice or circumstance. A contemporary American mystic might feel lonely because their deep introspections and inner experiences demand the quiet and space for reflection that fall outside of the capitalist logic of constant productivity and sociability. Mystics make decisions driven by intuition or spiritual insight and can seem "out there" to those who prioritize a different rationale for living. A few weeks ago, at my dad's seventy-fifth birthday party, my brother asked what was new as we all feasted on pizza. "Well, I'm trying to figure out how to buy this old Catholic church upstate so I can turn it into an alchemy school and quit my job at the university," I replied. What felt to me like a lighthearted life update was met with stunned silence. My dad stared at me, horrified. "You want to quit your *job*?" Everyone at the table looked uncomfortable.

Of course I wanted to quit my job and teach alchemy among the plants in rhythm with the Earth! What could be more exciting than an alchemy church? Quickly recognizing that this view would not be shared, I laughed inwardly and changed the subject. In my early twenties, I confided in my Gnostic teacher about feeling lonely on my path. It seemed like everything I said made my friends and family worried instead of happy for me. She clucked her tongue and told me that loneliness is a natural part of the seeker's experience but just beyond aloneness lies at-one-ness. She then grumbled, "Fuck 'em if they can't take a joke"—a phrase I return to often!

Separation as a mystical practice involves intentionally withdrawing from everyday life to gain clarity. When I first sat down to write this book, my mind was clouded with worries and perfectionism. I was so consumed with whether or not I could convey the genius of alchemy to you that I stopped writing altogether. In need of a reset, I decided to spend two weeks at a silent monastery, removing myself from speaking, phones, books, and writing and devoting myself instead to meditation and contemplation. After this period of separation, my mind was better able to return to the task of writing without so much worry. My words would do what they could to honor the tradition of alchemy, and in the silence between them, new meanings would emerge. Separation allows us to distill what is essential, shedding layers of unnecessary inner expectations and external influences.

Separation must be practiced with the utmost care both in the laboratory and in life. American culture overemphasizes separation in the form of individualism and independent responsibility to such a degree that loneliness and isolation plague most people, and many of us do not know where to turn when we need help. This hyperindividualism leads to a dangerous othering among humans, allowing them to separate themselves from shared humanity and even our home planet. We now have a billionaire class that knowingly destroys our ecosystems for capital gain and makes plans to colonize Mars rather than care for the vast web of life on Earth.

Understandably, in the alchemy courses I teach, people struggle when separation comes up; we've all been wounded by it. Yet, separation in a creative practice is one of the most crucial aspects of making good work. It's the process of cutting, splicing, editing, and refining that allows us to extract the "gold" from our creativity.

Crows are one of the primary symbols of separation. They are widely recognized for their intelligence, complex problem-solving abilities, and use of tools. Crows are naturally attracted to bright, reflective items like coins, jewelry, and bits of metal. Crows often scavenge these items, adding them to their nests or hoarding them in hidden spots. Crows will offer these shiny objects as gifts to humans who have been kind to them, and people who regularly feed or interact with crows may find the birds leaving small treasures in exchange for food or protection. This behavior demonstrates the crows' understanding of reciprocity and their capacity to form bonds. This behavior beautifully illustrates the alchemical concept of separation, which is not an end in itself but a precursor to the next phase of con-junction—the recombining of refined elements into a unified relationship.

I was recovering from a painful breakup when I first taught the Alchemical Imagination course. As I guided my students through the lesson on separation that season, I realized that my study of alchemy had given me the clarity I needed to break free from harmful relationship patterns handed down to me through genera-tions. I embraced the pain of separation as a necessary step in my own growth and committed myself to exploring the deep connections that can be made in solitude.

In response, the spirit of alchemy—which I speak to often—promised that if I was patient and took time to be a friend to myself, the practice would send me an alchemist to romantically partner with. There are so few practicing alchemists that I dismissed this flash of insight as an impossibility. But a couple years later, I was giving a talk on alchemical Mercury at a bar in Bushwick, Brooklyn. Afterward, a beautiful person qui-etly approached me and asked if I would join them for a walk in the Botanic Garden. I was hesitant, but they persisted. Eventually, over a year of courting, we found our-selves living in the forest, working together on spagyric preparations and alchemical distillation. It was pure magic, and I remembered alchemy's promise to me. Separation leads to refinement and recombination—it is not a stand-alone operation.

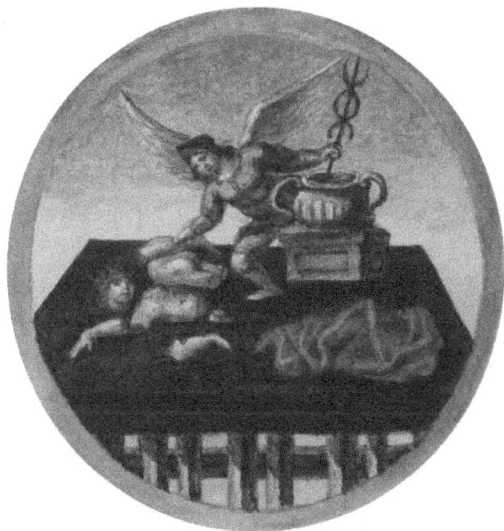

Separation is graphically depicted in this illustration by the dismembered body.
Once placed in the cauldron, the parts will undergo conjunction. From *Compendiolum
de praeparatione auri potabilis veri Philosophia hermetica*, by Federico Gualdi, 1790.
Mellon MS 131, Beinecke Rare Book and Manuscript Library.

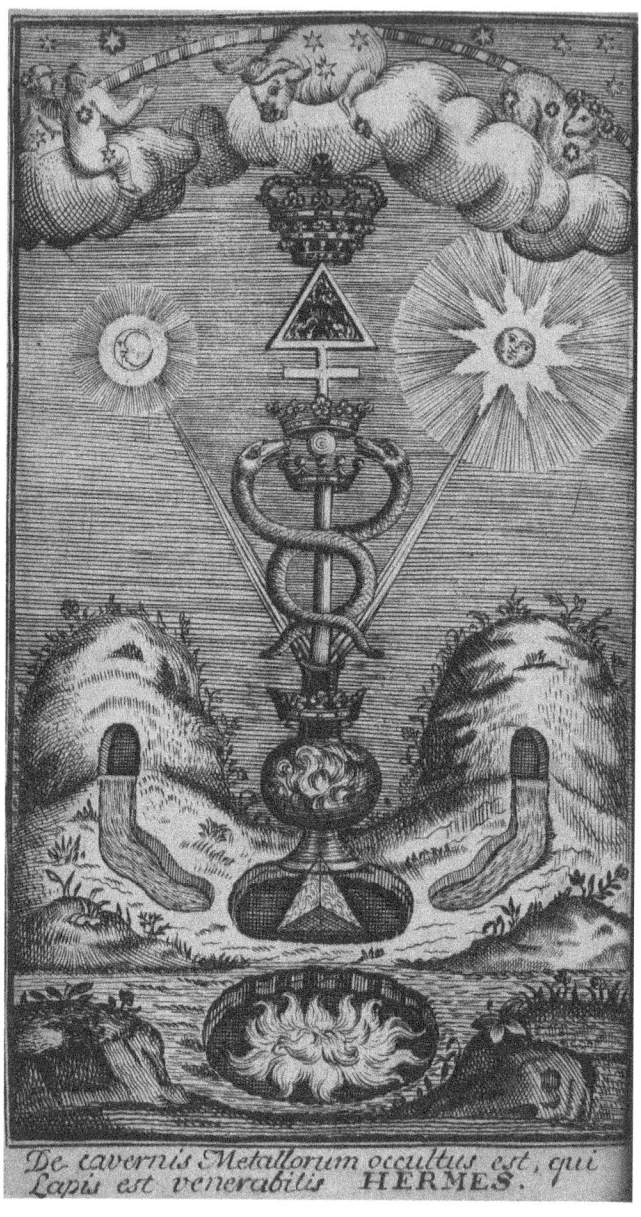

De cavernis Metallorum occultus est, qui Lapis est venerabilis HERMES.

The caduceus of Hermes. From *The Hermetical Triumph, or, the Victorious Philosophical Stone: A Treatise . . . Concerning the Hermetical Magistery*. Translated from the French of A.T. Limojon de Saint-Didier, which was translated from a German edition. Source: Wellcome Collection.

Separate the Earth from the Fire

THE TRIA PRIMA

Alchemy identifies three main components in matter, known by various names such as the Three Supernals, Supreme Trinity, Three Principia, Three Universals, Three Treasures, or the Tria Prima. According to alchemical tradition, these essential characteristics are extracted from a substance through separation and later recombined to create a more refined concoction. Paracelsus defined these three components as Sulfur, Mercury, and Salt.

Mercury is associated with the spirit, Sulfur with the soul, and Salt with the body. The soul (Sulfur)—symbolized by gold and the sun—represents an individual's unique essence, shaped by their personal experiences. The spirit (Mercury)—represented by silver and the Moon—is transpersonal and acts as the underlying blueprint or energy that connects the body to a broader, collective network of subtle forces. Mercury can be seen as a mediating force, bridging Sulfur and Salt. The body (Salt) represents the physical, material form resulting from the interaction of the soul and spirit.

The caduceus—a staff carried by Hermes in Greek mythology and by Hermes Trismegistus in Greco-Egyptian tradition—symbolizes the triad of body, soul, and spirit. This staff features two serpents entwined around a central rod, topped with wings or a pine cone, representing enlightenment. The serpent on the left signifies the spirit; the serpent on the right represents the soul; and the central staff is the body.

In Greek mythology, Hermes's staff was believed to possess mystical powers: it could awaken the sleeping and lull the awake to sleep. It eased the transition for those nearing death and restored life for the dead. For alchemists, the caduceus is key to unlocking the mystery of the Tria Prima, bringing us closer to understanding the fundamental forces of creativity and healing.

In your mind's eye, visualize holding a caduceus wand before you. See the staff in the center, standing tall and unyielding, flanked by two serpents, each coiling gracefully like DNA spirals around the staff. Observe how the serpents wind upward, intertwined yet separate, each with its own purpose and wisdom. Now, imagine that you are placing the caduceus gently on the ground in front of you. See the end of the staff sinking lightly into the soil.

Then focus your attention on the silver serpent whose head is on the left side at the staff's top. This is the serpent of the spirit and the Moon—the intuitive, subtle energy that flows through your being. Observe its movements, its undulating motions, as it coils with fluid grace. Feel the cool, receptive energy of the spirit rising from the left side of the staff. Now, shift your focus to the gold serpent, whose head is on the right side of the staff. This is the serpent of the soul and the Sun— the active, passionate energy that shapes your external words, actions, and intellect. Notice the warmth it radiates, the powerful energy current flowing upward along the right side. This serpent represents your drive, creativity, and ability to act in accordance with your will.

Now, place your attention on the center of the caduceus—the staff made of crystallized salt. This is the body, the result of the interaction between spirit and soul. Imagine the staff rising straight and true from the ground, signifying your physical body. Picture a light running from the base of the staff and lighting up the staff's top. Now imagine a light running from the base of your spine to your skull, lighting up your spine.

Focus on the wings or pine cone at the top of the caduceus. See how they glow with an ethereal light, representing enlightenment and awakening. In some alchemical traditions, it was believed that during enlightenment, the pineal gland located at the center of the skull would begin to glow and emit light from the eyes. See this happening for you now.

The serpent on the left brings cool, intuitive energy, while the serpent on the right carries warmth and drive. The central staff supports and grounds you. Feel the balancing power of the caduceus within you. Trust that, with each breath, you are aligning yourself with the deeper, creative forces of the universe.

Stay with this feeling for as long as you need, allowing the caduceus's wisdom to guide and center you. When you feel ready, slowly bring your awareness back to the space you are in, carrying your caduceus with you.

The Star Inside

CREATING A SPAGYRIC

Paracelsus introduced the concept of the spagyric—an herbal medicinal preparation designed to isolate and recombine the Tria Prima into a potent remedy. The term *spagyric* comes from the Greek words *spao* ("tear apart") and *ageiro* ("gather together"), meaning "to break down and then reunite." Creating a simple plant-based spagyric tincture offers a practical way to explore the alchemical process of separation, refining your extraction techniques and deepening personal meditations on the concept.

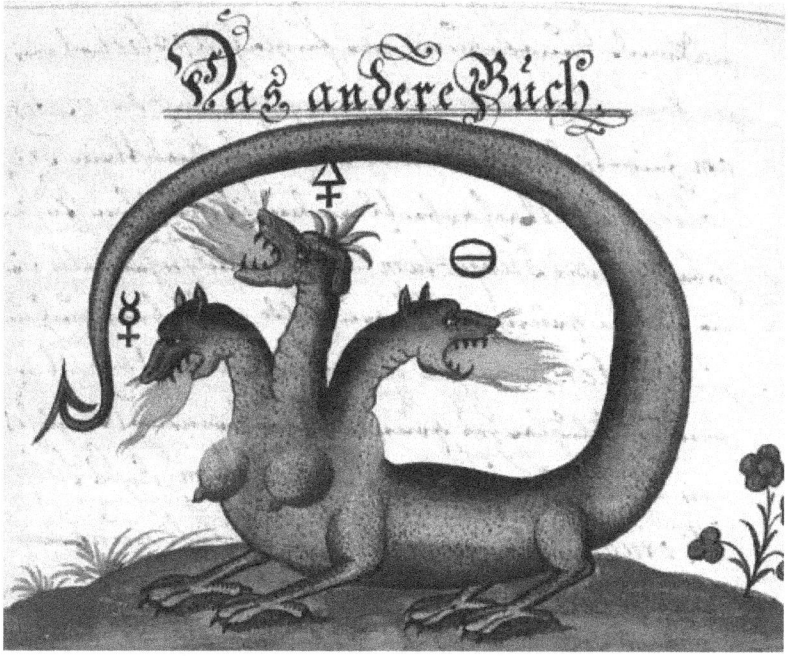

A three-headed dragon representing the Tria Prima. From *Clavis Artis*, Zoroaster, 1738. MS. Verginelli-Rota, Biblioteca dell'Accademia Nazionale dei Lincei, Roma, vol. 2, p. 7.

Spagyric medicines require a more extensive preparation than modern tinctures, as they must be made during specific planetary alignments. Paracelsus referred to the inner essence of plants as their "inner star," a concept rooted in the Doctrine of Signatures. In this framework, a plant's inner star is connected to the stars in the heavens, embodying the principle of "As Above, So Below." The inner star represents the essence of a being—the divine spark that gives it form and life. Paracelsus explained, "One must understand that the medicine must be prepared in the stars, and that the stars themselves become the medicine" (Pagel 1982, 72).

Each planet is believed to govern a specific organ or system in the human body and, by extension, the associated ailments. Each planet also governs plants that can support the corresponding body part or system. The spagyric process, including harvesting, cutting, sifting, drying, or extracting plant material, should be timed according to the planetary rulership of the plant. The planet's influence is strongest when it is highest in the sky during its planetary hour.

Practice Separation: Make a Solar Spagyric

INGREDIENTS

Dry Materials

- 2 ounces of dried chamomile

- 1 quart mason jar (Ensure the lid is plastic or line the inside with parchment paper, as the tincture should not come into contact with metal.)

- A filtering tool (e.g., coffee filters or muslin)

- A funnel

- An uncoated stainless steel tray, Corningware pan, or large silica crucible

- Tincture bottles with labels for storage

Wet Materials

- 1 quart of 190–200 proof alcohol (like Everclear) or 100-proof vodka (Traditionally, spagyric tinctures are made with alcohol. I'll provide a few alcohol-free options below. A typical dose of spagyric tincture is 15–30 drops.)

- 5 percent distilled white vinegar (alcohol alternative) (Vinegar-based tinctures are better suited for chronic conditions, as they are more cooling and suitable for long-term use. You can also use apple cider vinegar, which has a more pleasant flavor, but remember this will introduce an additional plant signature—Venus—through the apple ingredient.)

- Glycerin (alcohol alternative) (Glycerites are made with vegetable glycerin, an excellent alternative for those sensitive to alcohol or for use with children and animals. While glycerites are less potent than alcohol or vinegar tinctures, they are still effective. Vegetable glycerin is a clear, odorless liquid derived from oils like palm, soy, or coconut. Choose organic, non-GMO, sustainably harvested glycerin for the best-quality glycerite. Glycerin works best with fresh plants, as it is less effective at extracting constituents from dried herbs than alcohol or vinegar.)

We will work with chamomile, a solar herb linked to positive energy, for this exercise. I recommend sourcing the dried herb from a local grower or herb shop if you are unable to grow it yourself. If you gather fresh chamomile, dry it before using it unless you plan to make a glycerite. Whenever possible, it's preferable to start primary operations on the herb—picking, drying, mixing, and tincturing—on the planetary day and the associated hour. For chamomile, being a solar plant, the best day to work with it is Sunday, and the hour when the sun is highest in the sky is the time to start. I generally prefer to initiate the spagyric process as close to the New Moon as possible and complete it as close to the Full Moon as possible.

On a Sunday at high noon, place a dish of dried chamomile in front of you. Take the time to examine it closely, taking in all its details, growth patterns, shapes, and colors. Rub the herb between your fingers to become familiar with its weight and texture. Raise the herb to your nose and inhale deeply, taking in the odor. Hold your ears up to the plant and listen to it. Allow the plant to observe you in return and create a sense of familiarity and reciprocity with the herb.

Next, spend some time with your vessel. Take a moment to appreciate the empty space that will soon be transformed into a spagyric by the union of the herb and solvent. I enjoy lighting a candle and playing music that resonates with the feelings I want to capture in the medicine. For me, solar herbs benefit from joyful, upbeat music.

Crush the dried herb by hand into small pieces. It's essential to spend some time in physical contact with the herb. If you choose to use a mortar and pestle or a coffee grinder to powder the herb instead, hold the ground herb close to your heart for a while to create an energetic connection. Fill a jar about halfway with the chamomile. With focused intent, pour the menstruum over the herb until it is saturated, making sure not to overfill the jar; it should be about two-thirds full. Warm the jar with your hands and allow the herb to absorb the liquid, adding more solvent if necessary.

Once the herbs are fully covered with an ample amount of solvent and no longer seem to absorb much liquid, hermetically seal the jar. Shake the jar vigorously, then place it in a cool, dry area. Shake the jar once or twice a day to ensure proper mixing. Over time, the liquid will gradually darken. In alchemical terms, this color change represents the extraction of the Sulfur (the soul) from the plant's Salt (the physical matter) by Mercury—the spirit alcohol medium. Continue this process for three to four weeks, until the tincture reaches a deep, dark color.

Let no one else handle your spagyric, and be mindful of how you are feeling as the spagyric cures. The alchemist's attitude and emotions contribute to the tincture as much as the plant itself. This is not about creating a perfectly uniform emotional state while preparing the spagyric but rather about developing sufficient awareness of your own emotional and experiential states to notice how they influence the process.

Once the liquid has darkened sufficiently, open the jar and press out any remaining liquid from the plant material. Then, filter the solution until it is free of all plant matter. I prefer using unbleached coffee filters, but you can also use muslin. The resulting tincture contains the Sulfur (soul) of the herb—its essential oils and vegetable fats—along with the Mercury (alcohol, vinegar, or glycerin). Save the plant material left over after filtering, as it contains the dead Salts (caput mortuum) of the plant, which will later be reanimated. Lay the spent plant material out to dry on a nonmetallic plate or tray until fully dehydrated.

When sufficiently dry, place the caput mortuum in a crucible or metal pot; ignite the material; and let it burn. This is best done outside as it's a smoky process. Let the mass begin to roast and finally incinerate. When they've cooled, take the ashes and grind them to a fine powder. Some alchemists prefer to repeat this process a few times over until the ashes turn white. Experiment and see what works best for you. When the ashes are ready, combine the plant extract with the ashes. Shake vigorously, then hermetically seal the jar again. Place the jar in a dark location for three weeks, shaking it periodically.

After three weeks, filter the substance again and press out the remaining fluid. The spagyric now contains the Sulphur, the essential oils, waxes, and vegetable fats; the Mercury, the alcohol, glycerine, or vinegar; and the Salt, the resurrected body or ashes that contain the minerals within the plant. A spagyric contains the entire body of the plant and is therefore thought to have its full powers intact. Pour the liquid into separate tincture bottles for ease of storage and subsequent use.

Use the chamomile spagyric on a Sunday when the sun is highest in the sky. Find a quiet moment and hold the tincture bottle in your hand, feeling the potency of the plant's star contained within. I recommend administering between ten and thirty drops per dose. Once you've taken the spagyric, close your eyes and notice how the chamomile moves into your body, gently warming you from the inside outward. Feel the warmth spread across your chest, activating the heart and circulation. Notice the steady rise of sunlight in your body and allow it to flow to all systems that need this light. Take the spagyric every Sunday until it runs out, and notice how you feel before and after.

Creating spagyrics can profoundly enrich artistic practice by introducing exercises that help us foster a deeper connection with the soul of our materials and our understanding of the energy they carry in relation to our own energy. Making spagyrics also aligns our creativity with the macrocosm by encouraging us to pay attention to the movement of celestial bodies and how they influence what we produce. For example, we might edit and refine our work during a waning Moon, letting go of unnecessary elements, and then focus on adding to or expanding our work during a waxing Moon, when growth and creativity are supported by this celestial body. These connections are beautifully described in the *Corpus Hermeticum*:

> *Humanity looked in awe upon the beauty and the everlasting duration of creation. The exquisite sky flooded with sunlight. The majesty of the dark night lit by celestial torches as the holy planetary powers trace their paths in the heavens in fixed and steady metre—ordering the growth of things with their secret infusions.* (Freke & Gandy 1997, 63)

Practice Separation: Erasure Poems

Apophatic theology, also known as the via negativa (or "way of negation"), originated in the early centuries of Christian thought. This theological approach is based on the belief that human language and thought are insufficient to accurately describe the transcendent nature of the divine. Rather than stating what the divine is, we must articulate what the divine is not. The divine is not limited by time or space, subject to change, nor definable by any particular attributes that we can comprehend. By negating our descriptions of the qualities and characteristics of the world around us, we are led toward a deeper, more mystical understanding of the divine presence—one that can only be grasped intuitively beyond the reach of intellect or language.

Erasure poetry is an artistic form that reimagines existing texts by selectively obscuring or removing words to create new, distilled meanings. Through this process, the remaining words are often highlighted or framed as a poem, allowing the poet or artist to reveal hidden layers of meaning in the original work. The result can be left as it appears on the page or reorganized into structured lines or stanzas, transforming it into a more deliberate poetic form. Apophatic theology and erasure poetry both embrace the concept of revealing deeper truths through negation and elimination.

To create an erasure poem, print out a text that resonates with you. Use a pen, pencil, or digital tool to intuitively erase or cross out words and phrases. Once you've erased parts of the text, focus on how the remaining words fit together. Rearrange them if you feel called to. Pay attention to the spaces between words and phrases, as the absence is as meaningful as what remains. After refining the structure and flow of the poem, step back and consider the new meaning you've uncovered through the process of erasure, cutting, splicing, and distilling.

Agnes Martin

WHAT IS KNOWN FOREVER IN THE MIND

Agnes Martin (1912–2004), an American painter, is renowned for her minimalist works that convey a quiet sense of expansive space. Born in Saskatchewan, Canada, she moved to the United States in 1931 and pursued degrees in teaching. While studying, she encountered Zen Buddhism and Taoism, whose teachings on simplicity and mindfulness would profoundly shape her artistic approach. At thirty, while working toward her bachelor's degree, Martin became an artist. By the late 1950s, after establishing herself in New York, her work evolved into highly simplified geometric abstractions. These works gradually took the form of delicate, dynamic monochromes featuring subtle penciled grids on large square canvases. In 1966, her art was included in the *Systemic Painting* exhibition at the Guggenheim Museum, which spotlighted artists using reductive, systematic approaches to art-making.

In 1967, she ceased her painting practice and withdrew from the New York art scene, embarking on a journey across the United States and Canada. After more than a year of travel, she settled in a remote area near Cuba, New Mexico—twenty miles from the nearest highway and without electricity or neighbors. Here, she built a simple adobe hut and log cabin from local materials, embracing complete solitude. In 1972, Martin returned to her art and penned an essay titled "The Untroubled Mind," where she celebrated the transformative power of isolation, declaring that "solitude and freedom are the same" (Martin 1973a, 19). She emphasized that solitude is critical for artistic creation, writing, "To discover the conscious mind in a world where intellect is held to be valuable requires solitude—quite a lot of solitude. We have been very strenuously conditioned against solitude. I suggest to artists that you take every opportunity of being alone, that you give up having pets and unnecessary companions" (Martin 1973b, 18).

For over forty years, Martin's work remained focused on meditative paintings of grids and stripes. She believed this pared-down style could evoke profound, positive experiences in viewers, with each work created to invite a spacious, unhurried mindset. In the solitude of her studio, with her canvases facing the wall, Martin would sit in a rocking chair, waiting for inspiration. Sometimes, she would wait for weeks, months, or even years for an idea to emerge. When it did, the inspiration came to her fully formed and requiring no internal adjustments. Reflecting on this process, Martin said, "When I had the inspiration for the grids, I was thinking of innocence and the image was a grid. That was it. I thought, 'My god, am I supposed to paint that?'" (Princenthal 2018, np). Her transcriptions, while sometimes successful and sometimes not, were driven by crystal clear visions.

Martin's use of grids and lines, often executed over a light wash of color, was not about representing the visible world. She said, "My paintings are not about what is seen. They are about what is known forever in the mind" (Martin 1973a, np). Through her commitment to solitude, Martin distilled her practice to its most essential form, engaging only with what was necessary and inspired.

Martin's creative process is a profound example of the alchemical practice of separation, both in terms of removing the self from everyday life to gain insight and in her commitment to refining everything in her picture plane down to what is pure, essential, and aligned with a deep unseen truth.

Practice Separation: The Sacrament of Silence

Like Agnes Martin, I recommend that artists and alchemists periodically separate themselves from the world's noise, particularly from language and intellect. Silence creates the conditions necessary for learning to listen to the music of the world and attuning yourself to the subtler aspects of the divine, the natural world, and your own being.

I've experienced the power of this practice firsthand during silent retreats at the Insight Meditation Society. During these retreats, Noble Silence requires participants to refrain from speaking, reading, writing, or silently communicating with others through gestures. These constraints have a powerful ability to reduce mental chatter, creating space for clarity and focus.

It's important to recognize that silence isn't always a refuge; it can sometimes become a way to escape or suppress emotions. To prevent trapping your feelings in silence or using it as an escape, it can be helpful to first allow some sounds to emerge:

1. Decide whether you would like to sit or stand. Choose a posture that is both relaxed and grounded, enabling your breath and voice to flow freely.

2. Close your eyes and take a few deep, calming breaths to center yourself and quiet your mind.

3. Check in with yourself and notice if there is an area in your body where you've been holding emotional tension or discomfort. Where are emotions stored up that could use a release? This might be in your chest, throat, stomach, or any other area. Focus your attention on that spot.

4. Begin to create sounds that feel like they are massaging the area of tension. You can hum, laugh, fake laugh, cry, or make any sound that resonates with what you're feeling. Let your voice flow naturally—there are no rules here.

5. As you make sounds, pay attention to the emotional weight of them. Allow the vibrations to reach the tense area, letting emotions move through your body and voice.

6. When you're ready, gently bring your sounding to a close. Take a moment to sit in silence, noticing any shifts in your emotional state or physical body.

Noble Silence

A full twenty-four hours of Noble Silence offers a powerful opportunity to reset, clear mental clutter, and reconnect with your inner self before diving into your creative work. Ideally, this silence should take place in a quiet, undisturbed space at a time when interruptions are unlikely. However, if a full twenty-four hours isn't possible, shorter periods—whether fifteen minutes, an hour, or an afternoon—can still have a profound effect. The key is to carve out intentional time for quiet.

During this time, refrain from speaking, writing, reading, or even gesturing. Avoid all forms of communication, including verbal and nonverbal, as well as eye contact and hand gestures. The goal is to let go of any urge to react, analyze, or engage with the world around you. Focus on cultivating mindfulness by observing your environment, tuning in to your body's sensations, and noticing the thoughts that arise without judgment or attachment. When thoughts come, let them flow through you, noticing when you drift out into a story, and gently let the waves of your awareness wash back onto the shores of the present.

You can sit quietly, take mindful walks, stretch, or practice slow, intentional movements, depending on what feels right for you.

When your silence concludes, ease back into your creative work gently. Reflect on the experience—did any new insights, shifts in perspective, or innovative ideas arise during your time of silence? Did you gain a renewed sense of presence and clarity?

If you prefer a formal setting for this practice, numerous online and in-person Insight and Vipassana meditation groups offer instruction in sitting in Noble Silence. Many spiritual centers also provide spaces for silent contemplation if your home environment isn't conducive to conducting a period of Noble Silence. I often find refuge in New York City by slipping into a church for a half hour of contemplation.

IV.

Conjunction
THE ROSE, THE HEART,
AND THE CROSS

Zodiac: Capricorn ———————— **Planet:** Saturn

Images: Lovers' embraces, Cupid, Eros, filius philosophorum, the rose, the cross, the heart, the feather, the Sun and Moon embracing, roosters and hens, rams, satyrs, two white birds raising a crown to the heavens, red and white lions, two dragons sharing a single body

Material Applications: Combining, sticking and stitching together, amalgamating, alloys, collaborating, harmonizing, layering, love

> *After the chapter of natural Separation,*
> *By which the elements of our Stone be disseuered,*
> *Here follows the chapter of secret Conjunction,*
> *Which Natures repugnant joins to perfect unity.*
> *And so them knitteth that none from the other may flee,*
> *When they by fire shall be examined,*
> *They be together so surely conjugated.*
>
> —George Ripley, *The Compound of Alchymy*

In alchemical practice, conjunction is the process of recombining the elements separated in earlier stages into a new, unified substance. After calcination (burning), solution (washing), and separation (extracting), the next step is to bring together what remains. An example of conjunction in alchemy is the creation of brass. Brass is made by heating copper and zinc ore together in a crucible. The heat causes the zinc to vaporize, and the zinc vapor reacts with the copper, forming an alloy of the two metals. Alchemists referred to conjunction as the "Marriage of the Sun and Moon," symbolizing the union of two forces to create something new.

Imagery of conjunction typically shows the Sun and Moon in various positions of passionate embrace. The intense union depicted in the alchemical symbols for conjunction goes beyond physical pleasure or romantic magnetism; it represents the transcendence that can be achieved in merging. The couples in these images are often sinking into water or earth, signifying a spiritual fertility akin to the physical fertility of the Earth, whose "Father is the Sun and Mother is the Moon."

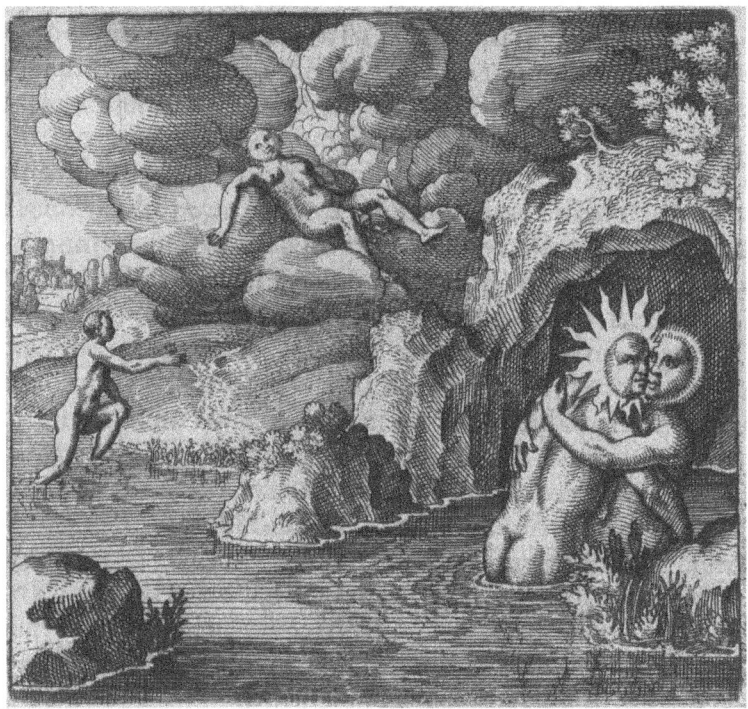

The Sun and Moon personified in a passionate embrace. Emblem 34 from *Atalanta Fugiens*, by Michael Maier, illustrated by Matthäus Merian. Oppenheim, Germany, 1618. Science History Institute Digital Collections, Science History Institute, Philadelphia.

The rose is a central symbol in the process of conjunction. It has long been integral to alchemy, with numerous texts bearing the title *Rosarium*, which translates from latin to "Rose Garden." As the Persian alchemist and poet Farid Attar wrote in the 12th century, "Mystery glows in the rose bed and the secret is hidden in the rose" (Attar 2019, 88). Fossilized roses dating back thirty-five million years have been discovered in Europe, and archaeologists have found petrified rose wreaths in some of the earliest Egyptian tombs. German alchemist Michael Maier (1568–1622) expanded on the symbolism of the red and white roses in his work *Septimana Philosophica*, describing the rose as "the first and most perfect of flowers" (Maier 1620, np).

The rose is tied to the most intimate aspects of the human heart, representing truths that cannot be easily expressed. The Latin phrase *sub rosa* ("under the rose") came to represent matters that should remain private, based on a tradition that originated in medieval times when red roses were hung on the ceiling in the meeting rooms of Hermetic societies such as the Rosicrucians, Freemasons, and alchemical guilds to indicate that their discussions were confidential.

Conjunction is also symbolized as an alchemical crucifixion, where the substance (or the alchemist) is fixed on a cross between the vertical axis of reality (the nonphysical) and the horizontal axis of reality (the physical). The heart is where the human body's horizontal (earthly) and vertical (divine) meet. When an alchemist is ready to explore the mysteries of the heart, they first ground themselves in the horizontal heart—the realm of earthly relationships and experiences.

Many alchemists engage in their work with a partner: Zosimos of Panopolis collaborated with fellow alchemist Theosebeia, while Nicolas Flamel worked alongside his wife Perenelle. Alchemical literature repeatedly emphasizes the importance of maintaining healthy, close friendships and working relationships as a spiritual practice. As the Gospel of Thomas, a Gnostic text, says: "Love your friends like your own soul, protect them like the pupil of your eye" (Meyer 2007, 30).

The horizontal heart is where emotional and relational dynamics with physical beings are explored, while the vertical heart connects us to celestial realms and nonphysical entities, such as angels, deities, ancestors, and energies. Alchemists often focus on understanding and refining their horizontal relationships before seeking initiation into vertical relationships with nonphysical realms.

In alchemical practice, the heart's mystery is central; the heart is seen as the origin of truth and the soul. This belief stems from the ancient Egyptians' deep reverence for the heart. In the Hymn to Atum, found on an Egyptian papyrus dating back to 300 BCE, the creator god states, "I conceived many living creatures. All were in my heart, along with their children and their grandchildren" (Faulkner 2016, 166). The heart was regarded not only as the organ that sustains life in an individual but also as the center of creation in the cosmos.

In Egyptian thought, the anatomical heart, known as *haty*, was considered the body's motor, while *ib* describes the heart as a metaphysical entity encompassing intelligence, memory, and wisdom. The ib was weighed upon death to determine the soul's fate.

Ma'at, in ancient Egyptian religion, is the personification of truth, justice, natural law, and the cosmic order. As a part of their judgment in the afterlife, the souls of the dead arrive at the Hall of Ma'at, where the ceremony of the weighing of the heart takes place to decide the fate of the deceased. The first part of the ritual is called the Negative Confession or the Declaration of Innocence, which requires the deceased to address each of the forty-two judges by their name and recite all the sins they have *not* committed. After this test, the deceased presents their heart to Ma'at's scale of justice, where the heart is weighed against a feather she wears tucked behind her ear. If the heart successfully balances with the feather, the deceased is presented to Osiris and granted eternal life in heavenly paradise. If the heart is heavier than the feather, it gets devoured, and the soul is destroyed.

The Egyptian Book of the Dead, an ancient collection of mortuary texts made up of magic formulas, was placed in tombs and read aloud over corpses to aid the deceased in the hereafter. To instruct the deceased in the weighing of the heart trial, the Book of the Dead says to address the heart this way:

> *O my heart which I had from my mother! O my heart which I had from my mother! O my heart of different ages! Do not stand up as a witness against me, do not be opposed to me in the tribunal, do not be hostile to me in the presence of the keeper of the balance, for you are my ka which was in my body, the protector who made my members hale. Go forth to the happy place whereto we speed, do not tell lies about me in the presence of the god; it is indeed well that you should hear!* (Faulkner 2016, 46)

Although these words are intended for a funerary rite, the message in this passage offers a valuable practice to the living. The core instruction is: do not lie about what you see in your own heart and do not turn against yourself no matter what is revealed. This requires honest self-examination and self-acceptance, even when facing difficult truths about ourselves. By confronting the full range of truths in your innermost heart without rejecting any part of yourself, you preserve your connection to your soul and resist inner estrangement.

Engaging in this inner process of conjunction is crucial, as it fosters clarity, presence, and an attitude of compassion, laying the groundwork for success in both external endeavors—such as work, relationships, and creative practices—and in the internal work of personal evolution.

Practice Conjunction

ENTER THE HEART'S MYSTERY

Find a quiet space and sit comfortably, closing your eyes. Place one hand on your chest and focus on the rhythm of your heartbeat. As you tune in to this pulse, let the word *welcome* gently rise in your mind. Repeat it slowly, allowing the word to sink in and open your heart, visualizing it unfolding like the petals of a flower, layer by layer. Its walls are soft and translucent, glowing with a gentle light. The chambers of your heart pulse with different aspects of your being—joy, sorrow, hope, and fear. Sit with these emotions, simply offering presence.

Say *welcome* again, and imagine yourself descending deeper into your heart, where a warm, steady light fills the space. Here, you are held in peace. Breathe deeply, drawing energy from your feet up to your head on an inhale and from your head to your feet on an exhale. Hold your arms out wide and move energy from fingertip to fingertip with your breath. Breathe up and down the spine and across your wingspan in turns. Find your heart at the intersection of this horizontal and vertical movement. Feel the energies of the earth and sky meeting there.

Now, imagine a child with glowing wings appearing before you. See their soft, radiant wings shimmering with iridescent colors. Gaze into their wise, joyful eyes and feel the light of their wings expanding within you, reminding you of the boundless love and possibility at the core of your heart. Open your hands in your lap, inviting the child's energy to fill you. Rest in the contentment of your being. When you're ready, gather your thanks for this experience into a single thought, word, or image, and offer it to the child. Close with a simple *yes*.

Take a notebook and pen and jot down any insights or experiences. What did you encounter in the innermost chamber of your heart?

Next, shift your focus to your creative practice. What parts of your work feel alive and vibrant, flowing effortlessly like gold? These might be moments when you are fully immersed in the process or feel connected to something greater than yourself. Write down what excites you and what feels aligned.

Now, focus on the parts of your practice that feel stuck or unpleasant—the "manure." This could include lack of motivation, technical challenges, feelings of rejection, or other emotional obstacles. Don't shy away from them; acknowledge them honestly.

Once you've examined both sides of your artistic practice—the gold and the manure—review your list and draw a circle around everything you've written.

Everything you've noted is part of your work. The moments of brilliance and the periods of struggle are intertwined, each nourishing the other.

Finally, draw a rose—a symbol of beauty, growth, and transformation—and offer it as a gift to your creative heart.

An Eye in Place of an Eye

ALCHEMICAL TRAVELING

Conjunction is the union of opposing forces or substances, a blending that creates a new, subtler element. This is symbolized by the *filius philosophorum*, the "child of philosophy," an image of a winged child representing the birth of a new consciousness or reality. Mystical conjunction is the marriage of the soul (what makes us unique) and spirit (what connects us to the All) necessary for true alchemical transformation. Out of this marriage emerges a third created being, a "child."

The arrival of the winged child of philosophy indicates that the alchemist is ready to ascend into the vertical realm of relationships with beings in nonphysical realms. This requires a shift in consciousness, where the alchemist's double body is activated, allowing a nonphysical avatar to detach from the physical form and explore worlds beyond the physical senses.

We learned about Sun Ra's ascent to Saturn in our discussion of the planetary spheres. In an interview with John Szwed, he describes the experience this way: "My whole body changed into something else. I could see through myself. And I went up ... I wasn't in human form ... I landed on a planet that I identified as Saturn ... they teleported me and I was down on a stage with them. They wanted to talk with me. They had one little antenna on each ear. A little antenna over each eye. They talked to me. They told me to stop [attending college] because there was going to be great trouble in schools ... the world was going into complete chaos ... I would speak [through music], and the world would listen. That's what they told me" (Szwed 1997, 88).

The techniques alchemists employed for what we might now call astral projection were designed to allow them access to dimensions beyond ordinary sensory experience. Alchemists can shrink themselves down to merge with the materials in their experiments, allowing them to understand their properties and what inner qualities they might possess that are not immediately apparent. Alchemists can also enlarge themselves, enabling them to journey beyond Earth as Sun Ra did, where they can interact with the cosmos on an experiential level. These methods are a practice of gnosis—a process by which you gain direct, experiential knowledge that can guide your work in ways that empirical observation and calculation alone cannot.

Practice Conjunction

TO MAKE A FOOT IN PLACE OF A FOOT

Jesus's words in the Gnostic Gospel of Thomas describe a process by which you can travel to nonphysical realms. In it, he says: "When you make the two into one, and when you make the inner like the outer and the outer like the inner, and the upper like the lower, and when you make male and female into a single one, so that the male will not be male nor the female be female, when you make eyes in place of an eye, a hand in place of a hand, a foot in place of a foot, an image in place of an image, then you will enter the kingdom" (Meyer 2007, 87).

This passage discusses the integration of dualities—such as inner and outer, male and female, physical and spiritual—into a single, unified whole. This integration represents conjunction, where opposites are reconciled and transformed, enabling the alchemist to access a unified reality. The author then describes the concept of creating an eye in place of an eye, a hand in place of a hand, a foot in place of a foot, and an image in place of an image. He refers to creating a nonphysical body that can travel to the Kingdom of Heaven while a person is still living.

This process can be understood through practicing techniques such as the alternate-body method, a form of out-of-body experiencing. By creating an energetic image or construct of the body and transferring consciousness into it, the practitioner can step outside their physical form and enter nonphysical planes of existence.

Find a quiet, undisturbed area where you can rest comfortably. Ensure that the space is free from distractions and that you can fully focus. Begin by taking a few deep breaths, allowing yourself to relax. Close your eyes and begin to bring your awareness to your physical form. Slowly scan your body from head to toe, noticing every part. Feel the sensations in your skin, the weight of your bones, the rhythm of your breath. Allow your awareness to settle into the feeling of your body as a whole.

Imagine a luminous field of energy surrounding your physical body. With each breath, this field becomes brighter and more distinct, radiating outward in all directions. Visualize this field of light as a shimmering, holographic projection filled with colors, textures, and movement. Picture your body forming a three-dimensional hologram in front of you, created from this light.

Within this hologram, create eyes that resemble your own, hands that look like your hands, and feet that mirror your feet. Continue filling in details. This holographic image of your body is a vibrant, living projection that reflects your physical appearance but is composed entirely of light and energy. Observe the features taking shape in the hologram. Once the image of your body is clearly formed, focus on merging your consciousness with it. Imagine your awareness gently shifting from your physical body into this energetic, holographic body, allowing you to exist in both forms.

Keep the nonphysical body within your room and start to move your holographic hands, feet, head, and face to interact with the environment. As you move, pay attention to how your holographic form interacts with space. Practice touching the floor and the ceiling. Explore listening, looking, tasting, and touching with this nonphysical body. When you are ready, gently guide your awareness back into your physical body. Visualize your consciousness traveling out of the holographic body and reconnecting with your physical form, grounding yourself back in the present moment. See the holographic body merging with you once more. Take a few deep breaths and slowly open your eyes.

If you'd like to extend your practice beyond the confines of your room, you can choose a short route between two points in a space where you won't be disturbed, such as from your bedroom to the hallway. Place four or five markers along the route at different spots to help you visualize these points clearly. Start by lying on your bed, then get up and physically walk to each marker, spending several minutes at each one to firmly imprint the location in your memory. Repeat this process five times.

Then, lie back on your bed and *mentally* walk through the same route you took before, making sure to spend the same amount of time at each marker as you did when you physically walked it. Practice this imaginative walk-through five times. Once you have completed these steps, repeat the entire process again. Aim to do this full practice once a day. Over time, your explorations may extend further and further. You can use these journeys to introduce new realms and ideas into your creative practice or to receive inspiration for your creative work, much like Sun Ra did.

Practice Conjunction

THE TELEPATHIC TELEPHONE

Consciousness, within this tradition, is understood as a boundless web whose interconnected lines allow for communication between minds. The transfer of wisdom from one mind to another transcends both physical distance and the constraints of time. Hermetic texts such as the *Corpus Hermeticum* are considered to be divinely inspired communications that surpass ordinary human authorship; they are believed to have been written by the gods themselves through the humans who have a mind-to-mind relationship with them.

Exercise 1: A Letter to Hermes

Find a quiet, sacred space where you can sit in stillness and write a letter to Hermes. You may choose to use one of his many epithets to address a specific aspect of the deity: Agoraios (Of the Marketplace), Dolios (Of Wiles), Epimêlios (Keeper of the Flocks), Kharidôtês (Giver of Joy), Dôtor Eaôn (Giver of Good Things), Eriounês (Luck-Bringing), or Promakhos (Champion). Be sure to offer gifts such as honey, incense, milk, olive oil, votive offerings, or water.

Once you've made your offering, sit in quiet contemplation and write your letter to Hermes, asking for guidance or insight. Make your request sincere and heartfelt. Remember that you are not just putting words on paper; you are engaging in a sacred dialogue with a divine force, a principal deity of alchemy.

When your letter is complete, offer it to the elements for transmission through what I like to call the "flaming fax machine." Burn the letter, inviting the energy of fire to assist in sending your message into the air, where it can reach the divine realms. Over the next few days, spend time in quiet contemplation and remain open to the response that comes. It may arrive in various forms—an unexpected insight, a dream, a meaningful encounter, or an unforeseen opportunity. Be receptive.

Exercise 2: The Telepathic Telephone

This exercise invites you to engage with creative mentorship across time and space. Choose an artist in your field who has passed away and whose work has influenced or inspired you. Place an image of this artist or their work on your alchemist's altar. You are setting up a direct line of communication with this mentor.

Next, find a communication device. You could seek out a vintage phone and decorate it in a way that feels personal by adding symbols, colors, or images representing the creative energy of the artists you wish to connect with. If a literal phone doesn't resonate, find a seashell, geode, discarded television antenna, or any other thing that feels right as a device to facilitate a conversation.

Make this communication object a focal point on your alchemist's altar. When you feel ready, call your artist using the phone. As you hold the receiver, speak aloud your questions, concerns, or desires for guidance in your work. You might hear something in response, or you might feel like you are leaving a voice memo.

After the call, place an offering in their honor on your alchemist's altar—perhaps a piece of art, a handwritten note, or a poem. This offering acts as a gesture of respect and acknowledgment of their influence in your creative life. Responses can come through subtle inspirations, serendipitous events, or creative break-throughs that feel guided. This practice cultivates trust that mentorship can still be accessed even across time, space, and death.

Vibrations of the Heart

MILFORD GRAVES

Milford Graves (1941–2021) was a pioneering American jazz drummer, educa-tor, and researcher known for his innovative contributions to music and holistic health. He was born in Jamaica, Queens, where he began playing the drums at age three. Graves developed a unique drumming style that blended elements of free jazz and African rhythms. His performances were marked by energetic improvisation; trombonist Roswell Rudd described Graves's playing as "like an anti-gravity vortex, in which you could either float or fly depending on your impulse"(Medwin 2009, np).

Graves was deeply interested in health and wellness, particularly the connec-tions between rhythm, sound, and the human body, what he called "biological music, a synthesis of the physical and mental, a mind-body deal" (Kilgannon 2020, np). He spent decades studying the heart, exploring its rhythms and how they relate to music and consciousness.

Graves eventually developed a modality called heart sound therapy, which involved using sound to influence the heart's natural rhythms to promote emo-tional and physical healing. He created computer programs to analyze the rhythms and pitches caused by muscle and valve movement in the heart. The pitches are programmed to correspond to notes on the Western musical scale. "When I hooked up to the four chambers of the heart, it sounded like four-part harmony," Graves said in a *New York Times* interview (Kilgannon 2020, np).

He began composing with the sounds by transcribing heartbeat melodies and using recorded fragments. He also realized he could help detect heart problems, and maybe even cure them. "A healthy heart has strong, supple walls, so the sound usually has a nice flow," he said. "You hear it and say, 'Ah, now that's hip.' But an unhealthy heart has stiff and brittle muscles that reflect in a high-pitched sound" (Kilgannon 2020, np).

In 2018, the same year a documentary about his life's work was released, Graves was diagnosed with amyloid cardiomyopathy, also known as stiff heart syndrome, and was given six months to live. "It's like some higher power saying: 'Okay, buddy, you wanted to study this, here you go,'" he told the *New York Times* shortly after his diagnosis. "Now the challenge is inside of me" (Kilgannon 2020, np). He lived for over two more years, during which he dedicated himself to continuing his study of the heart's music.

Watch the *Full Mantis* documentary about Milford Graves. Allow yourself to be fully immersed in its rhythms, visuals, and messages, observing how its energy resonates with your own heart and consciousness.

Afterward, create a work of art that directly depicts your heart using any medium that speaks to you.

V.

Putrefaction
ALL BENEATH THE MOON DECAYS

Zodiac: Sagittarius ——————— **Planet:** Jupiter

Images: Skeletons, corpses, skulls, graves, coffins, worms, Kronos, Saturn, scythes, dung, dung beetles, rotting flesh, maggots, murky water, black circles, birds diving downward from a pitch-black sky

Material Applications: Rotting, decomposition, decay, death, grief, mourning, time as a medium, ancestor tending

> *And Putrefaction may thus be defined, after philosophers sayings,*
> *To be the slaying of bodies,*
> *And in our compound a division of things three,*
> *Leading forth into the corruption of killed bodies,*
> *And after enabling them unto regeneration,*
> *For things being in the earth, without doubt,*
> *Be engendered of rotation in the heavens about.*
>
> —George Ripley, *The Compound of Alchymy*

Putrefaction is a decaying process that decomposes proteins, such as flesh and food waste, resulting in foul-smelling compounds like ammonia and fertilizers. In the biological decomposition that occurs after death, putrefaction is one of the later stages involving the breakdown of tissues, the liquefaction of organs, and the release of gases.

Medieval alchemists utilized putrefaction to decompose animal bones, urine, and other organic matter to release ammonia and volatile compounds, which were thought to possess medicinal properties. Decomposing manure was a use-ful—if fragrant—heat source for alchemists. By burying their vessels in decaying manure, they harnessed its steady heat to trigger a reaction known as digestion. This method was called *venter equinus*, or "the horse's bowels." Additionally, rotting manure was employed as a catalyst in producing perfumes, pigments, and medicines and was thought to be a vital ingredient for creating the Philosopher's Stone.

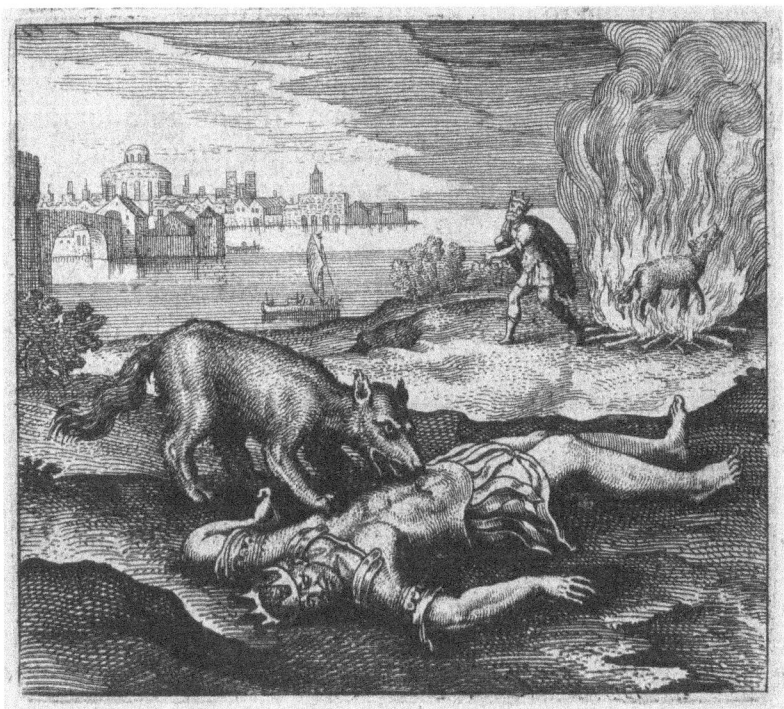

A wolf devours a fallen king, but the king is resurrected when the wolf is burned. Emblem 24 from *Atalanta Fugiens*, by Michael Maier, illustrated by Matthäus Merian. Oppenheim, Germany, 1618. Science History Institute Digital Collections, Science History Institute, Philadelphia.

In the interior laboratory, putrefaction occurs during moments of inner breakdown that ultimately lead to breakthroughs, primarily through the transformative power of grief. Grief and despair are essential states that bring us to thresholds where we lose ourselves and, in the process, gain a deeper understanding of who we are on the other side of this loss. Oscar Wilde wrote in his prison letter *De Profundis*, "Where there is sorrow, there is holy ground" (Wilde 2005, 42).

The Buddha experienced a profound awakening after encountering what are known as the Four Signs. Raised in a lavish palace, he had been shielded from the harsh realities of life until he chose to walk outside the gates at age twenty-nine. The four sights that changed his life were an elderly man, a person suffering from a disease, a decaying corpse, and a monk in deep meditation beneath a tree. These encounters forced him to confront the inevitabilities of aging, sickness, and death. As a result, he decided to leave his life of luxury and seek a spiritual path as a monk. The Buddha wanted to understand why people suffer and whether it was possible to end that suffering. He spent six years living a life of strict austerity and renunciation. Eventually, he felt that for him true wisdom did not lie in withdrawing from the world but in living a life of compassionate engagement with it, and he began to proselytize.

St. John of the Cross was a Spanish Roman Catholic priest, Christian mystic, and Carmelite friar. In 1577, when St. John was thirty-five years old, he was abducted by his own monastic brothers and incarcerated for nine months for attempting to reform their order. His prison cell—a stone room barely large enough for his body—had formerly been a latrine. His only robe rotted from his body in the heat of summer, and in winter he shivered in the rag that remained. Several times a week, the brothers brought him out to be flogged. Otherwise, he sat in the darkness, tracking the stars through a single small window high up in the wall of his cell.

Legend has it that while in this horrid place, he wrote one of his most famous poems: "The Dark Night of the Soul." In it, he wanders through a hellish darkness until he eventually embraces God as his light and lover and finds his faith renewed. The phrase *dark night of the soul* is often evoked to describe states of profound meaninglessness, lack of faith, and despair, in which the soul undergoes an intense, existential sorrow that pushes the seeker to release false attachments and simply be with what is. This process leads to an "unselfing," where the soul surrenders to the divine. After nine months of torture, St. John escaped from his cell and was nursed back to health by nuns. Once he recovered, he continued to champion reforms in his order undeterred.

Years ago, I organized an artist-in-residence session for Golden Dome in the forests outside Woodstock, New York. The residency centered on the Magician card in the tarot. I invited several artists who were also magicians to present their work, including Frank Haines, known for his intense and mystical performances timed to coincide with celestial events. When I asked Frank what themes artists interested in spirituality might want to explore, he answered "death" without hesitation. Frank brought a coffin he had specially built for the residency and placed it under an uprooted tree in the forest behind the house. At midnight, he performed a prayer at the entrance to the forest, inviting the attendees—who had not yet seen the coffin—to join him one by one to lie down in it, after which he would close the lid and throw some dirt on top. They were told to knock when they wanted to come out.

Frank's approach was gentle, and the serene forest setting created a peaceful and grounding experience for the participating artists. At one point, someone even drifted off to sleep inside the coffin and had to be softly awakened so another person could take their turn. When we gathered afterward, many artists shared that they had felt an exhilarating sense of freedom as they confronted their anxiety within the coffin, comforted by the presence of friends nearby. The coffin became both a literal and symbolic crucible—a space where we could face our deepest fears within the safety of a nurturing community.

Afterward, Frank left the coffin in the forest, where it slowly filled with water and became home to mold and fungus. Years later, he returned to lead another ceremony-class for the Empress card artist residency, this time centered on themes of life, nurturance, and the natural world. We gathered around the now-decaying coffin to reflect on the role of rot and decay in both mystical practice and the forest's life cycle—how fungi and microorganisms transform death into nourishment and renewal for all that grows.

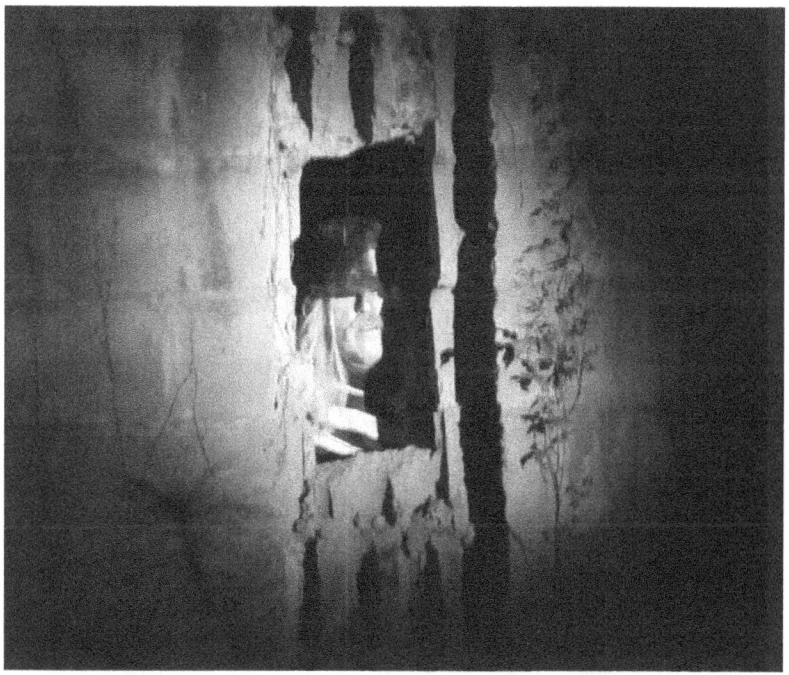

Mysteriously dressed in a top hat and peering through an opening in a stone wall, Frank Haines is the Magician in 2015. Photograph by Eliza Swann.

Putrefaction is an essential process in our ecosystems as it breaks down dead organic matter into simpler compounds and releases vital nutrients into the environment. These nutrients are then absorbed by plants and organisms, completing the nourishment cycle and supporting the ecosystem's overall health. The dominant culture in the United States attempts to stop rot in its tracks, thereby strangling growth. Falling leaves and animal carcasses are cleared from sight to a landfill before decomposing and returning their nutrients to the land where they fell. Our bodily waste is flushed away into our water supply.

Aging is considered undesirable, and people go to great lengths to prevent signs of aging on their faces. By extension, death is often seen as a failure, something to be resisted rather than embraced as a natural part of life. This aversion to putrefaction leads to an aversion to the psychic states that attend it, including fear, grief, loneliness, and despair. If these states of being are not accepted as a part of the natural growth system of the soul, we end up feeling worse. Artists must learn to survive loss—including loss of hope, reputation, money, self-belief, and faith—or we will hinder our ability to move in new directions.

Psychic putrefaction encompasses states of howling and desperate disillusionment, despair, and grief—the kind that comes out in sounds, not sentences. These are the moments when we can no longer hold it together, when inner pain erupts in a form that doesn't fit into the confines of our day-to-day life. Many of us don't have the space, permission, or support to fully express these feelings and are encouraged to suppress emotions that attend betrayal, loss of a loved one, or losing faith in a tradition or institution or in ourselves. Putrefaction encourages us to sit with these emotions and be consciously changed by them.

Practice Putrefaction

PSYCHIC PUTREFACTION AND THE POWER OF ROT

One powerful way to open the gates of psychic putrefaction and allow it to work its transformative magic is to sit with rot. There is a Buddhist practice called the Nine Horrible Notions, where an initiate contemplates the nine stages of decay by observing a rotting human corpse: distension, rupture, blood exudation, putrefaction, discoloration, animal consumption, dismemberment, reduction to bones, and parching to dust. We can adapt the Nine Horrible Notions exercise to explore the concepts of rot and decomposition by learning from mushrooms, nature's great decomposers.

There is a sacred balance between decay and renewal in our ecosystems, with fungi playing a key role in this transformation. Fungi secrete enzymes that break down complex organic compounds—such as carbohydrates and proteins—into simpler components, releasing energy in the process. These fungal decomposers and their bacterial partners absorb only a small portion of the nutrients and energy for their own use. Most of the energy and materials are transferred to the surrounding soil, air, and water. By studying these master decomposers, we can gain insight into the benefits that result from decomposition.

Order a mushroom kit with a fruiting block, and select a mushroom variety that intuitively feels like it can offer you some counsel. As you tend to your fruiting mushroom block each day, approach the process with mindfulness and reverence. Observe changes in textures, shapes, and colors. Feel the surface with your hands, acknowledging the life within. An unseen network of microscopic threads called mycelium will grow through the block, breaking down organic material and absorbing nutrients to produce mushrooms.

Eventually, you will observe the growth of the fruiting bodies. Notice their unfolding shapes. Reflect on the transformation within this small ecosystem, the birth of life from decay. As you get to know these mushrooms, ask them questions about their process. If you are using a medicinal mushroom variety, you can make a spagyric from the fruiting bodies using the recipe from the separation chapter and substituting the mushrooms for the chamomile.

Once the mushrooms release their spores, they quickly begin to deteriorate, softening, drying, or being consumed by insects and other decomposers. Take time to practice actively imagining into the breakdown of organic material. If you feel called to, howl some sounds that reflect your own inner putrefaction. See how the mycelium responds. Notice how you felt at the beginning of tending to your mushroom crop and how you feel toward the end.

In alchemy, we do not throw things away. Spent mushroom blocks are still rich in mycelium that adds a useful fungal punch to a compost pile or some soil. Bury the fruiting block or add it to a local compost bin. Spend some time with this transition.

Jakob Böhme

THE "ANTI-CHRIST SHOEMAKER"

Jakob Böhme (1575–1624) was a German mystic and philosopher. At fourteen, he began an apprenticeship as a shoemaker, a profession he pursued throughout his life. In 1599, he married Katharina Kuntzschmann, and they had six children together. Böhme was deeply spiritual and dedicated himself to prayer, Bible study, and the works of visionary thinkers such as Paracelsus, Johannes Weigel, and

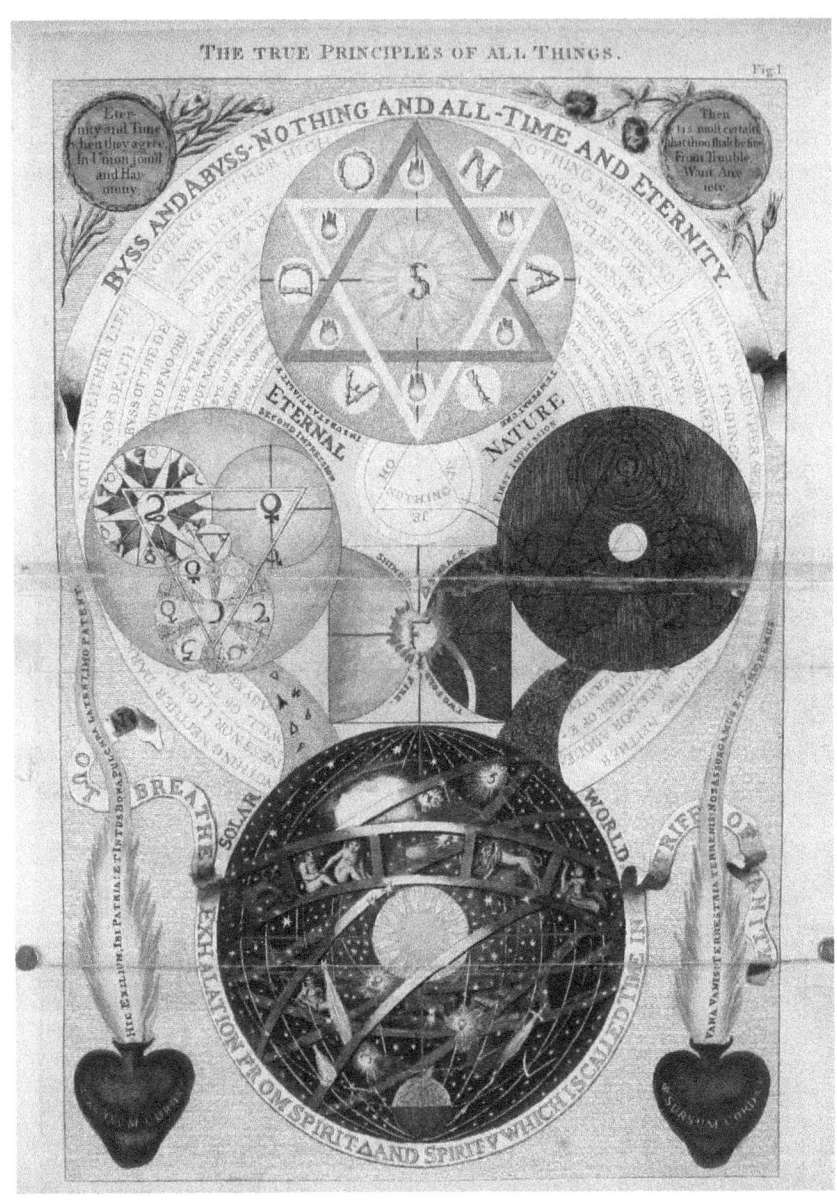

"The true principles of all things," fig. 1 from *The works of Jacob Behmen, the "Teutonic theosopher": to which is prefixed, the life of the author*, volume 3, by William Law, 1764 (hand-colored engraving). English School (18th century) / Bridgeman Images.

Caspar Schwenckfeld. Throughout his life, he experienced a series of mystical visions that profoundly influenced his beliefs. As a student of alchemy, Böhme regarded the imagination as humanity's central power—the source from which all creation flows—and he trusted his inner visions.

In 1598, while in a trance, Böhme saw himself surrounded by divine light and gained insight into the nature and virtues of the plant world. Two years later, in 1600, while contemplating sunlight reflected in a pewter dish, he received a revelation about the spiritual structure of the world. In 1610, another profound vision deepened his understanding of the unity of the cosmos, and Böhme was inspired to share his insights. He began recording his visions and philosophies, writing *Morgenröte im Aufgang* (*Dawn of the Day in the East*). The unfinished work was lent to nobleman Karl von Ender, who circulated copies. In 1619, he completed *De Tribus Principiis* (*The Three Principles of the Divine Essence*) after two years of work, followed by numerous other treatises, all hand-copied and shared privately among friends.

Through this secret circulation, he gained a growing network of friends, academic correspondents, and noble patrons. However, some of his increasingly radical ideas faced strong opposition, including from a local clergyman named Gregor Richter, who famously denounced him as the "Shoemaker Anti-Christ." During this period, Europe was experiencing significant political and religious fragmentation, including a philosophical shift from medieval to Renaissance cosmologies and the decline of feudal structures. Böhme believed his philosophy could heal this rift through what he called the dialectical principle: "In Yes and No all things consist" (Hegel 1995, 17).

He envisioned existence as unfolding in three interconnected realms. At the lowest level is the Dark Fire-World, which he called Hell, where all basic bodily impulses and the cravings that accompany them reside. He viewed this darkness as the very source of life. Above it is the Light World, or Heaven, where virtues and love emanate. He referred to these two realms, Hell and Heaven, as the Contraries, and their dynamic interplay—marked by contraction followed by expansion and rotation—creates motion and sparks divine energy. The Contraries, Hell and Heaven, are mutually essential; they exist simultaneously within God. Without the Opposition of Contraries in God, life itself could not exist. The third realm is the Outer World of Nature, which he saw as an "outbirth" or projection of the other two realms.

Böhme's work can be linked to the concept of putrefaction because he was unafraid to explore how Hell and its putrid qualities are integral to our transformation and spiritual evolution. Like other Christian alchemists, he viewed original sin (the theological concept in Christianity that humanity inherits a fallen, sinful nature due to the disobedience of Adam and Eve in the Garden of Eden) as something to celebrate. He saw it as a necessary step in the universe's development of consciousness.

Böhme's ability to surrender to the gravity of psychic putrefaction assisted him in persisting in his work despite considerable pushback from his contemporaries. Böhme's philosophies drew fire from the church authorities, who ordered him to stop writing. He obeyed for five years before he took it up again in secrecy, and his many admirers and adversaries soon caught wind of it. He raised the cockles of church authorities once more, and he was banished from his hometown and separated from his family. In exile, he continued to draw supporters with his writing and so was able to return home to his wife and children after a few years. Rather than viewing suffering as something to avoid, Böhme perceived it as a gateway to wisdom—a necessary purification that clears the path for deeper truths. However, suffering is not something we can carry alone. When we come together and allow our shared vulnerabilities to connect us, we can begin to transform our suffering into something meaningful. In the company of others, we find the strength to endure and the wisdom to see suffering as part of a larger process of growth and renewal.

Practice Putrefaction

ATTENDING TO THE DEAD

Start by selecting a cemetery to visit, and prepare to create art in collaboration with the space and the individuals buried there. Approach this activity as a way to honor the departed, using your creativity as a gesture of respect.

A few summers ago, I visited the grave of poet Frank O'Hara at Green River Cemetery in Springs, East Hampton, New York. I brought a bouquet of flowers and sat by his grave, singing to him and expressing my gratitude for the inspiration he had given me. I made a rubbing of part of a poem etched into his headstone, using pencil and paper. The inscription read, "Grace to be born / and to live as variously as possible."

Before leaving, I placed flowers on graves with eroded names, honoring the cemetery and those whose names may have been lost to time. Later, I sent the rubbing of the "Grace to be born" poem to a few friends who were expecting babies at the time, sharing O'Hara's beautiful words with an incoming new generation.

When you arrive at your chosen cemetery, take a moment to quietly observe your surroundings, allowing yourself to become fully present. Reflect on the lives of those buried there and the cemetery's history. As you explore, consider how you might make art out of this encounter—whether through writing, drawing, photography, or another medium.

As you complete your visit to the cemetery, leave a small tribute—flowers, a written note, or another meaningful offering—as a sign of appreciation.

VI.

Congelation
THE EAGLE AND THE TOAD

Zodiac: Scorpio ———————— **Planet:** Mars

Images: Snake nailed to a cross, an eagle chained to a toad or otherwise weighed down, a bird eating their own wings, Mercury bound in cords

Material Applications: Thickening, solidifying, slowing, adding weight or density, commitment, loyalty, and everyday practice

> *Of Congelation I need not much to write,*
> *But what it is, I will to you declare.*
> *It is the induration of soft things of colour white,*
> *And the fixation together of spirits which are flying,*
> *How to congeal, you need not much to care,*
> *For Elements will knit together soon.*
>
> —George Ripley, *The Compound of Alchymy*

In the alchemist's laboratory, congelation thickens or solidifies a liquid, transforming it from a fluid or semifluid state into a more solid or viscous form. To congeal a liquid using heat, you can reduce it by simmering or boiling, which allows water to evaporate and concentrates the remaining liquid. Cooling certain liquids can also cause them to congeal. Liquids like honey and vegetable oil become thicker as their molecules slow down in colder temperatures. As viscosity increases, some substances crystallize into solid structures, while others form a soft solid.

In alchemical practice, congelation is an essential method for "fixing the volatile." This process involves transforming a substance that is easily evaporated or changeable into a stable, solid, "fixed" form that resists heat and change and will be unaffected by fire. In creative practice, congelation marks the moment when ideas become tangible and solid, "fixing themselves" into form. Creative congelation happens more easily when we approach our work with enthusiasm and flexibility, allowing ourselves to release rigid expectations. In his guidelines for congelation, Ripley writes: "Congeal not into so hard a stone / As glass or crystal, which melteth by fusion / But so that it like wax will melt anon / Without blast: and beware of delusion." This reminds us to remain soft and agile as we bring our artwork to life.

Congelation in creative practice can be hindered when inflexibility turns our "volatile" ideas into something brittle rather than soft and yielding. Last year, I experienced this while writing a book of poetry. The time I spent letting words flow freely, watching them land on the page like a swarm of gleaming beetles, was one of the most joyful periods of creativity I've experienced. Once it was time to publish the book, however, perfectionism crept in, and what had once been an organic process became a rigid, grueling task. For the first time, I wondered how the poems would sound to other people, and I tore through them like a jackhammer in a field of wildflowers, trying to edit for an unknown reader who was judging the work harshly.

The image most commonly used to represent congelation is a snake (symbolizing renewal and the cycle of eternal return) nailed to a cross at the intersection of the earthly (horizontal) and divine (vertical) realms. In this position, the snake relinquishes its natural flow and changeability, becoming motionless. When we finalize a piece of art, we solidify it into a tangible form, sacrificing any other possible forms it could have taken and declaring it "finished." Once our work is completed and fixed into a shape, we subject it to judgment. But judgment is never fixed.

Emily Dickinson's poetry was disliked and misunderstood in her lifetime, remaining unpublished until a few years after her death. Publisher Thomas Niles once remarked that her poems "are quite as remarkable for defects as for beauties and are generally devoid of true poetic qualities" (Charters 1962, 2). Today, Dickinson is celebrated as one of the most significant poets in American literature. This shift in perception serves as a reminder that what is overlooked or undervalued in one moment can, over time, be recognized in an entirely new light. Ultimately, it is not for us as artists to determine the value of our work in the broader world. The path to successful congelation requires humility and the ability to let go of self-identification with how our work is received.

Reflecting on the symbol of a serpent entwined around a cross can help us release our attachment to the self in relation to our creativity. In alchemical terms, the self is often represented by a circle—a shape in which all points are interconnected, making it impossible to define where one begins and another ends, much

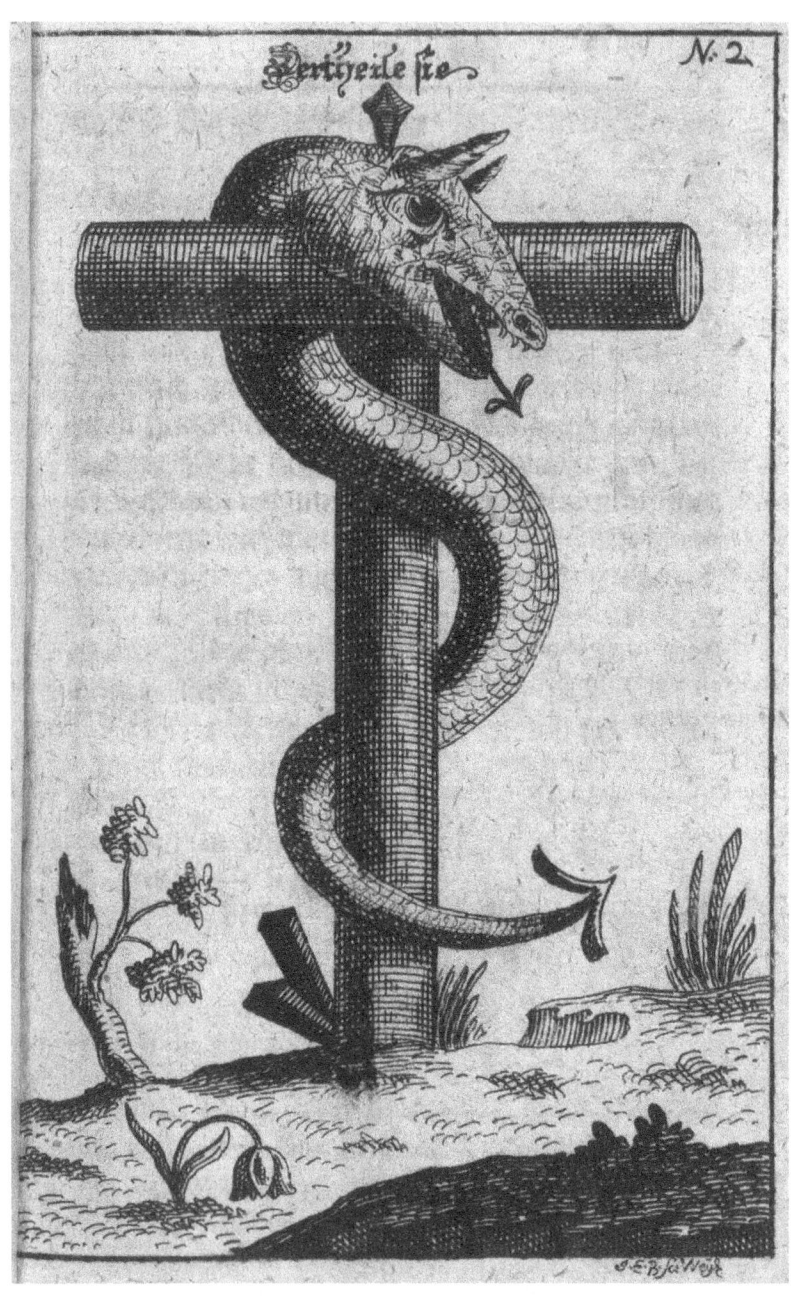

The snake on a cross. Image No. 2 from *Uraltes chymisches Werck*, by Abraham Eleazar.
Erfurt, 1735. Embassy of the Free Mind | Bibliotheca Philosophica Hermetica Collection.

like the serpent eating its own tail. Each point follows and precedes another in an endless cycle of becoming, with no clear beginning or end. In alchemical philosophy, you are someone, everyone, and no one at once. There is immense freedom in embracing this idea as an artist.

In the alchemical tradition, art is lightning that moves through the artist, who then grounds the energy into form. Once shaped into artwork, this energy takes on a life of its own, continuing on beyond the artist's control. This ongoing flow is a prayer in motion. Through the creative process, we draw the divine through ourselves and our work as part of an ever-evolving cycle. This passage from the *Corpus Hermeticum* describes epochs of creativity that come and go like waves in the sea:

> *This is the beginning of their living and becoming wise,*
> *according to their lot from the course of the cyclic gods.*
> *And this is the beginning of their being released,*
> *leaving behind great memorials of their works of art upon the Earth,*
> *and every generation of ensouled flesh,*
> *and every generation of the sowing of fruit,*
> *and every generation of every craftwork,*
> *all for fame unto the obscurity of the ages—*
> *all that is diminished will be renewed by Necessity. (Mead 1906, 11)*

Ingmar Bergman, the acclaimed Swedish director and screenwriter, is widely regarded as one of history's greatest and most influential filmmakers. Over his career, Bergman directed more than sixty films and documentaries, many of which he also wrote. He firmly believed that art had lost something essential when it became focused exclusively on the individual. In an excerpt from his *Four Screenplays of Ingmar Bergman*, he writes of art:

> *It is my opinion that art lost its basic creative drive the moment it was separated from worship. It severed an umbilical cord and now lives its own sterile life, perpetuating and deteriorating itself. In earlier times, the artist remained unknown, and their work was dedicated to the glory of God. They lived and died without being deemed more or less important than other artisans; terms such as "eternal values," "immortality," and "masterpiece" were not applicable in their case. The ability to create was seen as a gift. In such a world, a sense of invulnerable assurance and natural humility thrived. (Bergman 1960, 23)*

Perfectionism, fear of judgment, and egotism can make a creative work too stiff or rigid, hindering the process of congelation. Alternatively, congelation may fail if the work remains too vague and elusive to grasp. This lack of solidity can result from scattered attention, avoidance, procrastination, or the temptation to juggle too many projects at once, keeping the work in a constant flux. These distractions impede the consistent, focused effort necessary to solidify creative work.

When you find yourself struggling to congeal your creative work, the image of an eagle chained to a toad—an alchemical symbol for "fixing the volatile"—can offer valuable insight. In alchemical iconography, the eagle represents the divine or spiritual realm, soaring with inspiration and visionary ideas. This signifies the space where our creativity originates, echoing from the One Mind down to the material world. The toad represents the Prima Materia—the raw material of physicality and the grounding forces that give life to ideas. In this grounded space, the One Mind's ideas can take root and grow. This connection brings the energy and nourishment of the Earth into the sacred idea that wants to take form. The eagle, representing your creation, is not confined or limited; instead, it is being fed by the grounding forces of the material world. Through this connection, the work is prepared to take its place, having received the sustenance it needs to become fully realized, grounded, and capable of standing independently.

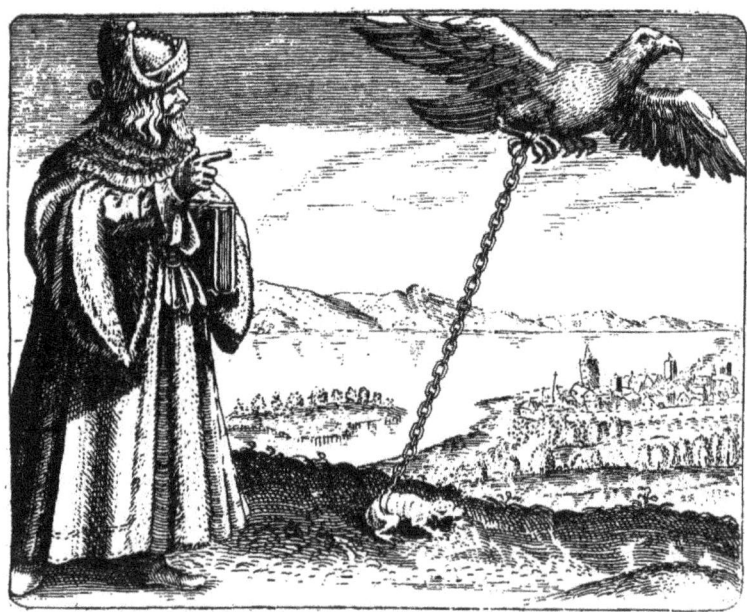

The eagle chained to the toad while Avicenna watches. From *Symbola Aureae Mensae Duodecim Nationum*, by Michael Maier, 1617. Courtesy Frankfurt University.

Practice Congelation

THE EAGLE AND THE TOAD

The engraving depicts Ibn Sīnā (c. 980–1037), commonly known in the West as Avicenna, a preeminent philosopher and physician of the Islamic Golden Age. Ibn Sīnā was influential in medieval European medical and scholastic thought and authored works spanning philosophy, medicine, astronomy, alchemy, geography, psychology, theology, logic, mathematics, physics, and poetry.

Meditate on the image of the eagle and the toad in this engraving to reflect on how the nourishment of congelation can enhance your creative practice.

▶ *What projects would I work on if I didn't feel they had to be well received?*

▶ *As a child, what was I told by my caregivers about my creative output?*

▶ *As a child, what do I wish I had been told by my caregivers about my creative output?*

▶ *What does the eagle have to say about my creativity? How about the toad?*

▶ *What opportunities do I feel frustrated about not getting? What does my inner eagle have to say about these missed opportunities? How about my inner toad?*

▶ *What does my creativity want or need at this exact moment? (Ask yourself, the eagle, and the toad this question in turns and note the differing answers.)*

▶ *Who in my life truly believes in my creative vision? Does the eagle believe in my vision? How about the toad?*

▶ *What limitations do I place on my creative practice, and why do I enforce them? Does the eagle agree with these limits? How about the toad?*

▶ *What does completion mean to me, and how do I know when a project is truly finished? Is it up to me? What does the eagle have to say about this? How about the toad?*

PRAYER AND PENITENCE

Zosimos of Panopolis was a high-ranking scribal priest, goldsmith, and alchemist. He played a significant role in creating temple statues, ensuring they were "ensouled" with divine spirits through the ritual preparation of the metals. In his text *Visions of Zosimos*, he describes the Egyptian statue-making ritual known as the Opening of the Mouth.

During this ritual, the statues of deities are subjected to violent acts such as smelting, chiseling, and engraving. Artisan priests perform these acts with a mix of reverence and horror. Once their work is completed, the priests vow that no further harm will come to the statues and seek forgiveness for the pain they have inflicted. This ritual illustrates a profound respect for both our materials *and* our creations, treating them as active, conscious participants in the creative process— an attitude we would benefit from reclaiming.

According to the World Wildlife Federation's "Living Planet Report," approximately 70 percent of the Earth's biodiversity has been lost to human extraction and resource consumption since 1970, and this trend is accelerating. If we treated everything on Earth as sacred, sought forgiveness, and reflected on our failures to honor the living world, humanity would shift toward a more sustainable and sacred mode of creativity. In the Hermetic tradition, thanksgiving, hymns, and silent contemplation align the artist's spirit with the divine, sensitizing them to the sacrifices made during the creative process.

In Egyptian alchemical practice, ingratitude was considered a serious offense that could burden the heart and lead to eternal suffering. Offering thanks before undertaking any creative or alchemical work was essential, as was asking for forgiveness and swearing to honor the artwork after it was completed. To introduce the concept of congelation into your creative practice, it is vital to approach your work with reverence, understanding that your efforts serve the divine.

Write a prayer of dedication and thanks to recite before doing creative work; this prayer can be as simple or elaborate as you wish. You may also include physical gestures, such as bowing your head or kneeling if they feel meaningful. I will provide a few examples of poems I have used as prayers. The goal is to establish a consistent ritual of offering your art to the divine before you begin, using words and actions that resonate with your purpose.

I like to light a candle and then recite this translation of a Sappho poem by Mary Barnard as a thank-you to the divine light of inspiration that visits me:

Thank you, my dear
you came, and you did
well to come: I needed
you. You have made
love blaze up in
my breast—bless you!

Bless you as often
as the hours have
been endless to me
while you were gone. (Sappho 1958, 47)

This Robert Bly translation of "Buddha Inside the Light" by Rainer Maria Rilke also makes for a wonderful prayer of thanks:

The core of every core, the kernel of every kernel,
an almond! held in itself, deepening in sweetness:
all of this, everything, right up to the stars,
is the meat around your stone. Accept my bow.
Oh, yes, you feel it, how the weights on you are gone!
Your husk has reached into what has no end,
and that is where the great saps are brewing now.
On the outside a warmth is helping,
for, high, high above, your own suns are growing
immense and they glow as they wheel around.
Yet something has already started to live
in you that will live longer than the sun. (Rilke 1981, 104)

Pay attention to how devotion and creativity become intertwined in your process as you step deeper into your role as an alchemist. Does prayer help you view your art as part of a divine cycle of inspiration and materialization? Does it enable you to move past perfectionism, scattered energies, or lack of clarity?

Paul Thek

I DO NOTHING OF MYSELF

The American Paul Thek (1933–1988) was known for his work as a painter, sculptor, and installation artist. Throughout his career, Thek exhibited a variety of installations and sculptural pieces across the United States and Europe.

In the 1960s, Thek and his partner, photographer Peter Hujar, became part of a dynamic circle of artists and writers. He developed a particularly close relationship with Susan Sontag, who dedicated her 1966 essay collection *Against Interpretation* to him. According to Sontag's biographer, the title and concept for the collection were inspired by a conversation with Thek. During this discussion, when Sontag began to analyze art in an overly intellectual manner, Thek interrupted her, saying,

"Susan, stop, stop. I'm against interpretation. We don't look at art when we interpret it. That's not the way to look at art."

Thek was a gay man and a devout Catholic—a combination that placed him in a deeply conflicted position. His sexuality clashed with the Catholic Church's rigid, anti-LGBTQ+ stance, while his faith set him apart from the secular art world, which often viewed religious devotion with skepticism or disdain. In New York's art scene, where individualism and the pursuit of material success, fame, and recognition are highly valued, Thek's more spiritual and communal approach to life and art stood in stark contrast.

Thek's artistic philosophy was rooted in early Christian sacred image theory, which held that an image's power came from its connection to a higher, divine source, not from the artist's personal creativity or expression. Thek viewed his work as a conduit to something greater than himself, opposing the dominant art world ethos that celebrated the artist as an autonomous, self-asserting creator.

He wrote in his notebook in 1975:

To wish that it may be known that "I was the author" is the thought of a man not yet adult.
Is the Holy Spirit any other than an intellectual fountain?
I do nothing of myself.
Not I but the wind that blows through me.
The secularization of art and the rationalization of religion are inseparably connected, however unaware of it we may be. (Aramphongphan 2021, 113)

In 1967, he received a Fulbright fellowship and moved to Italy, during which time he traveled extensively throughout Europe and worked on large-scale installations. Before leaving New York, Thek marked the end of his early career with a significant installation titled *The Tomb* (1967), which symbolized his rejection of the art-making methods he had previously used. The installation featured a life-sized effigy of Thek, painted pale pink, dressed in a suit adorned with jewelry, including a necklace made of human hair. His right hand—the hand he used to create his art—was severed, with the fingers placed in a nearby pouch, symbolizing his "silencing" as an artist. Surrounding the effigy were personal items such as pink goblets, letters, and earlier relics, giving the work the feel of an archaeological dig.

While in Europe, Paul Thek created installations he called *Processions*—immersive, often site-specific works deeply influenced by religious rituals and symbolism.

These installations used a diverse array of objects and materials to evoke a sense of a pilgrimage or spiritual journey.

After years of living a nomadic lifestyle, Thek returned to New York in 1976 and began teaching at Cooper Union. Despite personal struggles and difficulties in selling his work, he continued to exhibit his art nationally and internationally throughout the 1980s. Thek passed away on August 10, 1988, just a year after being diagnosed with AIDS.

Paul Thek's work exemplifies the alchemical concept of congelation—the idea that art is a material expression of the divine. He believed that the artist should not impose their will on the creative process but allow a higher force to guide it. In this view, art serves as a bridge between the earthly and the divine, with the artist's hands and vision acting as tools through which the divine manifests in the physical world. For Thek, creation was an act of humility—a way of allowing the sacred to flow through him, rather than a pursuit of individual expression or ego-driven achievement.

Take some time to study Thek's work, and see what you can learn about prayer from it.

VII.

Cibation

THE PELICAN IN HER PIETY

Zodiac: Libra ——————— **Planet:** Venus

Images: Feeding, nursing, suckling, watering flowers, tending the garden, the pelican vulning, birds drinking, birds feeding each other, alchemists offering elixirs to dragons and lions, and alchemists drinking elixirs from goblets and laboratory retorts

Material Applications: Feeding, tending, duration, using time as a material, resting, devotion, acts of service

> *Cibation is called a feeding of our dry matter,*
> *With milk and meat, which moderately you do,*
> *Until it be brought unto the third order.*
> *But give it never so much, that you it glut,*
> *Beware of dropsy, and also of Noah's flood:*
> *By little and little therefore you to it put*
> *Of meat and drink, as seems to do it good,*
> *That watery humours not overgrow the blood,*
> *To drink therefore let it be measured so,*
> *That you never quench it from that kindly appetite.*
>
> —George Ripley, *The Compound of Alchymy*

Cibation refers to the process of introducing a transformative or vital liquid into a substance or the alchemist's body to catalyze change or achieve a specific goal. The term originates from the Latin word *cibare*, which means "to feed" or "to nourish." When you consume a tincture, like the one we created during the separation phase, you are engaging in cibation. Just as the chamomile underwent alchemical processes to become more potent, consuming that tincture activates a similar transformative process within you. A parallel can be drawn to the Christian ritual of the Eucharist, where the faithful consume bread and wine, believed to have become the body and blood of Christ through consecration. Cibation reflects a similar concept applied to the elements of nature, where the alchemist becomes one with the powers they seek to harness by eating and drinking them, or by feeding their experiment, as you fed your spagyric spirits during the separation stage.

The most common image for cibation is a pelican feeding her young with blood that gushes from her own heart. This stems from a medieval belief that, in times of famine, a mother pelican would sacrifice her own blood to nourish her offspring—and sometimes to resurrect her dead young. While the origins of this belief are unclear, it may have arisen from the observation that pelicans regurgitate food for their chicks and appear to stab their own hearts when tucking their bills into their breast feathers. The pelican became a symbol of self-sacrifice and the nurturing mother, and it was also linked to Christ's sacrifice in Christian tradition. The image of the "Pelican in Her Piety," where the bird feeds her young, or the "Pelican Vulning," where she wounds herself, appears in church facades, alchemical manuscripts, and medieval heraldry.

Practice Cibation

COPPER OXIDE VENUS INK

A vital part of alchemical practice is mastering the art of feeding your materials—nurturing and sustaining a reaction over time to achieve the desired transformation. One of my favorite ways to connect with cibation as a laboratory practice is by creating copper oxide ink. The process yields a striking marbled blue ink with different layers of color that resemble a planet. To make this ink, however, you'll need an outdoor space where it can cure safely, as the fumes may cause respiratory irritation. A windowsill, rooftop, fire escape, or yard works well. It's essential to work in a place where children or animals won't accidentally interfere with the mixture. If you don't have access to a safe outdoor space, please skip this exercise. Your practice of cibation must remain nourishing, not harmful.

MATERIALS

- Glass container with a tight-fitting lid

- ¼ to ½ cup copper (wiring, copper sponges, or bits of copper tubing from the hardware store work well)

- 1 cup of white vinegar (then adding more as needed)

- 1 tablespoon of iodized salt (must be iodized, add more as needed)

- Spoon (that you will only use to make this ink) or a stick for stirring

- Rubber gloves

In alchemy, copper's conductivity and sensitivity to touch associate it with Venus, the planet of love, art, beauty, and sex. According to alchemical tradition, it's best to start this mixture on a Friday, Venus's day, and wear green or white, her colors. To pay tribute, you can place roses, incense, or milk with honey on your alchemist's altar. Adding music, prayer, and other devotional elements to the preparation of this ink will strengthen it.

When you're ready, put your copper pieces inside a large glass container that has a tight-fitting lid (but don't put it on just yet) and add white vinegar until the pieces are submerged. Add iodized salt and stir gently. Leave the mixture outside without the lid in a well-ventilated area away from pets and children. Each day, stir the mixture. (This is where cibation comes in.) Add more vinegar and salt if there has been any evaporation so that the copper pieces stay covered. The process could take anywhere from two to five weeks and will require consistent feeding.

Once you've reached your desired color, strain or fish out your copper pieces while wearing rubber gloves. Depending on the oxidation states you achieve, you may have anything from a forest green to a neon blue. Cap your mixture, and keep your finished ink capped when not in use. Shake each time before use, or play around with the layers that will naturally separate (darker, transparent color on top and a thicker, milkier color that gathers on the bottom). Copper ink, when allowed to dry in a small puddle from a dropper or paintbrush, creates a swirling effect that can look like the marbled surface of Venus. Experiment with using your Venusian ink to write letters or make paintings that align with subjects under Venus's rulership.

The Circulation of the World Soul

One of the most revered alchemical distillation devices is the Pelican—a glass retort that features two tubes connecting the neck to the body, which creates a reflux still. When a mixture is heated, vapors condense in the neck and flow back into the retort body through the tubes. This circulatory process allows alchemists to purify a substance. Beyond its practical function, the Pelican retort holds deep symbolic meaning, representing nature's cycles of giving and receiving. Working with the Pelican is believed to help the alchemist attune to the natural rhythms of life, correcting imbalances in both the material and spiritual realms.

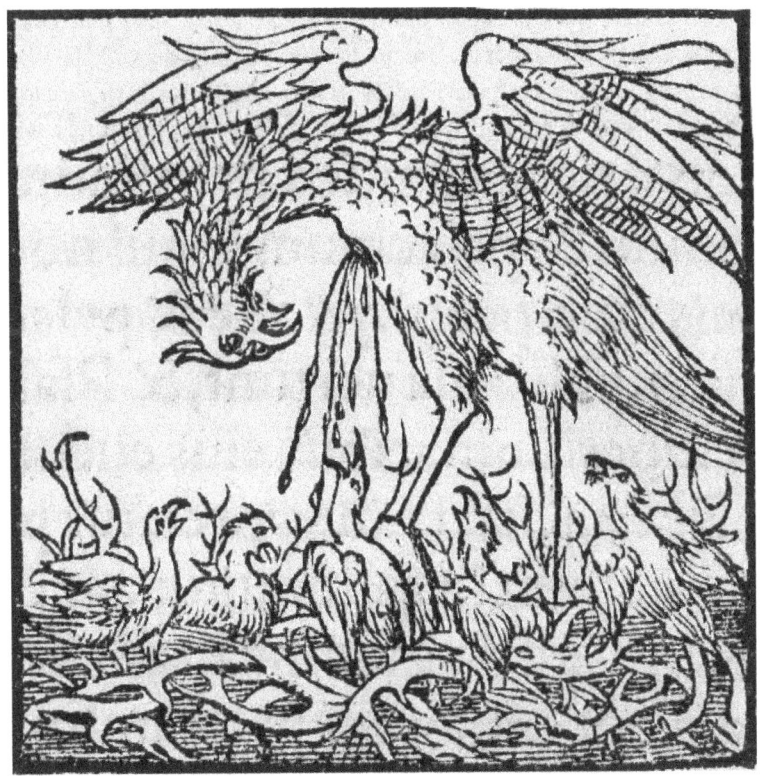

A medieval pelican feeds its brood with its own blood. "A Vulning Pelican" from *Historia Animalium*, by Conrad Gessner, 1555. Courtesy Kenneth Spencer Research Library, University of Kansas.

In alchemical thought, the world is viewed as a living entity animated by the World Soul, or Anima Mundi, with which we have an interdependent relationship. As Plato writes in *Timaeus*: "This world is indeed a living being endowed with a soul and intelligence . . . a single visible living entity containing all other living entities, which by their nature are all related" (Plato 2016, np). For alchemists, every experiment is done in collaboration with the World Soul. While the church seeks enlightenment in the ethereal realm, alchemists aim to uncover this hidden spark in the material world, revealing its divine light within their laboratories.

A society built on constant production, consumption, and extraction is destined to collapse. According to data provided by the Global Forest Watch, humans are cutting down approximately fifteen billion trees annually while only replanting around five billion, resulting in a net loss of about ten billion trees each year. At this rate, all trees could disappear within the next 300 years. As contemporary alchemists, we must confront the disruptions in our relationship with the World Soul. When spiritual leader Thich Nhat Hanh was asked, "What do we need to do to save our world?" he replied, "What we most need to do is to hear within us the sounds of the Earth crying" (Vaughan-Lee 2016, 33).

Anohni

IT'S TIME TO FEEL WHAT'S REALLY HAPPENING

Anohni (b. 1971) is a British American singer, composer, and visual artist known for her commanding voice and deeply emotive performances. She first gained widespread recognition with her 2005 album *I Am a Bird Now*, a soul-baring collection of songs that received critical acclaim and won the Mercury Prize, cementing her status as a singular voice in contemporary music. In 2016, Anohni released *Hopelessness*. Produced in collaboration with Hudson Mohawke and Oneohtrix Point Never, the record transformed club-friendly beats into vessels for grief, rage, and protest. *Hopelessness* confronts some of the most pressing issues of our time—climate change, drone warfare, mass surveillance, and institutional violence.

One of the standout tracks, "4 Degrees," serves as a chilling reckoning with ecological destruction and the emotional distance many people maintain from it. Anohni's voice rises with both anguish and irony as she sings about her own complicity in environmental collapse, challenging listeners to confront their own roles in the crisis. Throughout the album, the tension between beauty and devastation creates a powerful, unsettling experience—one that refuses easy answers and demands moral introspection.

For the 2025 Vivid festival in Sydney, Anohni staged performances at the Opera House under the title "Mourning the Great Barrier Reef." Coral reefs are among the planet's most vital ecosystems, supporting roughly a third of all marine species and playing a crucial role in carbon sequestration and in sustaining global oxygen levels, thanks to their symbiotic algae. While the Amazon rainforest is often called the Earth's right lung—responsible for generating around 20 percent of the planet's oxygen—the Great Barrier Reef, spanning an area half the size of Texas, could be considered the left. But this lung is in decline. Over the past nine years, the reef has endured six mass bleaching events triggered by unprecedented marine heat waves. Scientists warn that the collapse of coral reefs could set off a devastating chain reaction, pushing other ecosystems toward collapse and edging the planet closer to mass extinction.

In response to this ongoing ecological tragedy, Anohni has been contemplating what she described to the *Guardian* as "ceremonies fit for purpose" (Cain 2025, np). She notes that society knows how to mourn sudden catastrophes—through funerals, memorials, protests, or acts of resistance. But she asks, "What do we do in the face of a slower death?"

In a haunting twist of natural beauty, distressed coral often appears most stunning just before it dies. As they fluoresce—a defensive response to heat stress where corals emit vivid pigments—the reef glows with surreal brilliance. The subsequent stage of bleaching occurs when corals expel the symbiotic algae that provide them with their vibrant colors, leaving them ghostly white. This dazzling signal signifies a world unraveling, like Anohni standing at the center of the stage, singing. Anohni's art invites audiences not only to reflect but also to feel—to mourn, to rage, and to grieve.

What kind of artwork might you create to mourn the losses unfolding across our biosphere? How can your creative expression help your community carry this grief together? In today's world, we are often taught to grieve in silence—to carry our sorrow alone, behind closed doors, as if it were something to hide or be ashamed of. But ecological grief is not a private burden; it is a shared wound. Holding it in isolation only deepens the ache and distances us from one another. Grief must be seen, spoken, and held in community. In this time of accelerating environmental loss, we are all students of sorrow. Each of us must commit to an apprenticeship with loss, learning how to name it, express it, and ultimately share it.

Practice Cibation

THE WORLD SOUL VULNING

A simple way to connect with the World Soul is to lie on the Earth with your heart facing down, oriented toward the planet's core. When I lived in cities, I would bring a picnic blanket to the park and lie face down on it most days, regardless of the weather, to connect with the Earth on a heart-to-heart level. As you do this, you can close your eyes and tune in to the sensations of life happening beneath you, feeling the warmth of the planet's heart beating rhythmically through your body.

Let this quiet exchange remind you that you are part of a nurturing relationship with the planet. Many eco-theorists encourage treating the Earth as a beloved partner, attuned to its needs with a tender, loving heart. In this spirit, it can be lovely to kiss the ground or the trunks of trees, offering them affection and gratitude. Consider bringing gifts to the trees in your neighborhood or singing to them gently, consciously becoming a lover of the Earth.

When confronting grief about the disrupted flow of giving and receiving on our planet, I often turn to Joanna Macy's teachings for guidance. An environmental activist and Buddhist scholar, Macy developed the Work That Reconnects, a program that helps people reconnect with themselves, one another, and the Earth. This teaching is divided into four stages. It begins with Coming from Gratitude, which includes exercises for grounding and fostering empathy. Next is Honoring Our Pain for the World, where shared suffering is embraced, deepening compassion and connection with others. This leads to Seeing with New/Ancient Eyes, where the intertwined nature of social and environmental justice is recognized. Finally, there is Going Forth, where intentional action is taken based on unique gifts and circumstances (Macy & Brown 2014, np).

This dynamic process shifts individuals from feelings of isolation and despair to a deeper sense of interconnectedness and empowerment. Macy believes that by acknowledging the connection to all life, transformation of relationships can occur, leading to ecological and social healing.

Here are some journal prompts based on the Work That Reconnects to help you attend to the World Soul, which is also your own:

Some things I love about being alive on Earth are . . .
A place that was magical to me as a child was . . .
A person who helped me believe in myself was/is . . .
Some things I appreciate about myself are . . .
To be alive at this time of ecological crisis, what's hard for me is . . .
What I appreciate about living in this time of crisis is . . .
These are the ways I see myself participating in addressing this crisis . . .

Free and Easy Chemistry for Ladies

CIBATION AND THE NOURISHMENT OF OTHERS

Cibation, in the context of an alchemist's quest, signifies a phase of personal growth where the alchemist shares their teachings and discoveries with their community. This can be done through publishing, sharing artwork, teaching, or mentoring others. A hallmark of a realized alchemist is their generosity. By sharing their knowledge and experiences, these individuals play a vital role in healing the World Soul, assisting others in recognizing its presence and importance.

La Chymie Charitable et Facile en Faveur des Dames (*Free and Easy Chemistry for Ladies*) is a treatise written by the French alchemist Marie Meurdrac in the 17th century. It discusses the language, equipment, recipes, and processes for the alchemical preparation of medicines, including a fold-out plate with a reference table of alchemical symbols.

Meurdrac wrote this work specifically for a female audience and was aware that women often faced prohibitive costs and limited access to the equipment and supplies required for her procedures. In her text, she directly addresses the gender disparity in medicine and academia, stating, "If women were provided with the same education as men, they would equal them in knowledge" (Meurdrac 1656, np). She expresses her hope that the work will ultimately benefit the less fortunate by educating them in the preparation of medicines, particularly for women. Although she faced public ridicule for publishing this treatise, it became a bestseller, going through five French, six German, and one Italian edition.

Paracelsus famously criticized academic medical institutions and apprenticed with midwives, sorcerers, and village healers to perfect his craft, believing these individuals possessed a practical understanding of medicine grounded in the community rather than theoretical frameworks. He took an oath to "love the sick, each and every one of them, more than if my own body were at stake" (Jacobi 1958, 4), which was the guiding principle for his alchemical and medical practices.

In contrast to the academic doctors of his time, Paracelsus offered his lectures free of charge to anyone interested and presented them in German instead of Latin to ensure his ideas were widely understood. He even went so far as to publicly burn medical treatises in protest against a medical system that treated diseases rather than people, criticizing doctors for failing to communicate compassionately with their patients. He treated the poor for free and gave away any earnings from his wealthy clients, insisting that if medicine was not rooted in love, it was false. Ultimately, cibation speaks to the importance of establishing a continuous cycle of nourishment between the alchemist's output and their community.

Consider sharing your knowledge or skills with others. You could volunteer to read to children at a local library or hospital or create zines about a skill you excel in, such as cooking or gardening, and distribute them in your community. If you have expertise in crafts like woodworking or painting, consider hosting free workshops at community centers. For those knowledgeable about sustainable living, organizing events to teach composting or urban gardening can be impactful. The aim is to provide opportunities for connection, strengthening community resilience through generosity.

VIII.

Sublimation

UP TO THE VERY CIRCLE
OF ETERNITY

Zodiac: Virgo ———————— **Planet:** Mercury

Images: Birds flying upward, other flying figures, alchemists ascending mountains, ladders, towers, stairs, eggs, comets, wind

Material Applications: Invisible energies as mediums, space as a tool, flight, the language of the birds, inspiration, intuition

> *Fools do sublime, but you do not sublime so,*
> *For we sublime not in the way they do,*
> *To sublime truly therefore you shall not miss,*
> *If you can make the bodies first spiritual,*
> *And then your spirits (as I have taught you) corporeal.*
>
> —George Ripley, *The Compound of Alchymy*

Sublimation is when a substance transitions directly from a solid to a gas, bypassing the liquid phase entirely. In alchemical laboratories, this involves heating a solid material until it vaporizes without melting. A classic example is the sublimation of mercury. Mercury's primary ore, cinnabar—also known for producing the red pigment vermilion—undergoes sublimation when heated over an open flame. As the cinnabar is heated, it releases mercury vapor, which can be captured and cooled, condensing back into liquid mercury. In alchemical tradition, the vapors generated during this process are called the "Hermes Bird." The term *sublimation* comes from the Latin word *sublimis*, which means "high." This refers to the process in which a material changes from a heavy, earthbound solid to a light, sky-bound vapor.

Alchemical vessels were viewed as miniature representations of the macrocosm, with the lower section symbolizing Earth and the upper section representing Heaven. A typical depiction of sublimation features a bird rising from the lower part of an alchemist's glass retort to the top of the vessel.

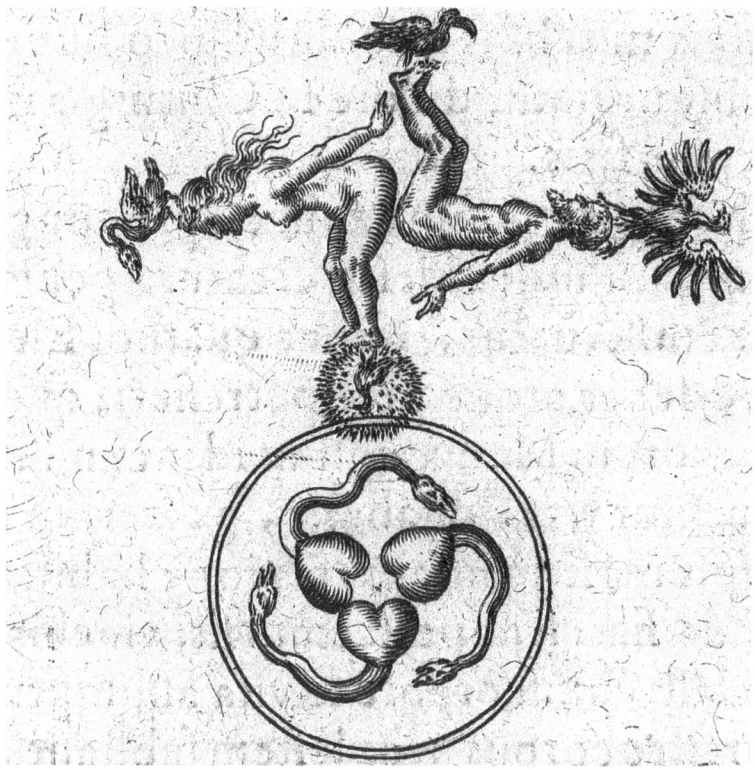

"IX Clavis" (Ninth Key) from *Musaeum Hermeticum Reformatum et Amplificatum,* by Basilius Valentinus, 1625. Courtesy Science History Institute Digital Collections, Science History Institute, Philadelphia.

Alchemical teachings as a whole have long been connected with birds. Thoth—the Egyptian god of alchemy, writing, and language—has the head of a long-beaked ibis. In the *Corpus Hermeticum,* Hermes Trismegistus instructs his students to: "Close your eyes and let the mind expand. Let no fear of death or darkness arrest its course. Allow the mind to merge with Mind. Let it flow out upon the great curve of consciousness. Let it soar on the wings of the great bird of duration, up to the very Circle of Eternity" (Hermes Trismegistus 1945, np).

The imagery of a bird soaring freely into the infinite captures the alchemist's quest for spiritual ascent and transformation. The "great bird of duration" symbolizes the alchemical process itself—an ongoing practice of refining the inner self and the outer world, elevating the soul toward a greater cosmic understanding. The saints and poets who claim that birds "praise God" with their songs are not mistaken; these melodies represent the song of life, a message from the divine to those on Earth, and a song of devotion from the Earth to the divine.

To avoid persecution, alchemists concealed their recipes in symbols, surreal imagery, and hidden ciphers. Some alchemists referred to this cryptic code as the "Green Language" or "Living Language," suggesting that it conveyed more than just words—it had the power to create. Over time, this form of communication became known as the Language of the Birds, which was regarded as a higher, more perfect language for expressing intuitive insight.

The Language of the Birds operated as a coded, high-frequency language beyond ordinary hearing range. In Abrahamic and European mythology, medieval literature, and occult traditions, this language is often described as a divine, angelic tongue—used by birds to communicate with the initiated, offering enlightened knowledge or wisdom.

Birds are often used as symbols to represent key concepts in the Great Work. Birds flying upward symbolize the volatilization or evaporation of substances, while birds descending indicate the fixation, condensation, or precipitation of materials. Birds shown both ascending and descending represent the process of distillation. A bird in a standing position typically indicates the type of alchemical operation being performed. The crow represents putrefaction; the rooster and hen symbolize the conjunction or union of substances; and the peacock heralds the end result of successful fermentation. The pelican represents circulation and distillation processes, while the eagle symbolizes sublimation. The Bennu bird or phoenix, a mythological bird reborn from fire, symbolizes the final stage of the Great Work: the creation of the Philosopher's Stone.

Practice Sublimation

BEGINNING WITH THE EGG

Scientists now believe that 13.8 billion years ago, the universe existed as a gravitational singularity—an incredibly small point from which all of creation emerged. This concept can be imagined in the form of the cosmic egg, which is a symbol found in the creation myths of various cultural and alchemical traditions. In alchemy, the cosmos is often represented as a serpent hatching from or coiling around an egg.

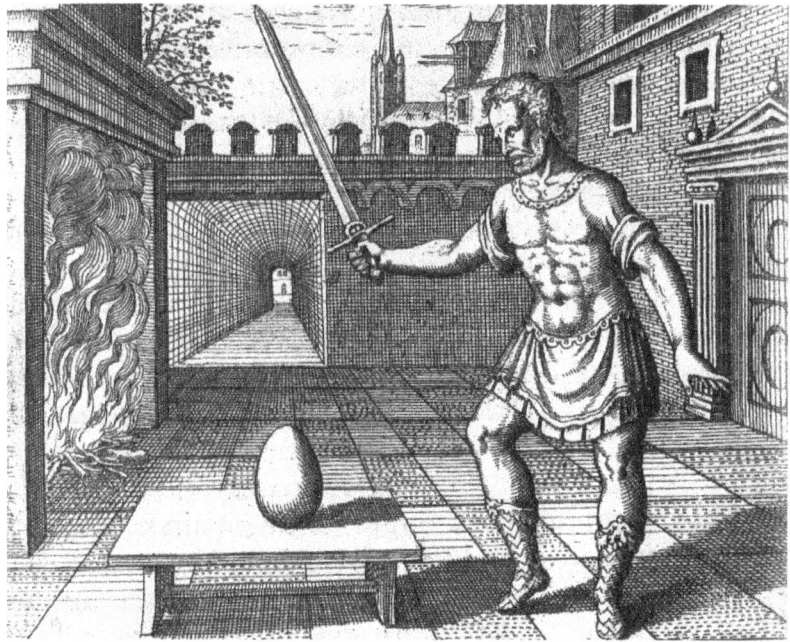

A soldier smites a large egg with a sword. Emblem 8 from *Atalanta Fugiens*, by Michael Maier, illustrated by Matthäus Merian. Oppenheim, Germany, 1618. Courtesy Science History Institute Digital Collections, Science History Institute, Philadelphia.

In one Greek myth, Nyx, the goddess of night, is portrayed as a solitary bird with dark wings, dwelling in an endless void. A gentle wind caresses her feathers, and together they create an egg. After some time, Nyx lays a golden egg and rests upon it for an age. Eventually, life stirs within the egg, leading to the emergence of Eros, the god of love. As the egg cracks open, half of the shell ascends to form the heavens, while the other half descends to create the earth. Eros names the sky Uranus and the earth Gaia, uniting them in love, which results in the creation of all Earth's creatures.

In some Egyptian creation myths, the cosmic goose known as Kenkenwer, or the "Great Cackler," is said to have laid the cosmic egg from which the world originated. The Egyptian god Geb, associated with farming and fertility, is often depicted with a goose on his head. In some versions of this myth, it is Geb who lays the cosmic egg from which the Sun rises each morning.

The Leiden Papyrus contains a song from Geb describing his own birth from an egg.

Behold, I rejoice on my standard, on my seat.
I am the Creator of Darkness, making my place in the limits of the Sky,
The Ruler of Infinity.
I am the Son of the Earth,
Sprung from the Egg of the World.
I rejoice in the Lord of the Palace.
My Nest is unseen; I have broken the Egg.
I am the Lord of Millions of Years.
I have made my Nest in the limits of the sky,
And descended to the earth as the goose who drives out all sins. (Griffith and
Thompson 1904, np)

Eggs have been used in various alchemical practices, such as creating binders for pigments in paint and preparing the Oil of Egg, where the oils from the egg yolk are cold-extracted. The Oil of Egg is believed to possess limitless curative powers in alchemical medicine. Today, it is primarily used to heal and regenerate the skin.

Beyond their practical uses, eggs are employed in meditative and contemplative exercises practiced by the alchemists to connect them with creative energy.

Begin by drawing an egg on a blank piece of paper. Focus on its shape—the gentle curves, smoothness, and weight. Let your hand move with intention, capturing the essence of the egg's form. Once you've completed your drawing, you can use it as a point of reflection or meditation, allowing yourself to consider the egg as a symbol of creation, transformation, and rebirth—a vessel containing infinite potential.

After your drawing is finished, create a physical version of your egg using materials that inspire you. You might sculpt it from clay, shape it from paper, carve it from wood, or even build it with fabric, metal, or found objects. Once your egg is complete, place it on your alchemist's altar. You can accompany this with a prayer or a quiet intention for renewal, growth, and transformation in your life. Use this egg as a focal point for meditating on the creation of the cosmos.

Practice Sublimation
THE LANGUAGE OF THE BIRDS

Observing and feeding birds are integral spiritual practices for alchemists. Messages from the divine are encoded in the movements of birds, and taking the time to observe them and watch their motions attunes us to their language and can open us up to new ideas in our art. Nikola Tesla, a famed inventor renowned for designing the alternating electric current motor and the Tesla coil, had a passion for birds, and he attributed his ability to harness ideas about the movements of electrical currents to observing them.

Throughout the streets of New York, Tesla would let out a soft whistle, and flocks of pigeons would emerge from the shadows, settling on his outstretched arms to be fed. He covered his windowsills with birdseed and always left his windows open, allowing the birds to come and go freely. He cared for injured birds, and on one occasion, he was arrested for trying to lasso an injured homing pigeon in the plaza near St. Patrick's Cathedral. Tesla told his biographer John O'Neill, "I have been feeding thousands of pigeons for years. But there was one pigeon, a beautiful bird, pure white with light gray tips on its wings; that one was different. It was a female. I would recognize that pigeon anywhere. No matter where I was, she would find me. When I wanted her, I only had to wish and call for her, and she would come flying to me. She understood me, and I understood her" (O'Neill 1944, 316–17).

Tesla said he and this pigeon could communicate telepathically. In 1922, he reported that his special pigeon had flown into his room to tell him she was dying. Before she passed away, he described a bright white light shining from her eyes, more brilliant than anything he had ever created with his electrical machinery. Tesla was heartbroken by her death and told his friends that at that moment, he felt his life's work was complete.

Find a spot to sit and offer seed to local birds. Watch their movements and listen to their songs. Sit in this place weekly so you become familiar with the types of birds that live in your area and how they operate. Each time you sit to observe the birds, ask yourself what you are learning by paying attention to them. Can you embody lightness, swiftness, boldness, or song more easily? Is their manner of movement a type of language? Do you notice patterns? Are you aware of what their different calls might signify?

Augury is the practice of using birds to predict the future by observing their behavior for omens. The individual who performs this practice, the augur, "takes the auspices" by interpreting these signs. The term *auspices* means "looking at birds," and the word *auspicious*, meaning "good omen," is derived from this practice. In ancient Rome, military augurs would throw bread or cake to a flock of chickens designated to predict the outcomes of military strategies. The omens were unfavorable if the chickens refused to come out or eat, cried out, flapped their wings, or flew away.

On a practical level, bird behavior can provide valuable insights into the local environment. Birds inhabit every ecosystem and are affected by various environmental disturbances, such as habitat loss, climate change, pesticides, and pollution of air, water, and land.

Additionally, bird behavior can give us clues about the weather. For instance, swallows have very sensitive ears, and when barometric pressure drops, they tend to fly low to the ground where the air is denser and more comfortable. Generally, when birds are flying close to the ground, it is often a sign of impending rain, while birds soaring high in the sky typically indicate fair weather.

You can begin your quest to learn augury by carefully observing local birds throughout a season. When it feels right, you can present a question out loud to the birds and wait to observe their movements to see if any insight is offered. This can be formalized into a specific response interpretation, as the Roman army created with their chickens, or left to act as a kind of poetic call-and-response relationship that opens intuitively.

BIRDCALLS, PHONETIC PATTERNS, AND VOWEL MAGIC

In ancient Greek and Egyptian magical traditions, specific combinations of vowels were believed to possess inherent cosmic power. Demetrius of Phaleron, the keeper of the Library of Alexandria in 297 BCE, reported that priests praised their gods by singing the seven Greek vowels consecutively (Ognjenovic 2014, np). Each of these vowels was associated with a planetary deity.

A (alpha, *a*) = Moon

E (epsilon, short *e*) = Mercury

H (eta, long *e*) = Venus

I (iota, *i*) = Sun

O (omicron, short *o*) = Mars

Y (upsilon, *u*) = Jupiter

Ω (omega, long *o*) = Saturn

In the Hellenistic world, written vowels were sometimes arranged into specific geometric patterns, believed to be powerful enough that they were licked or consumed in rituals so as to absorb their magical potency. Additionally, vowels were combined with visual imagery and organized into symbolic shapes, such as squares, triangles, wings, or diamonds. These visual patterns enhanced the power of the vowels, giving them iconographic significance and amplifying the magical effect of their recitation. It is thought by some scholars that the arrangement of these vowels was inspired by the language of birds, echoing the rhythms of their calls.

Step 1: Listen to a Birdcall

Go outside, preferably in the first hour of morning, and listen carefully for any birdsong you might hear. Close your eyes and focus on the subtle variations and repetitions in the sounds. Do you hear any vowels? How do these vowels change? Do some vowels seem more pronounced than others?

Step 2: Write Out the Phonetic Spellings

Transcribe the birdcall phonetically as you hear it. For example, if the bird sounds like "*zee zee zee zoo zee zee,*" write it down.

Step 3: Explore the Mystical Power of Vowels

Reflect on the vowels you've written down. How do you feel when you focus on each one? How does the sound of *ee* differ from the sound of *oo*? Write down your feelings or observations as you concentrate on them individually. For example:

Zee—high-pitched, sharp, and light, feeling expansive like air

Zoo—round, deep, and soothing, invoking calmness like water

Step 4: Create Visual Patterns

Now, transform the phonetic spellings into visual forms. For example, you could arrange the call "*zee zee zee zoo zee zee*" in the shape of a square to represent balance and symmetry, a diamond for transformation, or wings to evoke the soaring of birds. For example:

> zee
> zee zee
> zee   zee
>   zoo

Step 5: Recite and Meditate

Finally, recite the birdcalls aloud, following your created pattern. As you do so, consider the mystical properties of the vowels: their symbolic representation of natural forces and their harmony with the life around you.

This exercise connects your awareness to the rhythms in nature and the sacred power of language itself. How did arranging the call in patterns affect your perception of the sound? Did you notice any shifts in your experience as you recited the vowels aloud in their new visual forms? How does the connection between the birdcall and the magical nature of vowels expand your understanding of sound and silence?

Yves Klein

TO CAPTURE THE SUBLIME

Yves Klein (1928–1962) was a French artist who played a significant role in developing contemporary performance art, conceptual art, and minimalism. His diverse practices included painting, sculpture, performance, photography, music, architecture, writing, and plans for projects in theater, dance, and cinema. Klein shifted the focus of art from the material to what he called "immaterial sensibility." He referred to himself as "the painter of space" and aimed to achieve this through pure color, particularly an ultramarine blue of his creation—International Klein Blue (IKB). He believed that this color transcended dimensions and could encapsulate boundless eternity.

He eventually decided that he had to exhibit space itself unbounded by a frame and said in his notebooks, "Recently my work with color has led me, in spite of myself, to search little by little, for the realization of matter, and I have decided to end the battle. My paintings are now invisible and I would like to show them in a clear and positive manner, in my next Parisian exhibition" (Klein 1974, np). He began to leave galleries empty of objects during his exhibitions.

In 1960, Klein hired the photographers Harry Shunk and János Kender to make a doctored series of pictures of the artist leaping out of a window and appearing to fly entitled *Leap Into the Void*. Klein distributed a fake broadsheet at Parisian newsstands commemorating the photographs, in which he wrote, "Today the painter of space must, in fact, go into space to paint, but he must go there without trickery or deception. He must be capable of levitation."

Klein embodies the concept of sublimation by transforming his artistic processes from physical materials into intangible forms, utilizing air and space as the medium for his work. His goal was to dismantle traditional, materialistic forms of art and the art world itself, exposing their inherent contradictions and dissolving their boundaries.

Practice Sublimation

MAKE A DISAPPEARING ARTWORK

Create a "disappearing artwork" as a way to explore the concept of sublimation. How might you make a work of art with no physical form at all or with a form that vanishes over time? Perhaps you could concoct a fragrance that only lingers for a moment, make a sound that fades into silence, or craft something that only exists in the fleeting instant of its creation.

During the COVID quarantine, I began writing poems for my friends using invisible ink made from lemon juice. To create the ink, I squeezed the juice from a lemon into a small bowl and dipped a brush into it to write my poems on a piece of paper. Once the ink dried, the words became hidden. Each invisible poem included instructions to hold the paper over a flame, and as the heat worked its magic, the words would gradually reveal themselves, appearing letter by letter. Sometimes, the paper would catch fire, causing the poem to vanish completely before it was fully read.

I trained as a painter in art school, and I was often at odds with my teachers there about their insistence that I use "archival materials" which I could not afford and didn't feel conceptually aligned with. I painted on bedsheets and used house paints and other found materials that would degrade in time. The process of making lemon-juice poems reminded me that some of the most powerful moments of creation are those that exist only for a fleeting moment, never fully captured, and felt more deeply for their impermanence.

IX.

Fermentation
I AM THE UTTERANCE OF MY NAME

Zodiac: Leo ——————— **Planet:** The Sun

Images: Black suns, the sun emerging from a tomb, resurrection, rising from the tomb, spiritual fires, black eggs shining in the sun, a black circle in the middle of earth, a farmer planting gold coins in a black field, a yellow bird descending into a multicolored sea

Material Applications: Fermenting, resurrection, revitalization, naming, speaking, writing, renewal

> *For true fermentation as I tell you,*
> *Is the incorporation of the soul with the bodies,*
> *Restoring to it the kindly smell,*
> *With taste and colour by natural compacting together,*
> *Of things dissevered, a due re-integration,*
> *Whereby the body of the spirit takes impression.*
> *That either the other may help to have ingression.*

> —George Ripley, *The Compound of Alchymy*

Alchemists use fermentation to preserve food and create medicines, elixirs, pigments, fabric dyes, and perfumes. Fermentation involves allowing organic matter to undergo controlled decomposition and revitalization. In this process, alchemists place their materials in closed, dark containers and periodically add fermenting sugars to enhance the activity. As the material decays, it is revitalized by the action of digesting bacteria. Throughout this process, you can hear the ferments fizzing, feel them warming, and observe their growth, all of which indicate that life is occurring within the decaying matter. The imagery associated with alchemical fermentation evokes concepts of ascent and descent, death and resurrection. Fermentation is a process that "resurrects" decaying material and arrests the process of decomposition. Because of this, it was considered essential for creating the Elixir of Life, a medicine believed to grant immortality, eternal youth, and the ability to cure any illness.

Fermentation produces beverages that can be stored for long periods, which is crucial when fresh water or other perishable foods are scarce. Fermented drinks are regarded as both sustenance and, because they represent new life emerging from death, a source of spiritual awakening. They were often consumed during festivals honoring the gods or shared during rites of passage. The restorative powers of fermented foods were celebrated in antiquity; Cleopatra attributed her beauty to a diet rich in pickles, while Julius Caesar supplied his troops with fermented vegetables to enhance their physical and mental stamina.

Practice Fermentation

SOLAR DYEING WITH POMEGRANATE PEELS

In Greek mythology, Persephone (the daughter of Demeter, goddess of the harvest) was abducted by Hades, god of the underworld. Hades fell in love with Persephone and took her to his realm of death to become his bride. Heartbroken, Demeter withdrew her gifts from the world, causing the Earth to wither and fall into famine.

Eventually, a compromise was reached: Persephone would spend part of the year with Hades in the underworld and the rest with her mother on Earth. To seal the covenant, Persephone ate six pomegranate seeds, which bound her to the underworld for half of each year. Her descent marks autumn and winter, and her return brings spring and summer. The pomegranate's rich red seeds symbolize transition, transformation, and the bloody dance between life and death.

In alchemical tradition, the pomegranate is linked to Mercury, the swift messenger god who ferries souls to the underworld. Mercury embodies transformation and liminality, mirroring Persephone's eternal travels between life and death. To align with this energy, it's best to begin your pomegranate dye on Wednesday, Mercury's day. This dye is activated by the very first stages of fermentation and can be used to infuse fabric with the powers of death, resurrection, and Mercury's swift movements between them.

MATERIALS NEEDED

- Glass jar with a lid

- Cold water

- Natural fibers to dye (silk, wool, cotton)

- Pomegranate peels

- Spoon for stirring

Fill your jar with cold water to about half its height. If the lid of your jar is rusty, it will alter the color of the dye from a soft yellow to an olive green. Adding iron nails or iron shavings will produce a similar effect. You can experiment with iron additives, but be aware this will imbue the dye with the energy of Mars.

Add the fibers you wish to dye to the jar. Pomegranate peels contain a high amount of tannins, so no mordanting is necessary. Ensure there's enough space for the materials to move around for an even color. Add a heaping spoonful of ground pomegranate peels to the jar, adjusting the amount based on the jar size and desired saturation. Stir the mixture well with a spoon to combine. Partially screw on the jar lid to allow for air exchange; without proper ventilation, gas buildup could cause the jar to explode.

Place the jar in a warm, sunny spot to ferment. Let it sit for two to seven days, depending on how intense you want the color to be, stirring the mixture daily. Small bubbles will eventually appear, signaling the dyeing process is underway. The longer you leave the mixture, the deeper and more vibrant the color will become. Once you've achieved your desired hue, rinse the fibers thoroughly. You can repeat the process with the same material for a richer shade.

As you engage in this dyeing practice, I invite you to reflect on the myth of Persephone and the profound cycles of life and death the story describes. How might the act of dyeing this fabric with pomegranate connect you to transitions in your own life? How will you incorporate this fabric into an artwork or ritual?

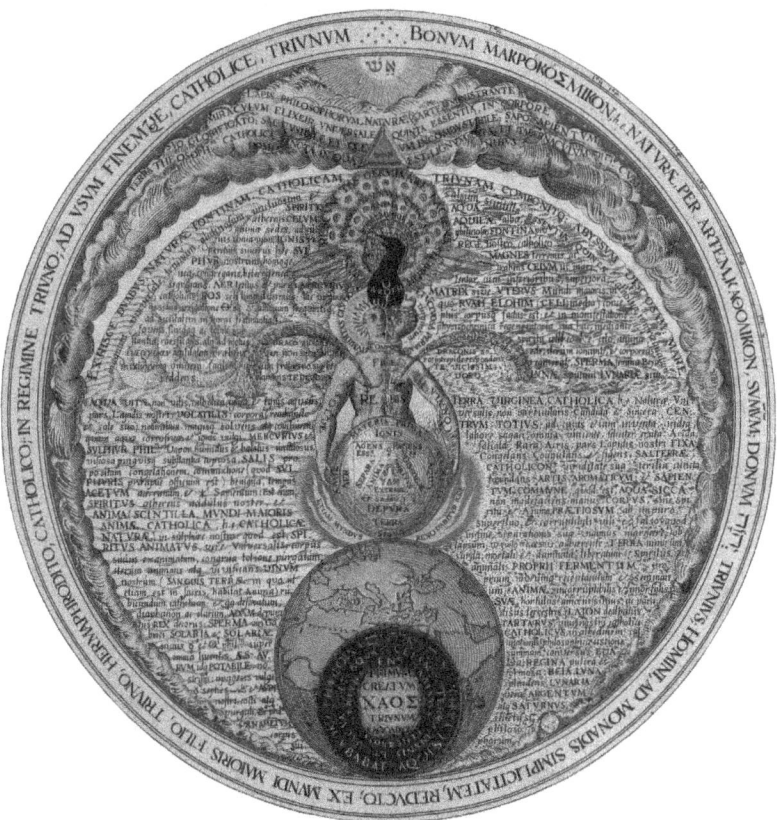

Plate 6 from *Amphitheatrum Sapientiae Aeternae Solius Verae*,
by Heinrich Khunrath, 1609. Courtesy of the Department of Special Collections,
Memorial Library, University of Wisconsin-Madison.

Lips Spitting

THE RITUAL OF NAMING

This image, created by the alchemist Heinrich Khunrath, illustrates the stages of
fermentation. The process begins at the center of the Earth, where organic materials decay within a black circle, symbolizing the initial stage of fermentation
when matter starts to rot and break down. As fermentation progresses, the materials rise into a flaming sphere, representing the warmth generated by microbial
activity. Above this sphere, an androgynous figure holds a fermentation flask,

while the figure's breasts flow with divine milk, symbolizing the phase when solids liquefy and transform. A black peacock with rainbow wings, inscribed with the word *Azoth*—an alchemical term for a universal remedy or solvent that facilitates transformation—emerges from the figure's head. At the pinnacle of the image, the peacock's tail unfurls, marking the stage of fermentation when the process is complete.

Heinrich Khunrath was a 16th-century German physician, Hermetic philosopher, and alchemist. A disciple of Paracelsus, Khunrath practiced medicine in several German cities and traveled widely. During his travels, he met the British occultist John Dee and his former partner, alchemist Edward Kelley. Influenced by Dee and the Paracelsian tradition, Khunrath aimed to develop a Christianized form of natural magic to uncover the secret Prima Materia that would grant humanity eternal wisdom, peace, and prosperity. Khunrath's most famous work is *Amphitheatrum Sapientiae Aeternae* (*The Amphitheater of Eternal Wisdom*), which delves into the mystical aspects of alchemy. First published in Hamburg in 1595, the book includes four circular, elaborately hand-colored plates enhanced with gold and silver, all designed by Khunrath.

Khunrath's biography remains shrouded in mystery, as he operated under several names—a common practice in alchemy. Traditionally, an alchemist's "true" name was never written down and only shared with a select group of initiated individuals, as this name was believed to possess the power to both create and destroy the alchemist. This practice has its roots in ancient Egypt, where a true name was thought to be connected to a person's spiritual essence. Keeping this name secret was crucial for protecting the individual from magical attacks. It was known only to the person themselves and their closest confidants, typically a parent and child or a devotee and their deity.

In Egyptian mythology, Ptah is the god of art and creation who communicated with Atum, the primordial god from whom all things originated. Ptah had the unique ability to bring other divine archetypes to life by knowing their names. By speaking true names, he was able to declare all of nature and every living creature into existence. The hieroglyph that represents Ptah depicts lips spitting, symbolizing the immense creative power of speech and naming.

During personal fermentation, an alchemist may choose a new name or receive one from a teacher. This name signifies the death of an old way of being and the birth of a new one. The name awakens the inner alchemist—aspects of themselves that carry knowledge of the alchemical tradition from past incarnations. Alchemists might also adopt multiple names for various purposes, such as publishing their work or sharing their practice. Each name reflects a specific connection to a person, deity, element, or aspect of the alchemical tradition, signaling the alchemist's lineage and deepening their connection to the art.

The Publick Universal Friend

YOU NOT BUSY BEING BORN ARE BUSY DYING

A year or two into my study of Hermeticism, my teacher gave me the name Emerald. I didn't think much of it then, assuming it was a corny reference to the Emerald Tablet, a text I hadn't taken the time to understand. Eventually, I parted ways with that teacher and forgot the name entirely. Nearly twenty years later, while preparing a lecture on the Gnostic Gospel of Mary Magdalene, I was drifting off to sleep, and as my eyes closed, an apparition of Mary Magdalene appeared at the foot of my bed. She reached into my chest and pointed to a glowing emerald within. "Emerald," I whispered before falling asleep.

A few weeks later, I officiated a wedding in Upstate New York, in the town where the Publick Universal Friend had lived and died. Born Jemima Wilkinson in 1752 in Rhode Island, they were one of eight children in a Quaker family. In 1776, the Friend fell ill with a contagious and deadly fever that spread throughout their community. At one point, they were declared dead but ultimately survived and emerged from the fever transformed. The Friend proclaimed they had been brought back to life by the Spirit of God as a new person, neither male nor female. This new identity, the Publick Universal Friend, was dedicated solely to serving God.

From then on, they would not answer to Jemima Wilkinson, instead using Publick Universal Friend, the Friend, or PUF. The Friend styled their hair short on top with ringlets in the back and dressed in a style that was seen as either androgynous or masculine for the period. They typically wore long, loose clerical robes, often in black, and accessorized with a white or purple cravat around their neck, similar to the fashion worn by men at the time.

Almost immediately after rebirth, the Friend began publicly preaching about their spiritual awakening. The Friend's Quaker group did not believe their story and dismissed them from the community, but PUF was not deterred. They traveled throughout the New England and Mid-Atlantic regions and continued to preach, slowly building their own community of followers who became known as the Universal Friends.

The Publick Universal Friend encouraged the Universal Friends to honor God's teachings, treat others as they wished to be treated, and pursue a righteous and peaceful life. The Friend's teachings were not radically different from those of other Quaker leaders, but their nongendered identity and insistence that they had a direct connection to God through their rebirth made them unique. Their meetings eventually attracted large crowds, and the Universal Friends established a town called Jerusalem in Upstate New York.

The Publick Universal Friend rejected ideas of predestination and believed that anyone, regardless of gender or race, could access God's light. They taught that God spoke directly to individuals, who had free will to choose their actions and beliefs, and they believed in the possibility of universal salvation. The Friend called for the abolition of slavery and persuaded followers to free enslaved people. The Friend owned few personal possessions, given mainly by followers, and never held property except in trust. The Friend also believed women should "obey God rather than men," and the most committed followers included about four dozen unmarried women, known as the Faithful Sisterhood, who took on leadership roles traditionally held by men.

In 1819, the Public Universal Friend died after years of declining health. Initially, members of the Society of Universal Friends buried the Friend's body in the basement of the house. Later, they moved the body to an unmarked location on the property. After the Friend's death, the society gradually disbanded.

When I visited the grounds of the old Universal Friends settlement, I entered into a deep meditation, allowing myself to fully connect with the energy of the place. As I meditated, I received a powerful message: I was urged to embrace the name Emerald as a commitment to my alchemical path and true self. The name felt like a bridge between my work in alchemy and the essence of who I was becoming. I use both my given name and Emerald interchangeably these days, embracing the fluidity between these two identities. Moving between them allows me to experience different facets of myself.

Practice Fermentation
NAME YOURSELF

Alchemists, with few exceptions, typically work under pseudonyms. The act of receiving or choosing a name is a powerful transformation—it represents a conscious rejection of external labels and expectations, allowing one's identity to align more closely with one's inner truth. In many spiritual traditions, naming signifies a rite of passage, marking a shift in consciousness or the beginning of a new life phase. It's an invitation to move beyond societal definitions and embrace a more intentional existence.

Take time to select your alchemist's name. Alchemists often choose names that connect them to teachers they resonate with—human, deity, plant, animal, or mineral. This name may change over time, with each shift symbolizing a rebirth. Naming yourself in this way is more than selecting a label; it's a formal commitment to honor the inner transformation you're experiencing.

Turiya Sings

ALICE COLTRANE AND FERMENTATION

Alice Coltrane (1937–2007) was a groundbreaking American jazz pianist, harpist, composer, and spiritual leader whose work combined music and mysticism. Initially trained in classical music, she became a prominent figure in jazz, often collaborating with her husband, the renowned musician John Coltrane. Their fusion of spirituality and sound resulted in some of the most beautiful musical compositions ever recorded.

After John's death in 1967, Alice Coltrane experienced a profound crisis marked by intense physical and metaphysical turmoil. She experienced severe weight loss, insomnia, high body temperatures, and vivid visions of hellish landscapes, which she later referred to as her "tapas." In Sanskrit, *tapas* signifies a type of heat generated through spiritual disciplines that involve austerity and self-discipline.

During this period, Coltrane endured excruciating physical symptoms, such as burns that scarred her skin and overwhelming sonic bombardments that strained her senses. She also underwent profound metaphysical revelations. These experiences included astral projections throughout the universe, hearing celestial music played on heavenly instruments, and witnessing cosmic wonders. A musical colleague introduced her to Swami Satchidananda, who guided her in receiving mantra diksha and studying Hinduism in the early 1970s. At this time, she underwent a mystical experience where she was directly initiated into sannyasa, a state of spiritual awakening characterized by a disinterest in material life and a commitment to peaceful, spiritual pursuits. She received the monastic name Turiyasangitananda, or Turiya for short, which she translated as "the Transcendental Lord's Highest Song of Bliss."

Turiya moved from New York to San Francisco in 1972, where she founded the Vedantic Center, and later relocated to Woodland Hills, Los Angeles. In 1983, Turiya established the Shanti Anantam Ashram, which was later renamed the Sai Anantam Ashram in the Santa Monica Mountains. In an interview with *Essence* magazine, she was asked why she gave up her recording career and famous name. She replied: "After fulfilling my Warner contract, I really wanted to go deeper into what the Lord had outlined for me to do. I felt that it was time for the next generation of musicians. And the music was changing, so I thought maybe my time is finished. Maybe this is sufficient" (Taylor 2020, np). At the ashram, Turiya would lead initiates in congregational chanting and kirtan. She developed original melodies from traditional chants and experimented by incorporating synthesizers and elements of gospel music into her compositions.

Throughout the 1980s and '90s, Turiya wrote books, available through her private publishing company, the Avatar Book Institute, that detailed divine communications she received. The first of these, *Endless Wisdom I*, was released in 1982, accompanied by a cassette of music titled *Turiya Sings*. Coltrane would release three more cassettes—*Divine Songs, Infinite Chants,* and *Glorious Chants*—alongside the books *Divine Revelations* and *Endless Wisdom II*.

Interest in her work grew in the 1990s, leading to the compilation album *Astral Meditations* and her comeback album *Translinear Light* in 2004. After a twenty-five-year hiatus from public performances, she returned for three U.S. concerts in the fall of 2006, culminating in a performance at the San Francisco Jazz Festival on November 4. Turiya passed away from respiratory failure in 2007 at age sixty-nine and is buried alongside John Coltrane in Pinelawn Memorial Park, New York.

Turiya experienced a huge resurgence in popularity following her passing. In 2017, Luaka Bop released *World Spirituality Classics 1: The Ecstatic Music of Alice Coltrane Turiyasangitananda*, a compilation featuring tracks from her recordings at her ashram. In 2021, Impulse! Records rereleased *Turiya Sings* under the new title *Kirtan: Turiya Sings*. Around this time, the bumper sticker "Keep Honking! I'm Listening to Alice Coltrane's 1971 Meteoric Sensation Universal Consciousness" began trending across the United States, reflecting a growing cultural interest in her work.

The Year of Alice in 2025 featured previously unreleased music, reissues, community programming, concerts, and a multimedia exhibit at the Hammer Museum. Curator Erin Christovale viewed the *Monument Eternal* exhibit at the Hammer as an opportunity to share Turiya's healing music with both fans and newcomers. The exhibit coincided with the republication of Turiya's 1977 autobiographical book, which inspired the title. Christovale notes, "In today's world, we seek healing and art that brings joy or liberation" (Mitter 2025, np).

Turiya underwent a profound transformation when she relinquished her old identity and famous name, allowing a new life defined by spiritual exploration and service to emerge. The continually renewed interest in her artistic legacy reflects the profound impact of her transformation and its lasting significance.

To honor Turiya, make a heartfelt offering on your alchemist's altar to her. Once your altar is prepared, find a comfortable place to lie down. Close your eyes, inhale deeply, and exhale slowly to center yourself. Play *Turiya Sings* and invite the music to move through you, instigating a transformation as you surrender to its essence, feeling it resonate within your mind and body, shifting your consciousness and expanding your awareness.

After the music concludes, take time to reflect on the experience. Grab some art supplies and create a piece of artwork that captures the emotions, thoughts, or visions that arose during your listening. Finally, sign your creative piece with a new alchemist's name, one that symbolizes your own rebirth and transformation.

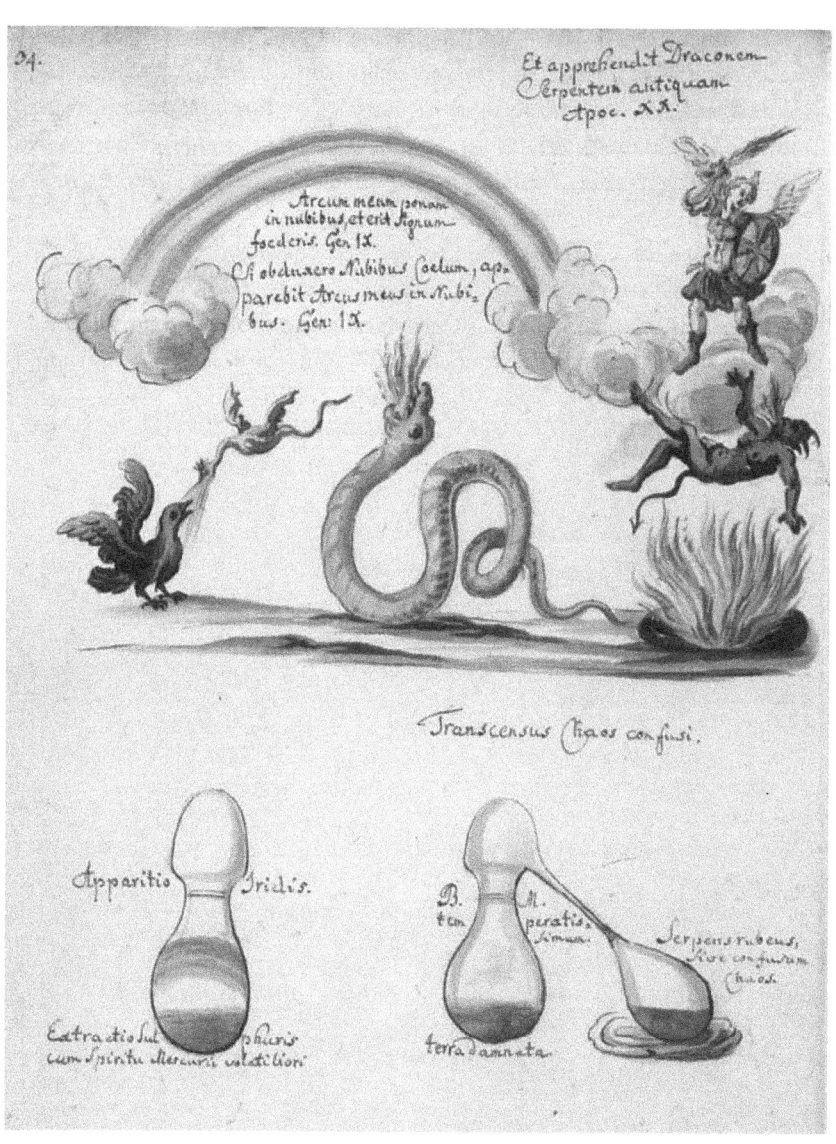

"And he seized the dragon," depicting one of the steps in creating a Philosopher's Stone. Figure 20 from *Thesaurus Thesaurorum*, 1725, MS. 4775. Source: Wellcome Collection.

X.

Exaltation
THE RAISING OF RAINBOWS

Zodiac: Cancer ——————— **Planet:** Moon

Images: Lotus flowers, edelweiss blossoms and other eightfold flowers, rose petals, rain, snow, ascending flames, rainbows in the sky, baptismal fonts, unicorns, white doves, and the ouroboros—a dragon devouring its own tail

Material Applications: Distilling, filtering, simplifying, streamlining, clarifying, jubilation, celebration, inspiration

> *If you therefore will exalt the bodies,*
> *First you augment them with the spirit of life,*
> *Till in time the earth be well subtilized,*
> *By natural rectifying of every Element,*
> *Exalting them up into the firmament,*
> *Then much more precious shall they be than gold,*
> *Because of the quintessence which they do hold.*
>
> —George Ripley, *The Compound of Alchymy*

Exaltation refers to the process of refining a material to its purest and lightest state, essentially "en-lightening" it. This en-lightening of materials in alchemy is achieved through various techniques, with distillation being one of the most significant methods. During distillation, a tool called an alembic is used to separate the components of a liquid mixture through selective evaporation and condensation. Originally, distillation was employed to purify drinking water, and alchemists drew inspiration from nature to design tools for this process.

During the day, the sun heats bodies of water, causing them to evaporate. The vapor then rises, cools in the atmosphere, and condenses into droplets, which fall back down as rain. Alchemical distillation employs an apparatus that mimics this natural process, composed of a pot, an alembic, and a condenser arm. During distillation, liquid is heated in the lower vessel—the pot—until it becomes vapor. This vapor rises into the alembic, where it cools in the bulb and then condenses as it travels down the arm of the condenser. Heavier impurities are unable to rise so remain in the lower vessel, allowing only the lightest water particles to pass through the alembic. This method effectively removes inorganic compounds, such as metals and nitrates, purifying the water to an impressive 99.5 percent.

A significant breakthrough in distillation occurred in the 11th century when the Islamic alchemist Ibn Sīnā invented the coiled cooling pipe. Over time, Islamic alchemists refined distillation techniques and enhanced their apparatuses to distill wine and other fermented liquids more efficiently. These advancements enabled the production of high-proof alcohol, which had a transformative impact on medicine. By the 13th century, the alembic and the production of *al-kohl* (alcohol) became well-known throughout Europe, significantly shaping scientific practices there. Alcohol is a highly effective solvent, extracting active compounds from plant materials such as leaves, roots, flowers, and bark. Its polar nature allows it to dissolve both water-soluble and oil-soluble compounds, making it ideal for extracting essential oils, flavonoids, alkaloids, tannins, and other bioactive substances from plants. This versatility makes alcohol an invaluable tool in the preparation of medicinal tinctures.

The Emerald Tablet suggests that the universe is undergoing a continuous distillation process—driven by cycles of ascent and descent—ultimately leading to the spiritualization of matter and an exaltation of the universe as encoded in these verses:

In truth, without deceit, certain and most veritable.
That which is Below corresponds to that which is Above,
and that which is Above corresponds to that which is Below
to accomplish the miracle of the One Thing.

And just as all things have come from this One Thing
through the meditation of One Mind, so do all created
things originate from this One Thing, through Transformation.

Its father is the Sun; Its mother the Moon.
The Wind carries it in its belly; its nurse is the Earth.
It is the origin of All, the consecration of the Universe;
Its inherent Strength is perfected, if it is turned into Earth.

Separate the Earth from Fire, the Subtle from the Gross,
gently and with great Ingenuity. It rises from Earth to Heaven
and descends again to Earth, thereby combining within Itself
the powers of both the Above and the Below.

Thus will you obtain the Glory of the Whole Universe.
All Obscurity will be clear to you. This is the greatest
force of all powers, because it overcomes every Subtle thing
and penetrates every Solid thing.

In this way was the Universe created.
From this will come many wondrous Applications,
because this is the Pattern.

Therefore am I called Thrice Greatest Hermes,
having all three parts of the wisdom of the Whole Universe.
Herein have I completely explained the Operation of the Sun. (Hauck 2003, 45)

The Emerald Tablet describes distillation as the process of separating a "subtle" or nonphysical essence from a "gross" or physical substance. In this process, the substance rises "gently from earth to heaven" before descending again, transforming from a dense state into a clearer, lighter form through repeated cycles of ascent and descent. This continuous refinement mirrors the universe's current expansion phase, where matter is spread across an ever-larger volume, leading to a decrease in density—an ongoing cosmic en-lightening in alignment with the process described in the Emerald Tablet.

Psychologically, exaltation represents a repeated cycle of separating and recombining the subtle and gross aspects of the personality. As we undergo these cycles of inner ascent and descent, our priorities gradually shift from valuing possessions and material security to prioritizing inner peace and clarity. This shift fosters a desire to "travel light," physically and emotionally. During this phase, the wisdom of living simply becomes clear, and a natural ease with letting go emerges. We begin to understand that simplicity creates space for openness to creativity. Embracing simplicity signals the soul's readiness to welcome the new and unexpected.

When I first began practicing laboratory distillation, I felt uneasy with the terms like *purity, lightness,* and *perfection* that often appear in alchemical texts to describe exaltation. Having struggled with disordered eating and body dysmorphia for much of my life, I was hesitant to engage with a system that seemed to place such high value on qualities like "purity" and "lightness," which felt inherently opposed to their counterparts—"dirtiness" and "heaviness." As I worked with plants to dis-till essential oils and hydrosols through repeated cycles of vaporization, I noticed a similar process unfolding within me. I began to experience greater clarity and flow, and the parts of myself clinging to false senses of security—both material and emotional—started to lighten up. I recognized that what was mine was my soul and that everything else would disappear.

I came to understand exaltation through the words of Thomas Merton: "In a world of noise, confusion, and conflict, it is necessary that there is a place of inner silence and peace; not the peace of mere relaxation, but the peace of inner clarity and love" (Merton 1961, 74). I strongly encourage anyone interested in alchemy to get a still and learn to extract essential oils and hydrosols from plants. When flowers, leaves, or herbs are steamed during distillation, the steam captures the volatile essential oils and the plant's water-soluble components, known as hydrosol. Extracting the "soul" of the plant through essential oils and the "spirit" through hydrosol is more than just a physical process; it fosters inner transforma-tion. Through this practice, I discovered a balance between my spirit's spontaneity and my soul's deliberate actions. Over time, my thoughts and actions became clearer and more honest.

Enlighten-Up

LAUGHTER EXERCISE

Learning to "enlighten" is nurtured by incorporating levity, laughter, and joy into your practices. In the book *Meditations on the Tarot*, the author encourages those studying mysticism to: "Learn at first concentration without effort; transform work into play; make every yoke that you have accepted easy and every burden you carry light!" (Anonymous 2002, 11). This approach is essential for making progress as an alchemist.

Engaging in laughter before starting your work can clear out stagnation and create a lighter frame of mind.

To initiate a laughter session, begin by clapping your hands together while chant-ing "ho, ho, ho" and "ha, ha, ha." This rhythmic clapping, ensuring full finger-to-finger and palm-to-palm contact, shakes up any rigidity or hesitation. Enthusiastic clap-ping and laughing sounds stimulate your diaphragm and generate positive energy, even when the laughter is false or forced. Allow your laughter to evolve, changing its sounds from low to high, and experiment with different noises.

As you laugh, move around and savor the moment. When you feel you've lightened up, begin your creative practice.

Practice Exaltation as Exhalation

THE MICROCOSMIC ORBIT

Alchemists use breath as a means to practice physical exaltation.

When you pay attention to your breaths, you discover that no two are alike. Nothing remains unchanged from moment to moment, and nothing physical has a fixed or permanent self. It is precisely because things are constantly transforming and we have no fixed self that freedom is possible.

Chinese alchemists use breath to circulate qi, or life force, using techniques that combine movement and breathwork to bring about profound improvements in mental and physical health. One such practice is the Microcosmic Orbit, a key exercise in Taoist energy cultivation. During the Microcosmic Orbit exercise, practitioners breathe energy up and down the spine, mirroring the alchemical circulation cycle from Above to Below, as well as the process of laboratory distillation. Continuous practice purifies the body's energy, fostering clarity and supporting the cultivation of the Golden Elixir, which, in the Taoist tradition, is produced by the body once the practitioner attains alchemical enlightenment. The following practice is adapted from *Healing Light of the Tao* by Mantak Chia (2008).

To practice the Microcosmic Orbit, start by sitting comfortably with an upright posture if possible. Focus on relaxing your body by softening any areas of tension, both mentally and physically, as you breathe gently into them. Close your eyes and take some time to release all the tiny little muscles around your eye sockets and forehead, relax the jaw, and allow the teeth to separate to help you settle in.

Next, visualize a flow of qi, or vital energy, gathering in your lower abdomen. As you inhale deeply through your nose, direct your awareness and the flow of qi to rise along the back of your spine. Imagine the qi traveling up the back of your body, moving from the base of your spine up between the shoulder blades and past the back of the neck to the crown of your head. When you reach the crown, visualize the qi collecting and expanding at the top of your head.

As you exhale, gently guide the energy to descend down the front of your body, from the crown of the head to the space between your eyebrows and then down to the lower abdomen, completing the circuit. Hold your breath at the base of the spine for a beat, and then cycle the breath up the spine and down the front of your body again. With each breath cycle, focus on the smooth, continuous flow of energy moving upward along the back and downward along the front, creating a loop of qi circulation.

After several rounds of this cycle, you can reverse the direction: inhale through the nose, guiding the energy up the front of the body, from the lower abdomen, up the belly, past the chest and face, up to the crown of the head; then exhale as you bring the energy down the back of the body, down between the shoulder blades, and back to the base of the spine. Repeat this for an equal length of time or number of repetitions as you did while breathing in the other direction. Try practicing this distillation of breath for ten minutes each morning and see if you notice a difference in your energy levels and clarity of mind as you go about your day.

Practice Exaltation
PILGRIMAGE

Pilgrimages to sacred sites are a transformative part of spiritual practice, blending physical travel with inner renewal. They represent a quest for deeper understanding, connection, and enlightenment within one's faith tradition; every step taken toward a sacred site clarifies and uplifts the spirit. In this exercise, you will pilgrimage to a work of art.

Choose a piece of artwork—in any medium—within a one-day trip from your home. Select a work that feels alive, stirs powerful emotions, and speaks directly to your soul. Both you and the artwork will be exalted by this experience, mutually uplifting and enlightening one another.

Plan your visit with intention. Choose a day that holds personal significance, dress in a way that reflects the essence of the artwork, and consider wearing fragrances that honor the spirit of the art.

The Ancient Greek term *agalma* refers to a beautiful gift offered to the gods meant to win their favor through its exquisite beauty. Approach your visit as if *you* are the agalma—offering yourself fully, with complete attention and presence, as a tribute to the artwork.

In my early twenties, I made a pilgrimage in the early days of spring to Emily Dickinson's home, a poet whose work I've loved deeply and constantly since childhood. I dressed in white, as Dickinson did, and read her poems on the bus ride there, whispering each word aloud as a prayer to Saint Emily. Upon arriving at her house, I kissed the trees in her yard in a clockwise circle before entering the front door. The lilacs—those ancient shrubs—were in full bloom, their fragrance mingling with the fresh green grass and the warm yellow ocher of the house's painted exterior. I walked into the house, alight with the season and Emily's words. I can't fully explain the intimate, unspoken exchange between my soul and her poems in the home where she lived and wrote—I still carry the soft and sacred light of that day inside as a place to refresh and renew myself.

Once you've completed your pilgrimage, reflect on how the experience deepened your understanding of art as a living entity. Write about how this consecrated journey helped you connect with the work more intimately. Did the artwork reveal something new? Did it speak to you in unexpected ways? What was that exchange like? How did it feel to offer yourself fully to the work? How has your own creative flow shifted in response?

The Distilled Sound of William Basinski

William Basinski (b. 1958) is an American composer, clarinetist, saxophonist, sound artist, and video artist, best known for his pioneering work in ambient music and experimental sound. Raised in a Catholic family in Texas, Basinski had early mystical experiences with music, particularly at St. Anne Church in Houston. In an interview with the *Guardian*, he described churches as "musical instruments" and "incredibly sophisticated machines" (Beaumont-Thomas 2019, np), highlighting the deep connection between the sacred, space, and sound in his sensibility.

Classically trained as a clarinetist, Basinski studied jazz saxophone and composition at the University of North Texas in the late 1970s. Influenced by minimalists like Steve Reich and Brian Eno, he began experimenting with tape loops and reel-to-reel tape decks, creating meditative and melancholic compositions built around short melodies played in repetition. Throughout the 1980s, Basinski expanded his artistic practice, generating an extensive archive of experimental works using tape loops, delay systems, found sounds, and shortwave radio static.

In August and September of 2001, Basinski began working on *The Disintegration Loops*, a series of four albums that would become his most iconic work. Basinski set out to digitize his earlier tape loop recordings—tapes that had aged and begun to deteriorate. As he did, he realized the tapes were falling apart, and as the tapes played, sounds were gradually being erased. Rather than discard the damaged recordings, Basinski chose to embrace the decay, allowing the loops to continue playing and capturing the process of their disintegration.

The result is a haunting, meditative work where short, melodic loops gradually unravel, like an abandoned house yielding to the rain seeping through its cracks. Over time, rhythms emerge and fade as the loops' original structures give way, creating an elegiac and deeply moving soundscape. The disintegration of these tapes mirrors the process of distillation—where something pure, refined, and essential emerges from repeated rinsing. In this case, Basinski distilled divinity from dust, turning the frailty of his decaying tapes into an exploration of mortality, memory, and time.

Play *The Disintegration Loops* in your creative space and allow its haunting, meditative sounds to transform the atmosphere into an exalted space. As you listen, reflect on how the unfolding of time reveals new depths, strips away the superfluous, or uncovers hidden beauty in your own practice. Consider how you might distill intentions, materials, and emotions in your work—how could you allow your process to become clearer, lighter, or more honest? Let the gradual unraveling of the loops inspire you to embrace change and imperfection in your practices.

XI.

Multiplication
THE ECSTATIC ECHO

Zodiac: Gemini ——————— **Planet:** Mercury

Images: Litters of young animals, lions kissing or caring for their young, dragons breathing life into vessels, flames spreading

Material Applications: Repetition, anaphora, patterning, rhythm, iteration, echo, making multiples

> *Multiplication is therefore as they do write,*
> *That thing that does augment medicines in each degree,*
> *In colour, in odour, in virtue, and also in quantity.*
> *And why may you multiply this medicine infinitely,*
> *Forsooth the cause is this,*
> *For it is fire, which kindled will never die,*
> *Dwelling with you, as fire does in houses,*
> *Of which one spark may make more fire this way,*
> *As musk in pigments and other spices more,*
> *In virtue multiplied, and our medicine right so.*

> —George Ripley, *The Compound of Alchymy*

Multiplication in alchemy refers to the process of enhancing the quantity or potency of a substance through repeated operations. Each cycle builds upon the previous one, amplifying the substance's properties and producing a more concentrated and powerful version of the original material over time. For instance, alchemists might repeatedly distill fermented liquids to increase their alcohol content while removing impurities. Alchemy is frequently viewed as a practice aimed at the multiplication of metals, particularly through the creation of alloys and compounds. For example, Egyptian alchemists discovered that alloying gold with copper made it more work-able for jewelry making and effectively increased the amount of usable gold. They also found that cadmia vapors could produce brass with golden hues, thereby "mul-tiplying" the appearance of gold. In 1404, King Henry IV of England enacted the Act Against Multipliers, specifically targeting alchemists' attempts to transform base metals into gold and silver. This law aimed to protect the royal treasury and prevent economic instability that could arise from the circulation of counterfeit coins.

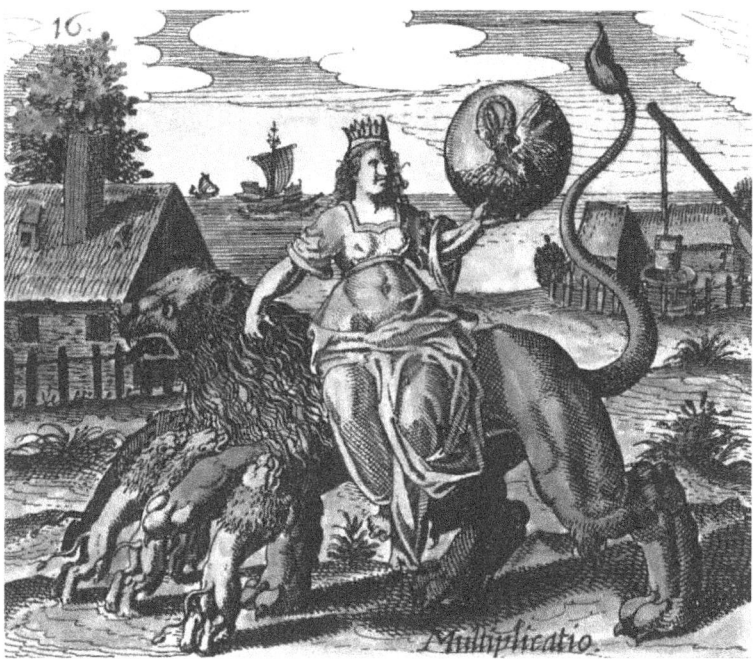

Figure 16, "Multiplication," from *Ioannis Danielis Mylii T. & Med. Candidati Wetterani Hassi Philosophia Reformata, Continens Libros Binos : I. Liber in Septem Partes Diuisus Est: . . . II. Liber Continet Authoritates Philosophorum. Apud Lucam Iennis*, by Johann Daniel Mylius and Lucas Jennis, 1622. Rare Books Division, Department of Special Collections, Princeton University Library.

In our personal practices, multiplication can strengthen our mind, body, and spirit through repetitive exercises. Just as the alchemist works to increase the potency of a substance, we can engage practices designed to amplify our own energy and powers of concentration through reiteration. For example, one of my teachers gave me the task of repeating my first name aloud for two hours. "Which one?" I asked. "I have three different names I use." "One hour for each then," she replied.

By the end of this intense practice, I had immersed myself so deeply in the sound and meaning of my names that I began to perceive each one as a note in a larger musical composition. This shift significantly expanded my understanding of myself, allowing for greater flexibility and freedom in thinking of a "self" altogether. I began to dissolve into something greater than the constraints of these names with each repetition. Engaging in practices of repetition can help us transcend the limits we place on our sense of possibility, enabling us to explore new realms of experience. Many spiritual exercises involve repetitive movements, breathing techniques, or chanting. The Sufi poet Bulleh Shah beautifully captures this idea in his poem:

> *By repeating the name of the Beloved,*
> *I have become the Beloved myself.*
> *Whom shall I call the Beloved now?*

In sacred poetry and chant, the repetition of names, phrases, and invocations is a powerful tool to build divine energy and increase spiritual power. An early written example of this can be found in the work of Enheduanna, a Sumerian priestess and poet, widely considered the first known author in history. She was the daughter of King Sargon of Akkad and is best known for her hymns dedicated to the goddess Inanna. Her work played a central role in ancient Mesopotamia's religious and cultural life and used repetition to strengthen the spiritual power of her verses. In her "Exaltation of Inanna," Enheduanna utilizes the multiplication of the sacred number seven to enhance her invocation.

> *Powerful Mistress, seizer of the seven divine powers!*
> *My Heavenly Lady, guardian of the seven divine powers!*
> *You have seized the seven divine powers!*
> *You hold the divine powers in your hand!*
> *You have gathered together the seven divine powers!*
> *You have clasped the divine powers to your breast! (Hallo 1997, np)*

In antiquity, names were multiplied to enhance their potency. The title Trismegistus, from Hermes Trismegistus, means "Thrice-Great" and signifies an elevated status. It derives from the Egyptian phrase *aa aa*, meaning "great, great," used as an epithet for Thoth in late hieroglyphics. By amplifying Hermes's power with the title Trismegistus, or *aa aa aa*, the deity's influence was magnified so well that, over two thousand years later, we continue to study his teachings as outlined in the *Corpus Hermeticum*.

Multiplication is a powerful and versatile tool in creative practice, although its use is deceptively simple. One application is the rhetorical technique known as anaphora. Derived from the Greek words *ana* ("repeat" or "back") and *pherein* ("to carry"), anaphora involves repeating a word or phrase to embed it in the listener's mind. This repetition creates a rhythmic cadence that draws the audience in and reinforces memory. In times when oral communication dominated over written text, anaphora was essential for ensuring that key messages endured long after they were spoken.

In his book *Trance: From Magic to Technology*, Dennis Wier defines a simple trance as a mental state induced by cognitive loops. These loops consist of an object—such as a thought, image, sound, or intentional action—that repeats for long enough that various cognitive functions are hindered. Repetitive auditory stimuli, including singing, chanting, or rhythmic sounds, can induce trance states. Similarly, the repetitive flickering of light or the rhythmic progression of images can lead to this altered state of consciousness.

A trance state is characterized by a reduced awareness of external stimuli and an enhanced ability to imagine. People in a trance may experience changes in their sense of self, perception of time and space, and bodily sensations. This state is often used to enhance mystical and artistic experiences.

The challenge of using multiplication creatively lies in finding the right balance in repetition. Skillful multiplication entails applying a repeated motif in a dynamic and engaging way, allowing it to develop and build energy rather than becoming monotonous and diminishing energy.

Practice Multiplication

JOE BRAINARD AND THE ANAPHORIC EPIC

Joe Brainard (1942–1994) was an American artist and writer closely associated with the New York School, a group of artists and poets active in Manhattan during the 1950s and '60s. His multidisciplinary practice spanned assemblage, collage, drawing, painting, book and album cover design, theatrical sets, and costume design. Brainard's work is characterized by a distinctive blend of wit, intimacy, and philosophical depth, often engaging with themes that range from the banal to the transgressive in the same breath. He destabilizes conventional hierarchies of subject matter by granting equal attention to the trivial and the profound, the erotic and the innocent, the confessional and the camp.

One of Brainard's most celebrated works is *I Remember*, a 150-page memoir that breaks from a traditional narrative structure by employing anaphora. Each sentence in the book begins with the phrase "I remember," capturing a series of personal memories from his childhood in Oklahoma in the 1940s and '50s, as well as his adult life as an openly queer artist in New York City in the 1960s and '70s. Combining seemingly trivial details with more profound revelations, Brainard (2001, 119) creates a poignant and complex portrait of his life, where the particular and the universal coexist in a nuanced way. *I Remember* has become a highly influential work, inspiring numerous homages and adaptations, and remains a key text in the genre of experimental memoir.

Here's an excerpt from *I Remember*:

I remember green Easter egg grass.
I remember never really believing in the Easter bunny. Or the sandman. Or the tooth fairy.
I remember bright colored baby chickens. (Dyed) They died very fast. Or ran away. Or something. I just remember that shortly after Easter they disappeared.
I remember farts that smell like old eggs.
I remember one very hot summer day I put ice cubes in my aquarium and all the fish died.
I remember dreams of walking down the street and suddenly realizing that I have no clothes on.
I remember a big black cat named Midnight who got so old and grouchy that my parents had him put to sleep.
I remember making a cross of two sticks for something my brother and me buried. It might have been a cat but I think it was a bug or something.
I remember regretting things I didn't do.
I remember wishing I knew then what I know now.
I remember peach-colored evenings just before dark.
I remember "lavender past." (He has a . . .)

To create your own anaphoric poem, start by selecting a simple phrase that will begin each line. Then, reflect on memories, observations, or thoughts related to this phrase, and begin writing lines that start with those exact words. As you write, let the repeated phrase build on itself. Each line should add depth, expanding on the previous ones and enriching the poem's overall meaning. This repetition will create a smooth flow, allowing the content to evolve and become more complex as you continue. Once you have finished, read the poem back to yourself and reflect on how the repetition has invoked and intensified your meanings.

God's Not Dead, He's Bread

SISTER CORITA KENT

Sister Corita Kent (1918–1986), a Roman Catholic nun and artist, was a trailblazer in 20th-century American art. She became renowned for her vibrant and evocative screenprints, which uniquely blend elements of popular culture, religious iconography, and social commentary. Her faith, dedication to social justice, and innovative applications of color, typography, and form made her an influential voice in contemporary art. One of the most striking features of her work is her use of repetition and multiplication.

Frances Elizabeth Kent was the fifth of six children born to devout Catholic parents. After graduating from Los Angeles Girls High School in 1936, Kent followed her older sister Ruth into the Sisters of the Immaculate Heart of Mary in Los Angeles, close to their family home. Before beginning her postulancy that summer, she attended classes at the Otis Art Institute.

Upon entering the novitiate, she adopted the name Sister Mary Corita, meaning "Little Heart," and became the assistant instructor in the art department at Immaculate Heart College. In 1951, she earned a master's degree in art from the University of Southern California and discovered the medium of silkscreen printing. Before she received her degree, another sister submitted her silkscreen print *The Lord Is With Thee* to a competition at the Los Angeles Museum of History, Science, and Art, where it received first prize.

Kent continued her printmaking practice, eventually moving away from traditional religious imagery and adopting a pop art style. Her work featured abstract shapes and commercial imagery, focusing on social justice issues such as protesting the Vietnam War and advocating against racial inequality in the United States. She specialized in brightly colored silkscreens that combined bold, gestural brushwork with layers of printed text.

By the early 1950s, her distinctive aesthetic and teaching style had garnered widespread recognition, attracting clergy members from across the country to study at Immaculate Heart College. Her students were drawn to her innovative methods, which included assignments like creating two hundred drawings in one session or spending three hours drawing their arm without looking at their work.

In the late 1950s, the Los Angeles archdiocese began to criticize Immaculate Heart College for its perceived liberal stance. Prominent guest speakers at the college—figures like John Cage, Buckminster Fuller, and Charles and Ray Eames—were labeled as "communists," and Kent was singled out as "particularly troubling," with her art described as blasphemous. Representatives from the chancery office repeatedly contacted her superiors to voice their concerns about her work and the college's activities.

In the summer of 1968, Kent took a leave of absence and eventually left the sisterhood to live independently in Boston. After 1970, her art shifted toward a sparser, more introspective style, influenced by her new environment, secular life, and battle with cancer. Kent remained active in social causes until her death. By the time of her passing, she had created nearly eight hundred serigraph editions, thousands of watercolors, and countless public and private commissions, all conveying powerful messages of love and justice.

Sister Corita Kent's chosen medium was the multiple, a generous format that allowed her work to challenge the exclusivity of the art market and embrace a more democratic, inclusive approach. Repetition in her art was more than a stylistic choice—it was central to her faith. Kent sold editions of her multiples to raise funds for causes close to her heart and used both the content and the proceeds from her work to convey messages of social justice and peace. Her repetition mirrors meditative practices in the Catholic tradition, where cycles of actions and recitations—such as saying prayers like the Hail Mary or counting rosary beads—help center the mind.

Similarly, Kent's art used repetition to bring viewers into a reflective, meditative state. Kent's innovative approach to multiplication enabled her to engage with the world in a way that was both intensely personal and profoundly universal, solidifying her as a distinct voice at the intersection of art, spirituality, and social activism.

Practice Multiplication

MULTIPLY THIS MEDICINE INFINITELY

To work with repeated images in visual art, start by selecting a symbol, object, or image from the alchemical tradition that you find in this book. Once you've chosen your image, make multiple prints of it—either by printing copies or by drawing the same image repeatedly. Next, arrange the copies on a sheet of paper to create a collage. As you repeat the image, experiment with different variations in size, color, placement, or orientation. You can overlap the images, shift their positions, or cut and reassemble them to introduce depth and dimension. Pay attention to how the repetition of the image affects the overall composition. Does it create rhythm or tension? Does the meaning of the image evolve as it gets repeated? Can you collapse or expand time with repetition? Could you shift your reality by repeating images? How?

XII.

Projection
RAYS OF LIGHT SPREAD FULL WIDE

Zodiac: Taurus ———————— **Planet:** Venus

Images: The Rebis, Hermaphrodite, the Androgyne, meteorites, two-headed eagles, a golden egg, gold coins

Material Applications: The creation of gold, the Elixir of Life, the realization of a divine art form

> *In Projection it shall be proved if our practice be profitable,*
> *Of which it behoves me the secrets here to move,*
> *Therefore if your tincture be sure and not variable,*
> *By a little of your medicine thus you may prove,*
> *With Metal, or with Mercury as pitch it will cleave,*
> *And tinge in Projection all fires to abide,*
> *And soon it will enter and spread full wide.*
>
> —George Ripley, *The Compound of Alchymy*

Projection is the final stage in creating the Philosopher's Stone, an object whose nature and capacities differ across alchemists and alchemical traditions, and whose lore describes seemingly limitless applications. The Philosopher's Stone grants the alchemist boundless knowledge, allowing them to be fluent in all languages, including those of animals and natural forces. With the Stone, the alchemist can foresee all possible pasts and futures, reading the threads of time in all their patterns and permutations. The Stone can also transmute any material it touches, enabling unlimited shape-shifting. Alchemists can grind parts of the Stone into a powder known as the Powder of Projection, which can be sprinkled onto metals to transform base ones into noble ones. When the Stone is made into an elixir, it confers eternal youth and the ability to cure any illness. In alchemical symbolism, projection is often represented by the Rebis—a being that embodies all masculine and feminine qualities, as well as everything in between and beyond.

Projection signifies a state of spiritual enlightenment in which the alchemist transcends the illusion of separation from the divine. Here, the alchemist becomes absolute, from the Latin *absolutus*, which scholar Michael Inwood defines as "not dependent on, conditional on, relative to or restricted by anything else; self-contained, perfect, complete" (Inwood 1992, 71). The transformation of matter is only possible to the extent that the alchemist's inner state permits it, and the Philosopher's Stone cannot be brought into being until the alchemist believes in their own potential to create it. The production of the Stone marks the moment when the alchemist has learned to embody a deep understanding of alchemical reality. In a seeming paradox, the alchemist cannot step into the power of projection until they yield their individuality and its limitations and learn that true power only emerges when it is in service to the greater whole. Any attempt to create the Stone from a place of vanity will be thwarted. Only the forces of love can revive the Stone after each of the harrowing stages it passes through to become real.

This is beautifully illustrated in an ancient Egyptian myth involving Isis, the most powerful magician in the Egyptian pantheon. Ra, the sun god, had drawn too near the world in his desire to be close to it. His searing heat dried up rivers, scorched the air, withered crops, and killed livestock. As the people suffered—starving, weeping, burning, and pleading for relief—Ra continued moving closer to the world, driven mad by an urge to touch its surface. Isis was compelled to act on humanity's behalf and, therefore, was able to initiate the process of projection.

Isis fashioned a magical serpent from dust and Ra's own spittle, placing it in secret along one of Ra's well-traveled paths. When Ra passed by, the serpent struck, injecting him with a poison that Ra could not cure himself as it contained part of his own essence. Isis offered to heal him under one condition: Ra had to reveal his true name, a sacred and tightly guarded secret that would grant her equal power to his own. Ra agreed. He pressed his heart against hers and pulsed his true name into her with his last heartbeats, passing his power and immortality into her along with it. Isis then cured Ra and, with her newfound strength, compelled him to withdraw his scorching hot body from the Earth, allowing the planet to heal and the people to recover.

The motivation required for the successful creation of the Philosopher's Stone is embodied in Isis's transformative act. Just as she was able to take Ra's power of immortality into herself to restore balance and healing to the greater whole, the alchemist can only create the miraculous Stone in a manner that transcends personal ambition.

In alchemical apprenticeships, the methods for achieving projection are kept secret until the alchemist has completed rigorous initiations that test the strength and purity of their heart. The phrase "As Within, So Without" emphasizes that inner transformation must be reflected in outward actions of service. This concept serves as the horizontal counterpart to the maxim "As Above, So Below." While "As Above, So Below" connects us heart to heart with the divine, "As Within, So Without" connects us heart to heart with all beings on Earth. In a state of alchemical enlightenment, there is no separation between "us" and "them."

Nicolas Flamel (1330–1418) was a French bookseller, scribe, and alchemist who longed to create the Philosopher's Stone. Flamel's bookstore was filled with alchemical texts, and according to legend, one day, a young man came to him offering a rare alchemy book for sale. The book was distinctive, with an ancient copper binding engraved with mysterious diagrams in Greek, Hebrew, and an unknown script. Its pages were gilded and divided into groups of seven, with three sections separated by pages displaying strange, unintelligible diagrams. The title page credited its author as "Abraham Eleazar—Prince, Priest, Levite, Astrologer, and Philosopher."

According to his diaries, Flamel followed the instructions of Abraham Eleazar and was able to create the Powder of Projection, changing a half-pound of mercury first into silver and then into pure gold. Simultaneously, as Flamel put it, he "accomplished the same transmutation in my soul" (Lenglet du Fresnoy 1742, np). After only three transmutations of mercury into gold, Flamel was rich beyond his dreams, yet he kept almost none for himself. He and his wife Perenelle built almshouses, churches, burial grounds, and hospitals. At nearly all his charities, Flamel commissioned strange stones or plaques containing alchemical symbols to be placed at their entrances.

Flamel continued his lifelong work of copying manuscripts and studying alchemy but quickly lost interest in the pursuit of gold. Having witnessed many of his fellow alchemists fall into ruin due to their obsession with wealth, he locked away Eleazar's book and never revealed its secrets. He chose to live the quiet life of a scholar, writing many essential texts on the practice of alchemy. He and Perenelle lived prolonged, active lives, reaching their eighties, with their legacy remaining alive long after their physical bodies had returned to dust. The book was never found.

In mystical practice, the greatest achievements come to those who attain selflessness, and alchemical gold is only granted to those who do not seek to keep it for themselves. The selflessness required to obtain the Philosopher's Stone is one of the great mysteries. One might ask, "If I let go of my sense of self, how can I pursue anything at all?" This paradox challenges both our everyday logic and our deepest attachments.

For many of us in the United States, our lives are centered on individualism, competitiveness, and the pursuit of success for "I," "me," and "mine." From an early age, we are taught to compete, to strive, and to win against others who must lose. As demonstrated repeatedly in the lives of the alchemists and artists featured in this book, it is only those willing to relinquish their worldly name and reputation in pursuit of enlightenment who achieve immortality—leaving behind their insights for the benefit of the All.

In Indian alchemy, *siddhis* are extraordinary powers that arise through deep meditation, disciplined yogic practice, and spiritual awakening. They are considered manifestations of a practitioner's deep mastery over their body, mind, and consciousness but are viewed as by-products of the yogi's path rather than the ultimate goal. In book three of the Yoga Sutras, Patanjali lists a variety of siddhis (Patanjali 1990, 377). Some examples of these include *anima*, the ability to become as small as an atom, or *mahima*, the ability to expand one's body or consciousness, becoming infinitely large. There is *laghima*, the power of lightness, enabling the practitioner to become so light that they can float, and *garima*, the ability to increase one's mass beyond ordinary physical limits. There is also *prapti*—the ability to obtain any object, material or spiritual, from anywhere in the universe. The list goes on, describing powers of projection that allow the yogi to manipulate matter in miraculous ways.

However, Patanjali warns against seeking these siddhis, as they can lead to attachment and hinder the attainment of kaivalya, or liberation. He argues that while these powers may indicate an awakened spiritual state, they can actually serve as obstacles to achieving samadhi. For this reason, he emphasizes that siddhis hold no significance on the path to liberation. Patanjali highlights the risks of displaying these powers and the dangers they pose to their possessor, as a yogi may be tempted to use their abilities for influence instead of remaining devoted to their spiritual practice.

When I was in my mid-twenties, a dear friend and I spent a few months in Benares, India, studying Sanskrit and yogic meditation with a renowned scholar. During our meditation sessions, he would describe how the solar and lunar channels of energy move up and down the body's meridians. As part of the practice, he would walk around the room and tap us on the head and neck at various points during our meditation to stimulate energy flow—or so I thought. One afternoon, I cracked my eyes open and noticed he was standing far away at the front of the classroom, at the blackboard, with his eyes closed. Yet his finger was still tapping my left temple! I peeked during several other sessions and realized that he had never physically walked around the room at all during meditation. He could project his energy!

I didn't mention any of what I'd observed to him, but during one of our final lessons, he looked at me sharply and said that siddhis, or powers of projection, arise spontaneously when one practices these disciplines. He warned me not to fixate on them, advertise them, or become attached to them. Siddhis are physical manifestations of spiritual power, but they will tarnish the souls of those who grasp at them. "Focus on atman, your true self," he said, gesturing to a vast horizon with his hands. *Atman*, a Sanskrit word rooted in terms meaning "essence" or "breath," refers to the true nature of consciousness, which is constant and unchanging, unlike the fluctuating individual self. He explained that if I focused on the vastness of consciousness instead of my limited individual self, I would gain the wisdom to perceive the nature of the universe, which is One, and this was the goal.

Practice Projection

THE UNIFIED FIELD

In ordinary consciousness, we perceive ourselves as a separate, subjective "me" that observes objects, thoughts, emotions, and events. This creates a sense of distinction between ourselves and the world around us. Alchemy, however, allows us to exist in a state where the boundaries between the self and the universe dissolve.

As modern science advances, it increasingly provides insights into this alchemical reality. One significant insight comes from Dutch cardiologist Pim van Lommel, whose exploration of near-death experiences challenges traditional understandings of consciousness. Van Lommel's research revealed that patients who had been clinically dead often reported vivid memories of events that occurred while they were unconscious. His studies led him to hypothesize that consciousness is nonlocal and interconnected, suggesting that the brain does not originate consciousness but functions as a transceiver, receiving information from a timeless, remote space that can be accessed even without brain function (Van Lommel 2013, 7–48).

Physicist David Bohm proposed that the universe operates as an undivided whole through the metaphor of a hologram. A hologram presents an image of wholeness because, in its structure, every part of the holographic plate contains information about the entire image. Even if the hologram is divided into smaller pieces, each piece can still reconstruct the whole picture, though with some loss of resolution. Bohm described the cosmos as "Undivided Wholeness in Flowing Movement," implying that reality is an interconnected movement of forms, patterns within patterns, all reflecting the same underlying imprint.

According to Bohm, what we perceive as the world around us is merely a projection of a deeper, more fundamental reality. This deeper level, which he called the "implicate order," is the true origin of creation, from which all phenomena emerge—interconnected and indivisible (Bohm 1980, np).

KNOCK KNOCK! WHO'S THERE?

Sit comfortably and take a few deep breaths, allowing your body to relax and settle into the present moment. Begin by gently bringing your awareness to the sensations in your body. Feel the weight of your body pressing into the surface beneath you, the subtle pulse of life in your limbs, the rise and fall of your chest with each breath. Observe these sensations without judgment, simply allowing them to come and go. Notice the temperature of your skin, the tension in your muscles, the softness or hardness of the surfaces beneath you.

Now, ask yourself: *Who notices these sensations? Who is it that is aware of this experience in the body?* Gently explore the source of your awareness. As you sit with these questions, the answer may not come in words, but instead as a feeling of presence that is quietly aware. Continue to rest in that awareness.

Shift your focus to the emotions arising within you—notice how these emerge, how they shift, and how they change. Observe them as they are, without trying to change them, simply witnessing as they come and go. Label each one if possible with terms such as: "annoyance," "agitation," "aversion," "happiness," "peace."

Now, ask yourself again: *Who notices these emotions? Who is the one experiencing this inner landscape?*

Next, allow your attention to move to the thoughts that pass through your mind—the chatter, the judgments, the plans. Notice how these thoughts appear, take form, and dissolve like clouds in the sky.

Ask yourself once more: *Who notices these thoughts? Is there a sense of witnessing behind the thoughts, a part of me that is simply observing them without getting caught in their content?*

Finally, take a moment to step behind the noticing itself. Go deeper than the thoughts, emotions, sensations and even the noticer. *What is it that is aware of the thoughts, the emotions, the sensations?*

Sit with this sense of awareness, this presence that has no form, no beginning, and no end. In this quiet presence, notice that there is no need to do anything, no need to seek anything. Feel the stillness that arises in this recognition, and let yourself rest here.

The Body Contains Jewels

Stones found within the body, such as bezoars (solid clumps of undigested food or hair that occur in the intestines), were referred to as the Lesser Stones in alchemy and were thought, in some traditions, to be crucial in the creation of the Philosopher's Stone. Medieval physicians believed these masses protected the body against poison and used them in various healing remedies.

Ancient Egyptians, observing stones in the "large snake" (the intestines), sought out similar formations in the "small snake" (the brain), where they discovered the pineal gland. This small pine cone–shaped gland became a symbol of spiritual awakening. In many traditions, the pineal gland is seen as the center of enlightenment, thought to connect the physical and spiritual realms. Some believed that when awakened, the pineal gland could actually light up in the brain, causing a glow to emanate from the eyes, which would signify heightened awareness and spiritual illumination.

Techniques were developed by Chinese, Indian, and Egyptian alchemists to align the energies of the lesser anatomical Stone in the gut with the greater anatomical Stone in the brain in hopes of creating an immortal body. For Taoist alchemists, the human body is a sacred laboratory for transformation and mystical evolution. They view the organs as vessels for purifying matter and generating psycho-spiritual essences, which are essential for physical health and spiritual cultivation.

A specific set of Taoist exercises sometimes referred to as "cultivating the body beyond the body," involves directing the breath from the lower cauldron in the belly to the middle cauldron in the solar plexus and finally to the pineal gland, located at the center of the skull, just behind the eyes. When performed correctly and repeatedly, the circulation of energy causes the pineal gland to release nectar that gathers in the mouth.

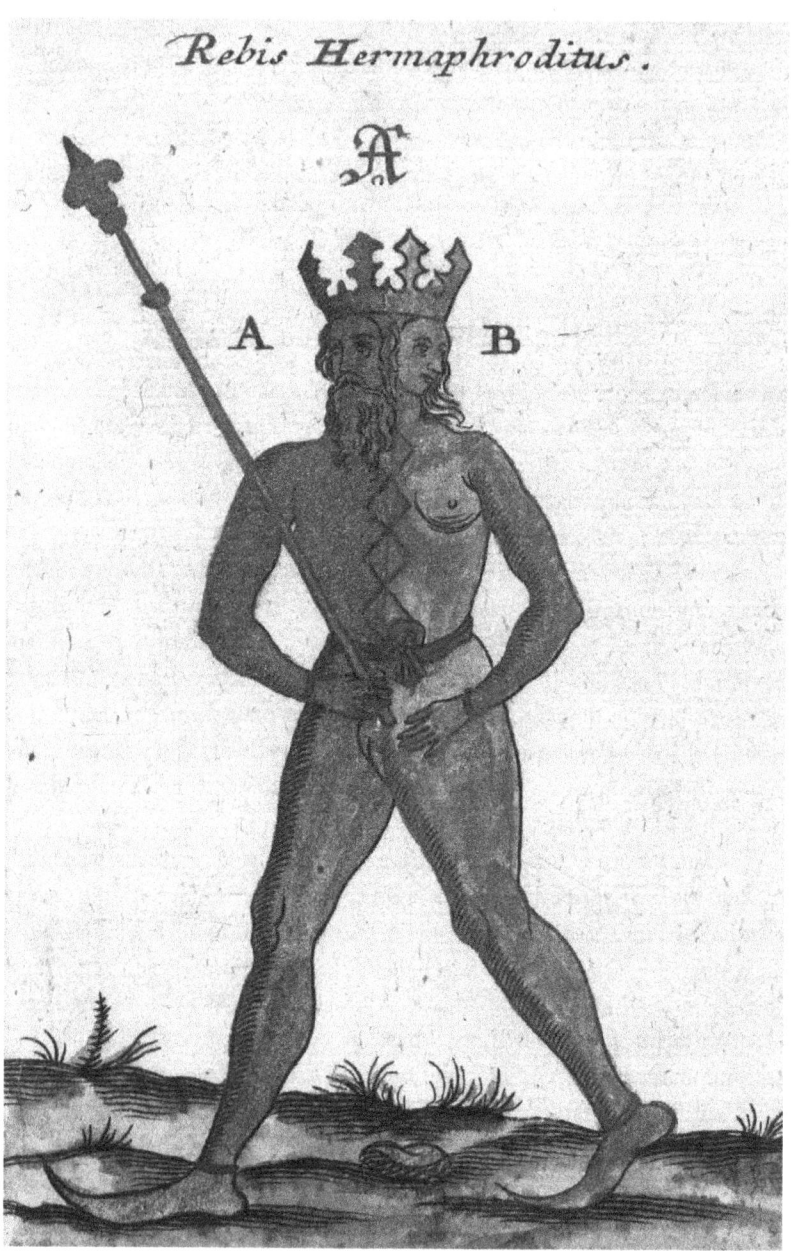

A king portrayed as hermaphrodite, half man/half woman. *Rebis Hermaphroditus*, hand-colored engraving by Johann Michael Faust, 1706. Getty Research Institute, Los Angeles (1385-531).

The brain then emits two lights—one golden, the other silver—that descend to the belly and merge. The light impregnates the nectar, and a being made of light begins to form and rise. At this moment, the mortal body ceases to breathe, and the immortal light body begins to respire. When this "body beyond the body" is ready, it ascends to the brain, where its luminous light merges with ultimate consciousness.

The Rebis

ENLIGHTENMENT IS NONBINARY

Out beyond ideas of wrongdoing and rightdoing,
there is a field. I'll meet you there.
When the soul lies down in that grass,
the world is too full to talk about.
Ideas, language, even the phrase "each other"
doesn't make any sense.

—Rumi

Alchemists perceive themselves as embodying all qualities—masculine and feminine, hot and cold, dry and wet, murky and clear—without succumbing to the allure of polarity. In Buddhism, equanimity (in Pali, *upekkha*) is one of the Four Immeasurables or four great virtues (along with compassion, loving-kindness, and sympathetic joy) that the Buddha taught his disciples to cultivate. This quality of being allows practitioners to remain balanced and grounded amid life's fluctuations.

The term *upekkha* is derived from the prefix *upa*, meaning "over" or "all around," and the root *ikh*, which means "to look" or "to see." This combination highlights the capacity to perceive situations clearly, akin to the expansive view from the summit of a mountain, allowing us to view the full picture without bias. Upekkha is associated with the ease that arises from understanding a broader perspective.

The Emerald Tablet expresses that all matter on Earth is born of the synergy between its father (the Sun) and its mother (the Moon). The alchemist interprets this to signify that they themselves encompass both solar and lunar qualities, integrating the full spectrum of masculinity and femininity within their being. This harmony of opposites is represented by the Rebis, or Rebis Hermaphrodite, a powerful symbol in Western alchemical traditions.

The Rebis is typically depicted as a human figure with two heads sharing one body: one head appears masculine, representing the Sun, while the other appears feminine, representing the Moon. In some portrayals, the figure may possess both masculine and feminine physical traits on a single head and body. The Rebis often has wings, symbolizing spiritual elevation. Yet they stand grounded—either on the earth or atop the back of a dragon—representing the alchemist's bridging of the Above and Below, the union of the spiritual and material realms in the enlightened practitioner.

In ancient Greek mythology, Hermaphroditus, the child of Hermes and Aphrodite, was depicted with both masculine and feminine physical traits. Hermaphroditus is one of the members of the Erotes, a group of winged love gods. In Ovid's version of Hermaphroditus's origin story, the female nymph Salmacis falls deeply in love with Hermaphroditus, who is male. In her desperation, she prays to the gods, asking that they never be separated. The gods answer her prayer by merging their bodies, transforming them into an androgynous form. Ovid frames this transformation as a punishment, portraying Hermaphroditus as an emasculated man who lives in torment.

Other Greek and Roman traditions depict Hermaphroditus as being born with both masculine and feminine qualities from the outset. In these origin stories, Hermaphroditus embodies the epitome of beauty and balance. Renaissance alchemists revered Hermaphroditus as a deity of enlightenment—for the alchemist, a "both/and" existence is ideal.

The both/and mindset refers to the ability to hold two seemingly contradictory qualities or truths simultaneously, transcending binary thinking to embrace complexity and mystery. For example, alchemists seek to balance the spiritual and the material, pursuing both inner enlightenment and physical transformation, without seeing the two as separate or conflicting.

Alchemy's focus on transformation, transcending binaries, and embracing dualities closely aligns with the fluidity that is central to many queer experiences. My belief that alchemy lends itself to a queer interpretation has been criticized by some scholars who argue that I am imposing a modern concept on a tradition that didn't have such a framework. Nevertheless queerness has always been a part of the human story—it is not a new concept, nor is my interpretation of alchemy as supportive of the queer experience a novel one. Queen Christina of Sweden, a 17th-century alchemist, was openly gender nonconforming and; she wore both masculine and feminine attire, had female lovers, and rejected the idea of taking a husband or producing offspring. Christina was educated as a royal male would have been, receiving lessons in religion, philosophy, Greek, and Latin. She was fluent in six languages and an accomplished natural scientist. Alchemist Johannes Franck described her reign as the fulfillment of Paracelsus's prophecy of a golden age brought about by alchemy.

Forrest Bess

HERE IS A SIGN

Forrest Bess was born in 1911 in Bay City, Texas, and demonstrated a passion for art from an early age. He enrolled at the University of Texas to study architecture—a compromise with his parents, who hoped he would pursue a more practical career. Bess found traditional education stifling and preferred spending his time in library stacks. Seeking a more fluid and experiential education, he chose to travel and immerse himself in art, ultimately dropping out of school in 1932. In 1941, after the United States entered World War II, Bess enlisted in the military. During his service, he suffered a violent assault related to his queer sexuality, leading to a mental breakdown. Bess took a leave of absence and later transferred to a convalescent hospital where he taught painting.

After the war, Bess sought solitude to recover from his traumatic military service and retreated to Chinquapin, a remote area on the Texas coast. Accessible only by boat and lacking electricity or phone service until the late 1950s, Chinquapin offered peace. In Chinquapin, Bess worked as a commercial fisherman while painting in his spare time. He often experienced vivid visions and dreams, which he translated into his artwork. As his work evolved, he began to exhibit his paintings, earning solo shows at museums in San Antonio and Houston.

During a trip to New York to find an art dealer, Bess met Betty Parsons, who agreed to represent him. From 1949 to 1967—one of his most productive periods—Parsons organized six solo exhibitions of his work at her gallery in New York City. During the early years of Abstract Expressionism, Bess's biomorphic paintings aligned well with Parsons's roster of artists, which included Jackson Pollock and Mark Rothko. Through painting, Bess developed an intensely private symbolic language, influenced by Jungian notions of the unconscious.

An avid reader of mythology, anthropology, and sexuality studies, Bess saw painting as an integral part of his lifelong metaphysical inquiry. This quest culminated in an extensive personal thesis exploring the merging of masculine and feminine energy within an individual. Bess hoped to display this research alongside his paintings, but Parsons declined the request. His desire to present both his art and theories together was only fulfilled after his death.

In the 1950s, Bess began lifelong correspondences with art historian Meyer Schapiro and sexologist John Money. These letters, later donated to the Smithsonian Archives of American Art, revealed that Bess's paintings were part of a broader personal practice. Drawing from alchemy and Carl Jung's philosophies, Bess proposed that achieving physical androgyny was the key to immortality. To pursue this goal, Bess underwent a series of surgeries to create an androgynous body, believing this transformation would lead to enlightenment.

At one point, Bess suggested to Parsons that he exhibit photographs of his surgeries instead of his paintings. Parsons declined and distanced herself from him, marking the beginning of a gradual decline in both his health and artistic output. Bess passed away at the age of sixty-six in a nursing home in Bay City, Texas, following a stroke. After his death, he was largely forgotten by the art world.

Bess's reputation as a visionary painter of extraordinary power was revived in 1988 when Hirschl & Adler Modern held a show featuring sixty-one of his works. This renewed interest in Bess's art continued with the release of *Forrest Bess: Key to the Riddle* in 1999, a documentary exploring his life and work, which later became a book of the same title. In 2012, the Whitney Biennial further cemented his legacy with a curated presentation of Bess's late 1950s paintings alongside archival materials.

Today, Forrest Bess is recognized as a unique figure in the art world whose work defies easy categorization and is deeply rooted in his intensely personal vision. Bess transcended boundaries—both artistic and societal—long before his time. Like many alchemists, Bess was ahead of his era, leaving future generations to gradually understand and appreciate his groundbreaking perspective after his death.

Practice Projection
FASHIONING THE REBIS

In the European alchemical tradition, the Rebis figure is often depicted as an androgynous human form that combines both masculine and feminine elements, symbolizing the harmonious blending of opposites.

Create your own interpretation of the Rebis—a symbol of unity beyond binaries that feels true to you. It could be an abstract swirl of energy, two intertwining elements, or even a field of lines—whatever visual representation speaks to you of a unified state of being.

Once you've created your image, place it on your alchemist's altar and offer something to it—perhaps a flower or a simple prayer. Gaze upon your creation and ask the Rebis to reflect yourself back to you.

Where do you feel internal polarities that are misaligned? Where might you be holding on to divisions that keep you from flowing together? Invite the Rebis to show you where you can soften and move beyond these polarities and into a deeper state of wholeness.

The Philosopher's Stone

Now is the time to begin the work of creating the Philosopher's Stone. There are many paths you can take in this pursuit. You might follow in the footsteps of John Dee, crafting a cipher that weaves together the mystical principles of alchemy and invites deeper insight into the nature of reality through art. Emerald School offers yearlong immersions that explore the intersection of art and alchemy, providing a rich environment for such exploration. Another path may lead you to study the sacred art of making Eastern Orthodox icons—many of its techniques are rooted in alchemical tradition.

You could also choose to work directly with traditional laboratory methods, studying the ancient recipes of the *Compound of Alchymy*. At the time of writing, both Robert Bartlett and Brian Cotnoir are offering courses in foundational alchemical lab techniques.

Alternatively, you may feel called to seek the Philosopher's Stone within your own mind and body. If your focus is inner transformation, disciplines such as somatics or qigong might open powerful new pathways for growth and understanding.

Remember, this sacred endeavor is a practice that may span many lifetimes, requiring commitment, patience, and a willingness to explore the depths of both the material and spiritual worlds. The search for the Philosopher's Stone urges you to seek the deeper truths that govern existence itself.

The next step in your alchemical practice in the here and now is to reach out to fellow alchemists—whatever that means for you. You might seek a mentor; discover a community of like-minded, creative people; or deepen your relationship with the plants and animals in your surroundings. Despite the common image of alchemists working in solitude, transformation never occurs in isolation; it flourishes in clusters, nurtured by generosity and shared purpose.

May your alchemical work be enriched by the connections you form and the wisdom you share. May you travel well and find nourishing communities, and may your quest bring laughter, compassion, peace, liberation, and insight into this world.

XIII.

The Recapitulation
INTO THE ART WITH FULL POWER

So to bring this treatise to a final end,
And briefly to conclude all these secrets here,
Diligently look at, and attend to your figure,
Which contains in it all these secrets great and small,
And if you conceive it, both theoretically and practically,
By figures and colours, by scripture plain,
It wisely conceived, you may not work in vain.
Consider first the latitude of this precious stone,
Beginning in the first side noted in the West,
Where the red man and the white woman be made one,
Espoused with the spirit of life to live in rest . . .

—George Ripley, *The Compound of Alchymy*

When I was in second grade, I auditioned for the school play—*The Wizard of Oz*—absolutely convinced I'd be cast as Glinda the Good. I'd watched the movie so many times I could recite every word, my tiny voice twinning with the 1939 soundtrack until I drifted off to sleep—only to pick up right where I'd left off when I opened my eyes. Each morning, I'd twirl out of my room singing, "She brings you good news, or haven't you heard / When she fell out of Kansas, a miracle occurred!" I wasn't pretending—I *was* Glinda, a big pink moon orbiting through my apartment, setting everything right with my big pink magic.

So when the cast list went up and all the lead roles were handed to sixth graders, I stared in disbelief at my name next to "ballerina Munchkin (1 line)." My brain cracked like thunder, and in a blazing inferno of seven-year-old fury, I made a solemn vow: if they wouldn't let me be Glinda onstage, I would be her for real—an *actual* good witch: that's who I was, I knew it. From that moment on, spells and magic weren't a game or a fantasy; they were a calling. As Glinda reminds Dorothy, "You've always had the power, my dear. You just had to learn it for yourself."

Years later I began to understand this early claiming of my magic was the work of alchemy. In that defiant vow, I had unknowingly invoked my future. And so it was that years after that first vow, when I was given my magician's name—*Emerald*—I was finally being handed the key to the Emerald City.

Alchemists call this kind of reflection on the patterns in our lives the Recapitulation—the spiral-like return to earlier stages of transformation, not to relive earlier experiences but to refine them. This practice includes reviewing past experiments to integrate new insights, correct mistakes, and refine one's approach. In the inner laboratory, it means revisiting the past—not just in this life but also lives before—to find the places where knowledge has been buried and energy left behind.

To return to the center, to the self, we must commit to fearlessly knowing what we know. I *am* a good witch. This is Gnosis: a soul-deep knowing that does not arrive through logic but through recognition. It's through this faith that we glimpse the Philosopher's Stone—not as something distant or yet to be forged but as something that was always there, quietly pulsing at the heart of our becoming. As Hermes writes in the *Corpus Hermeticum*:

> *Gnosis is no beginning; rather it is to us the first beginning of Its being known*
>
> *. . .*
>
> *'Tis very hard, to leave the things we have grown used to, which meet our gaze on every side, and turn ourselves back to the Old Old [Path].*
>
> *Appearances delight us, whereas things which appear not make their believing hard. (Mead 1906, 14)*

The role of the alchemist is to imagine and reshape the evolutions of the world—to recreate reality again and again through intention and creativity. Alchemists work by casting spells of awareness, shifting the material realm by tuning their attention to what is unseen. They learn to "see with both eyes": one eye on the visible, the tangible, the known; the other on the subtle, the fluid, the emergent. Through this way of seeing, the alchemist seeks truths that liberate—not just themselves but also all those drawn into their orbit. This liberation asks us to believe in what "appears not"—at least, not yet.

Your Alchemical Future

It is the year 3060. You wake in the early light and walk barefoot into a laboratory, feeling the warmth of the World Soul beneath your feet. You pause to sing with it as you light the fire in the room's tall stone athanor. As the blue-green flames rise, you gaze out the window and see children dressed in robes of many colors, planting sacred herbs and flowers in communal gardens with plants grouped according to their astrological signatures. Beings gather beneath open-air structures that belong to no one, as horses graze the wildflowers that line the wide pathways between free bookstores serving hot bread slathered in raspberry jam. A harpsichord concert is taking place inside a ceramic dome, the sounds chiming and ringing out into the air, thick with every imaginable bird. Horse manure is shoveled into the gardens and into pits where alchemical flasks are sealed and buried, cooking up perfumes and medicines in the warm mire.

Zeno of Citium, queer lover of nature and founder of Stoicism, once described an ideal society as one without marriage, without laws, without private property. You smile, realizing his vision from three thousand years ago has come to life. And beyond that, there is no longer "you" and "me"—only ever-changing variations of "us." Food, medicine, knowledge, and shelter are freely given. Language has shifted into telepathy, surfacing into sound only when the vibration and music of voices bring pleasure. The forests have returned—green cathedrals alive again with species once thought extinct, their songs spiraling through the air like spectral gladioli.

In a clearing stands a great temple to the alchemical arts, forged from unimaginable rainbow metals and gemstones devised long ago in your glass retorts—materials that hum and glow like a bioluminescent coral reef. In one of the temple's inner courtyards, you spend your afternoons swimming in a sacred fountain beside alligators and blooming lotuses. Your heart is steady as a mountain and light as a petal. As you do the backstroke, a heron clacks its beak to encourage you, and you can hear someone playing a theremin off in a field somewhere. Electricity now spontaneously erupts, evoked through willpower and deep feeling and not wires or generators.

Plants have swallowed up pavement and travel is accomplished through wishing, though this technology sometimes lands people in unexpected time zones and unknown geographies. After your swim, you attend a class teaching the art of regulating body temperature so that you never need to wear a coat unless you want to. As you practice, a baby deer nuzzles your toes, enjoying the heat you are learning to generate with the universal mind-fire.

You move through the day within this miraculous pattern; your alchemy a part of a living experiment, blazing at the edges of being, shaped by devotion. This

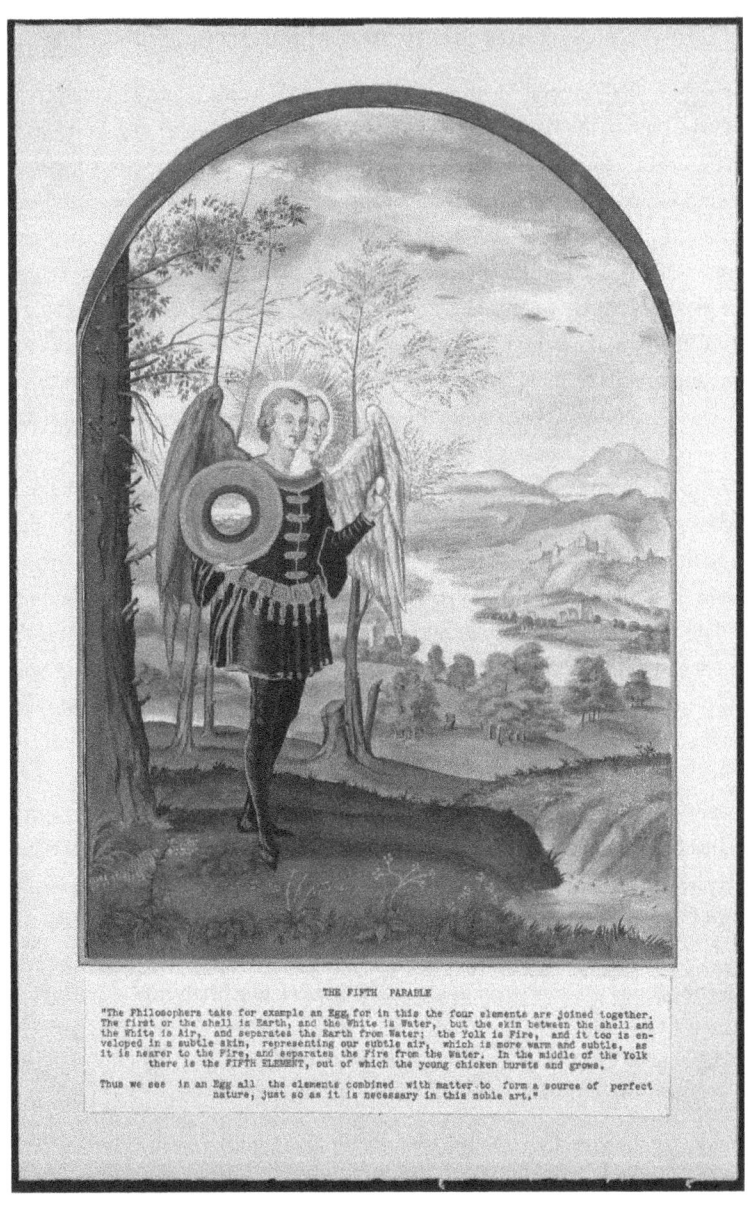

THE FIFTH PARABLE

"The Philosophers take for example an Egg, for in this the four elements are joined together. The first or the shell is Earth, and the White is Water, but the skin between the shell and the White is Air, and separates the Earth from Water; the Yolk is Fire, and it too is enveloped in a subtle skin, representing our subtle air, which is more warm and subtle, as it is nearer to the Fire, and separates the Fire from the Water. In the middle of the Yolk there is the FIFTH ELEMENT, out of which the young chicken bursts and grows.

Thus we see in an Egg all the elements combined with matter to form a source of perfect nature, just so as it is necessary in this noble art."

With one red wing, another white, and black garments, the androgyne contains the three phases of the work in one. The mirror in its right hand reflects nature. The egg in its left is known as the Philosophical Egg, because it contains all four elements at once.
The Hermetic androgyne; representing the stages of the alchemical Work in One.
Watercolor painting by E. A. Ibbs. Source: Wellcome Collection.

world was not built by domination or hatred but with holographic spirals of care and attention that continuously bloom. You, the alchemist, are one of the beings who imagined us here. Through horrific wars and unbelievably cruel greed—you brought us here. Elders tell appalling tales of something called patriarchy and its hateful warmongers who went to Mars to colonize it and became shards of glass on its scorching surface. Those who did not learn to work their inner fires were consumed by them, becoming brittle and breaking.

This radiant future was not dreamed into being by any one person alone. The practices of alchemy help awaken our awareness of interconnectedness, revealing that nothing exists in isolation and that our fates are intertwined.

Through trust, we learn to trust. Cultivate trust in your vision of what is possible, and tend to the flowers of trust in your community. From the *Corpus Hermeticum*:

> *When shall I sing a hymn to you? One cannot detect in you time or season.*
> *For what shall I sing the hymn—for what you have made or what you have*
> *not made, for what you have made visible or what you have kept hidden? And*
> *wherefore shall I sing the hymn to you—for being something that is part of*
> *me, or has a special property, or is something apart? For you are whatever I*
> *am; you are whatever I make; you are whatever I say. You are everything, and*
> *there is nothing else; what is not, you are as well. (Copenhaver 1995, 20)*

APPENDIX

Recapitulation Inventory

Take note of the stages that need further cycles of attention.

Calcination, in the alchemical laboratory, involves burning away impurities from solid objects. In the internal laboratory, this is the process of incinerating outdated beliefs and rigid structures, encouraging us to confront areas in our lives where inflexibility has led to stagnation or collapse. Guided by Mars, the planet of conflict and action, calcination prompts us to reflect on personal struggles and the role of anger in our lives. Mars teaches that, like fire, anger can destroy stagnation and corrupt systems, but it must be wielded with care.

Suggested Ritual: Construct a ceremonial fire or funeral pyre and burn something that represents inner tyranny to symbolize the release of rigid beliefs, making way for renewal.

Questions to Explore:

▶ *Where am I rigid internally? Where am I a tyrant?* This tyrant can insist on strange things, like being "nice" all the time.

▶ *What are the rigid structures in my chosen field (e.g., the art world)?*

▶ *Did I experience spiritual or scientific rigidity in my household growing up (including atheism)?*

▶ *Where does fear exist in my life? In my creative practice?*

▶ *Who or what has been critical of my creativity?*

▶ *Where does fire or heat show up in my creative process?*

Solution in the alchemist's laboratory involves submerging the calcined materials in a bath to remove ash and detritus. In the internal laboratory, solution is a stage of softening and releasing resistance by letting emotions flow. At this stage, we are encouraged to let water teach us to release dualistic thinking structures, such as "me" and "them" or "wrong" and "right," as we begin to move away from polarizing thought patterns.

Suggested Ritual: Engage in a water ritual—immerse yourself in a bath, stream, or ocean to surrender any calcified internal defenses.

Questions to Explore:

▸ *What is a "flow state," in my understanding?*

▸ *What is the difference between doing and being as a creative person?*

▸ *What resistance in my life can I dissolve with softness, gentleness, and peace?*

▸ *Where does guilt show up in my life? Where does it show up in my creative practice?*

▸ *How can I learn to trust my own process?*

▸ *In what areas of my life am I holding on too tightly, and how can I soften?*

▸ *Where do fluids or fluidity show up in my creative practice?*

In the laboratory, **separation** involves extracting, cutting, and dissecting materials to isolate what is essential. Internally, it is the process of clarifying, eliminating distractions, and refining focus. This stage supports the establishment of healthy boundaries, helping us see the "inner star" of our creative or spiritual work. Once we've softened and dissolved, separation allows us to get clear about what matters. Ruled by Saturn, this phase draws on decisive, assertive energy—not for destruction but for discernment.

Suggested Ritual: Engage in practices of silence and solitude to find clarity.

Questions to Explore:

▸ *What boundaries need to be set in my life to promote clarity and focus?*

▸ *Where are there messes in my creative practice? Where are there messes internally? How do I work with mess?*

▸ *Where is the energy of disagreement placed in my life right now? What do I refute?*

▸ *How can I create space for clarity by paring down or cutting back?*

▸ *Where does cutting or splicing come into my creative practice?*

In the laboratory, **conjunction** refers to the fusing or blending of multiple materials to create a new substance. Internally, this stage invites us to explore relationships of all kinds—between self and other, body and spirit, inner and outer life. By examining the dynamics of attraction and repulsion, we begin to better navigate the relational complexity inherent in creative and spiritual work.

Suggested Ritual: Engage in a devotional practice. This could include building an altar to your ancestors, offering fruit or flowers to a deity, or performing a divinatory practice that opens you to guidance from the realm of spirit.

Questions to Explore:

▸ *Who do I admire artistically, and why?*

▸ *What artists am I jealous of, and why?*

▸ *What kind of community or personal support would help my creative growth?*

▸ *Are the relationships in my life supportive of my creativity?*

▸ *Where does shame or embarrassment show up in my creative practice?*

▸ *Are there creative ancestors I can reach out to for guidance?*

▸ *Are there nonhuman beings I can reach out to for assistance and collaboration?*

Putrefaction invites us to engage with themes of decay, death, and grief. In the external laboratory, decomposition becomes a catalyst for transformation. Internally, this stage urges us to confront impermanence, to witness how grief opens us to deeper connections and truths. Ruled by Jupiter, the planet of expansion and growth, putrefaction teaches us to embrace decline and impermanence as necessary aspects of our life cycles.

Suggested Ritual: Meditate with the dead—this could mean visiting a cemetery or taking time to honor a deceased animal, insect, or tree with a ritual.

Questions to Explore:

▸ *What do I think about my own mortality?*

▸ *Do I think about my legacy or the traces I leave behind me?*

▸ *How do I work with time, death, and the natural cycles of decay in my creativity?*

▸ *Do I think of grief as an acceptable emotion for me to have?*

▸ *Where is the energy of grief showing up in my life right now? Does it have an outlet?*

Sublimation in the laboratory is the process by which a solid is converted directly into a gas, bypassing the liquid stage. In the internal laboratory, sublimation involves seeking inspiration from the invisible, immaterial realms, with Mercury assisting you in creating relationships with these subtle energies. This stage invites you to connect with unseen forces that guide creative work, such as space or air.

Suggested Ritual: Feed and observe birds daily. This quiet, attentive act can open your perception to the invisible forces in nature and the dynamics needed to make flight possible.

Questions to Explore:

▶ *How does the unseen or invisible guide my creative practice? How is it represented in my work?*

▶ *How do I understand nothingness? Can I make creative work about it?*

▶ *Where do air and space fit into my creative practice?*

▶ *What can birds teach me about creativity?*

In the lab, **fermentation** is a stage where microorganisms transform organic matter into a stable, living substance—something that does not decay. In the internal laboratory, this is a time of resurrection and renewal, where dead or stagnant parts of ourselves are revived and reanimated. Guided by the Sun, fermentation brings warmth, clarity, and vitality. This is a phase of sacred rebirth, where we give voice to what has long been buried. Naming—whether a project, self, or part of your creative identity—is a ritual act that restores power and vitality.

Suggested Ritual: Give yourself a new name that feels authentic to you at this moment, and take note of how it feels. You do not need to share this name with anyone.

Questions to Explore:

▶ *What aspects of my life or creative process feel dead and must be brought to life again?*

▶ *What kinds of art inspire me and make me feel alive?*

▶ *How do I use language to describe myself?*

▶ *How can I utilize language to enhance my creative processes? Is there a new way to approach language here?*

▶ *Which microorganisms are involved in my creativity?*

Exaltation in the laboratory involves refining, distilling, or filtering substances to "en-lighten" them. In the inner laboratory, exaltation brings ascent and expansion, with the Moon supporting us in finding clarity and joy in the act of creation itself. Here, we learn to lighten up and let go.

Suggested Ritual: Try practicing ten minutes of voluntary laughter every day for a few weeks and see if you can find more levity in your work as a result. If it's difficult for you to laugh on command, mimic the expressions of laughter by making sounds such as "hee-hee ho-ho" for ten minutes.

Questions to Explore:

▸ *Am I confident in my creative work? What would more confidence allow me to do?*

▸ *Where does confidence come from?*

▸ *How do I use laughter to make spiritual progress?*

▸ *Where does joy come into my creative practice?*

▸ *What appearances am I willing to shed to pursue my creative path?*

In the laboratory, **multiplication** refers to the process of repeating an operation—such as distilling wine multiple times to make a strong spirit—in order to amplify its power, strength, or potency. Internally, this stage reveals the value of repetition, rhythm, and refinement. What we repeat becomes who we are. Guided by Mercury, the planet of language, movement, and transformation, multiplication invites us to harness the energy of recurrence. Certain patterns, when consciously practiced, build momentum, resilience, and mastery.

Suggested Ritual: Engage in daily repetition rituals—such as reciting a mantra, chanting, or using prayer beads. Let repetition be an act of devotion rather than habit.

Questions to Explore:

▸ *How does repetition shape the structure of my creativity?*

▸ *What patterns can I identify that lead to expansion in my life?*

▸ *What patterns lead to contraction?*

▸ *What recurring motifs exist in my creative practice?*

▸ *What recurring behaviors get in the way of my creativity?*

▸ *What recurring behaviors strengthen it?*

In the laboratory, **projection** is the ultimate expression of realized potential, resulting in a Philosopher's Stone capable of limitless powers of transformation and healing. Internally, this stage represents the embodiment of wisdom, when the alchemist no longer seeks transformation but becomes the agent of it. Projection reveals that true mastery is not in control, but in alignment—with purpose, with truth, with love. Guided by Venus, the planet of art, beauty, and harmony, projection invites us to extend the fruits of our inner work into the world. It is not the end of the alchemical journey but its integration. Here, belief is not fantasy—it is creative force. The Philosopher's Stone emerges only when the alchemist wholly trusts their capacity to transmute, not from a concept of self but from devotion to the All. What we project from within becomes our contribution to the whole.

Suggested Ritual: Acts of service where we ask for no acknowledgment or thanks can help us to move more freely into an expanded state of unified consciousness.

Questions to Explore:

▸ *What is "me"? What is not "me"?*

▸ *What beliefs limit my capacity to create a Philosopher's Stone?*

▸ *How does my art reflect unified fields and limitlessness?*

▸ *What will I lose if I allow the serpent to close the circle, showing me eternity? What will I gain?*

BIBLIOGRAPHY

Aftel, Mandy. 2001. *Essence and Alchemy: A Natural History of Perfume*. North Point Press.

Ana Mendieta: A Retrospective, exh. cat. 1987. Essays by Petra Barreras del Rio and John Perrault. New York: The New Museum of Contemporary Art.

Anohni. 2016. *Hopelessness*. Secretly Canadian.

Anonymous. 2002. *Meditations on the Tarot: A Journey into Christian Hermeticism*. Translated by Robert A. Powell. Tarcher/Penguin.

Aramphongphan, Paisid. 2021. "An Artist in the Secular World: Paul Thek's Relics." *American Art* 35, no. 1 (Summer).

Atkins, Anna. 1973. *Photographs of British Algae: Cyanotype Impressions*. 1843. Reprint. Dover Publications.

Attar, Farid ud-Din. 2019 *The Conference of the Birds*. Translated by Sholeh Wolpé. Penguin Classics.

Ault, Julie, ed. 2007. *Come Alive! The Spirited Art of Sister Corita*. Distributed Art Publishers.

Bartlett, Robert Allen. 2009a. *Real Alchemy: A Primer of Practical Alchemy*. Ibis Press.

Bartlett, Robert Allen. 2009b. *The Way of the Crucible*. Ibis Press.

Bashō, Matsuo. 1997. *The Narrow Road to Oku*. Translated by Donald Keene, illustrated by Masayuki Miyata. Kodansha USA.

Basinski, William. 2002. *The Disintegration Loops*. Temporary Residence Limited.

Beaumont-Thomas, Ben. 2019. "'I Wanted to Be David Bowie': Music Maverick William Basinski." *Guardian* (10 April), *www.theguardian.com*.

Bergman, Ingmar. 1960. *Four Screenplays of Ingmar Bergman*. Translated from the Swedish by Lars Malmström and David Kushner. Simon and Schuster.

Beuys, Joseph. 1982. "'I Put Me on This Train!' An Interview with Joseph Beuys: *Art Papier*, vol. 1." Neugraphic, *www.neugraphic.com*. Accessed 13 July 2025.

Bohm, David. 1980. *Wholeness and the Implicate Order*. Routledge.

Böhme, Jacob. 1920. *The Confessions of Jacob Böhme.* Compiled and edited by W. Scott Palmer, with an introduction by Evelyn Underhill. Methuen & Co.

Brainard, Joe. 2001. *I Remember.* Granary Books.

Bruno, Giordano. 2021. *On the Infinite, the Universe, and the Worlds: Five Cosmological Dialogues.* Translated by Paul Summers Young. Black Letter Press.

Budge, E. A. Wallis, trans. 1967. *The Book of the Dead: The Papyrus of Ani.* Dover Publications.

Cage, John, and Thomas McEvilley. 1993. *Dove Bradshaw: Works 1969–1993.* Sandra Gering Gallery.

Cain, Sian. 2025. "'People Can't Imagine Something on That Scale Dying': Anohni on Mourning the Great Barrier Reef." *Guardian* (25 April), *www.theguardian.com*.

Cameron, Julia. 1992. *The Artist's Way: A Spiritual Path to Higher Creativity.* TarcherPerigee.

Campbell, Karen, ed. 1991. *German Mystical Writings: Meister Eckhart, Hildegard of Bingen, Jakob Böhme, and Others.* Continuum.

Carlos, Wendy. 1984. *Digital Moonscapes.* CBS Records.

CERN. 2025. "ALICE Detects the Conversion of Lead into Gold at the LHC." 8 May, *home.cern*.

Charters, Samuel. 1962. *The Letters of Emily Dickinson: A Reminiscence by Thomas Wentworth Higginson from "The Atlantic Monthly" October 1891.* Smithsonian Folkways Recordings. PDF file. Smithsonian Folkways, *folkways-media.si.edu*. Accessed 27 Oct. 2025.

Chia, Mantak. 2008. *Healing Light of the Tao: Foundational Practices to Awaken Chi Energy.* Destiny Books.

Coltrane, Alice. 2021. *Kirtan: Turiya Sings.* Produced by Ravi Coltrane. Impulse! Records/UMe. CD.

Coltrane, Alice. 2025. *Monument Eternal.* Akashic Books, Ltd.

Cooke, Lynne. 1990. "John Baldessari." *Burlington Magazine* 132, no. 1048 (July): 512–13.

Copenhaver, Brian P., trans. 1995. *Hermetica: The Greek Corpus Hermeticum and the Latin Asclepius.* Cambridge University Press.

Cotnoir, Brian. 2017. *Alchemy: The Poetry of Matter.* Khepri Press.

Dee, John. 2001. *John Dee's Hieroglyphic Monad.* Weiser Books.

Del Popolo, Antonino. 2021. *The Invisible Universe: Dark Matter, Dark Energy, and the Origin and End of the Universe.* World Scientific.

Dickinson, Emily. 1981. *The Letters and Poems of Emily Dickinson*. Edited by Richard B. Sewall. Harvard University Press.

Dunham, Hayden. 2021. "Pippa Garner and Hayden Dunham on the Struggle of Being Inside Bodies." *Interview Magazine* (19 May), *interviewmagazine.com*.

Edinger, Edward F. 1985. *Anatomy of the Psyche: Alchemical Symbolism in Psychotherapy*. Open Court Publishing Company.

Edou, Jérôme. 1996. *Machig Labdron and the Foundations of Chöd*. Snow Lion Publications.

Eliot, T. S. 1976. *Four Quartets*. Annotated and edited by Helen Gardner. Faber and Faber.

Faulkner, Raymond. 2016. *The Egyptian Book of the Dead: The Book of Going Forth by Day*. Edited by Ogden Goelet and Carol Andrews. Chronicle Books.

Flamel, Nicolas. 2009. *Theory and Practice of the Philosopher's Stone*. Martino Fine Books.

Fludd, Robert. 1976. *Utriusque Cosmi Historia*. Frankfurt, 1617–1621. Facsimile edition, Adam McLean.

Freke, Timothy, and Peter Gandy, trans. 1997. *The Hermetica: The Lost Wisdom of the Pharaohs*. Tarcher/Putnam.

Friedman, Susan Stanford. 1981. *Psyche Reborn: The Emergence of H.D.* Indiana University Press.

Fulcanelli. 1984. *The Mystery of the Cathedrals and the Esoteric Interpretation of the Hermetic Symbols of the Great Work*. Translated by Mary Sworder, revised ed. Brotherhood of Life.

George, Demetra. 2019. *Ancient Astrology in Theory and Practice: A Manual of Traditional Techniques*. Rubedo Press.

Griffith, Francis Llewellyn, and Herbert Thompson, eds. 1904. *The Demotic Magical Papyrus of London and Leiden*. British Museum.

Grimes, Shannon. 2018. *Becoming Gold: Zosimos of Panopolis and the Alchemical Arts in Roman Egypt*. Rubedo Press.

Halberstam, Jack. 2011. *The Queer Art of Failure*. Duke University Press.

Hallo, William W. 1997. "Sumerian Canonical Compositions. A. Divine Focus. 1. Myths: The Exaltation of Inanna," in *The Context of Scripture, I: Canonical Compositions from the Biblical World*, Leiden/New York/Köln.

Hauck, Dennis William. 2003. *The Emerald Tablet: Alchemy for Personal Transformation*. Penguin.

H.D. 1973. *Trilogy*. New Directions.

Hegel, Georg Wilhelm Friedrich. 1995. *Lectures on the History of Philosophy: Volume III: Medieval and Modern Philosophy*. Translated by E. S. Haldane. University of Nebraska Press.

Hermes Trismegistus. 1945. *The Corpus Hermeticum*. Translated by G. R. S. Mead. The Shrine of Wisdom.

Horsfield, Kate. 1987. *Ana Mendieta: fuego de tierra*. Produced with Lyn Blumenthal.

Inwood, Michael. 1992. *A Hegel Dictionary*. Blackwell.

Jacobi, Jolande, ed. 1958. *Paracelsus: Selected Writings*. Bollingen Series XXVIII, Princeton University Press.

John of the Cross. 1959. *Dark Night of the Soul*. Translated by E. Allison Peers, 3rd rev. ed. Image Books.

Jonas, Silvia. 2016. *Ineffability and its Metaphysics: The Unspeakable in Art, Religion, and Philosophy*. Palgrave Macmillan.

Kilgannon, Corey. 2020. "A Jazz Drummer's Fight to Keep His Own Heart Beating." *New York Times* (5 August), www.nytimes.com.

Kinniburgh, M. C., ed., and Diane di Prima. 2023. *The Catalog of the Diane di Prima Occult Library*. TKS Books.

Klein, Yves. 1974. *Yves Klein, 1928–1962: Selected Writings*. Translated and edited by Barbara Wright. Tate Gallery.

Langford, Thomas A. 2015. *Giordano Bruno: Philosopher/Heretic*. Routledge.

Lao Tzu. *Tao Te Ching*. 1988. Translated by Stephen Mitchell. Harper Perennial.

Lao Tzu. 1998. *Tao Te Ching: A Book About the Way and the Power of the Way*. Translated by Ursula K. Le Guin, with an introduction by Ursula K. Le Guin. Shambhala.

Leiden Papyrus X. ca. 3rd century CE, Leiden University Library, Papyrus Collection, Leiden, Netherlands.

Lenglet du Fresnoy, Nicolas. 1742. *L'Histoire de la philosophie hermétique*. Vol. 3, Coustelier.

Ma, Anandamayi. 2002. *The Essential Sri Anandamayi Ma*. Translated and edited by Thomas A. Blomberg. State University of New York Press.

Macy, Joanna, and Molly Young Brown. 2014. *Coming Back to Life: The Updated Guide to the Work That Reconnects*. New Society Publishers.

Maier, Michael. 1620. *Septimana Philosophica: Qua Ænigmata Aureola De Omni Naturæ Genere a Salomone Israëlitarum Sapientissimo Rege, & Arabiae Regina Saba, Nec Non Hyramo, Tyri Principe, Sibi Invicem in Modum Colloquii Proponuntur & Enodantur*. Typis Hartmanni Palthenii.

Maier, Michael. 1992. *Atalanta Fugiens*. Translated by H.M.E. de Jong, edited by Hildemarie Streich. Inner Traditions.

Malone, Tyler. 2022. "She Is Her. I Am Her: H.D.'s Autobiographical Novel Asks: What's in a Name?" *Paris Review* (7 November), *www.theparisreview.org*.

Martin, Agnes. 1973a. "The Untroubled Mind." In *Agnes Martin*, edited by Ann Wilson. Institute of Contemporary Art, University of Pennsylvania.

Martin, Agnes. 1973b. "What We Do Not See If We Do Not See." In *Agnes Martin*, edited by Ann Wilson. Institute of Contemporary Art, University of Pennsylvania.

Mayer, Bernadette. 1984. *Utopia*. United Artists Books.

McEvilley, Thomas. 2001. *The Shape of Ancient Thought: Comparative Studies in Greek and Indian Philosophy*. Allworth.

McEvilley, Thomas. 2003. *The Art of Dove Bradshaw: Nature, Change and Indeterminacy*. West New York, NJ: Mark Batty Publisher.

Mead, G. R. S., trans. 1906. *The Corpus Hermeticum: Initiation into Hermetics; The Hermetica of Hermes Trismegistus*. London: Theosophical Publishing Society.

Medwin, Marc. 2009. "Milford Graves: Time Piece." All About Jazz (22 June), *www.allaboutjazz.com*.

Meginsky, Jake, and Neil Young, dir. 2018. *Milford Graves Full Mantis*. Criterion Channel, *www.criterionchannel.com*. Accessed 13 July 2025.

Merton, Thomas. *New Seeds of Contemplation*. New Directions Publishing, 1961.

Meurdrac, Marie. 1656. *La Chymie Charitable et Facile, en Faveur des Dames*.

Meyer, Marvin, ed. 2007. *The Gospel of Thomas: The Hidden Sayings of Jesus*. HarperOne.

Meyer, Marvin, and Willis Barnstone, trans. 1997. *The Essential Gnostic Gospels*. Shambhala.

Mitter, Siddhartha. 2025. "Alice Coltrane: Artist Muse and Sonic Healer." *New York Times* (7 February), *www.nytimes.com*.

Montano, Linda. 1988. *The Art/Life Institute Handbook*. Women's Studio Workshop.

Montano, Linda. 2005. *Letters from Linda M. Montano*. Edited by Jennie Klein. Routledge.

Moyer, Paul B. 2015. *The Public Universal Friend: Jemima Wilkinson and Religious Enthusiasm in Revolutionary America*. Cornell University Press.

Ognjenovic, Igor. 2014. "Greek Vowels and the Chaldean Planets." Academia.edu, *www.academia.edu*.

O'Neill, John J. 1944. *Prodigal Genius: The Life of Nikola Tesla*. Ives Washburn.

Orpheus. 2013. *The Orphic Hymns: Text, Translation, and Notes*. Translated and edited by Apostolos N. Athanassakis and Benjamin M. Wolkow. Johns Hopkins University Press.

Ovid. 1986. *Metamorphoses*. Translated by A. D. Melville. Oxford University Press.

Pagel, Walter. 1982. *Paracelsus: The Man and His Reputation, His Ideas and Their Transformation*. Princeton University Press.

Pagels, Elaine. 1979. *The Gnostic Gospels*. Random House.

Patanjali. 1990. *The Yoga Sutras of Patanjali*. Translated by Sri Swami Satchidananda. Integral Yoga Publications.

Paul Thek: Paintings, Works on Paper and Notebooks, 1970–1988. 1998. The Arts Club of Chicago.

Philostratus. 2005. *The Life of Apollonius of Tyana*. Edited and translated by Christopher P. Jones, introduction by C. P. Jones. Harvard University Press, Loeb Classical Library vols. 16–17.

Plath, Sylvia. 2004. *Ariel*. Edited by Frieda Hughes. Harper Perennial Modern Classics.

Plato. 2016. *Timaeus*. Translated by Peter Kalkavage, 2nd ed. Focus Philosophical Library.

Princenthal, Nancy. 2018. "Art 'Requires a Relaxation of Control': How Agnes Martin Gave Up Intellectualism to Harness Her Inspiration." *Artnet News* (31 December), *news.artnet.com*.

Rilke, Rainer Maria. 1981. *Selected Poems of Rainer Maria Rilke*. Translated by Robert Bly. Harper & Row.

Rilke, Rainer Maria. 1996. *The Book of Hours: Love Poems to God*. Translated by Anita Barrows and Joanna Macy. Riverhead Books.

Ripley, George. 1973. *The Twelve Gates*. Edited by John Ferguson. Chymical Publications.

Ripley, George. 1991. *The Compound of Alchymy*. London, Printed by Thomas Norton, 1591. Reprint, edited by Stanton J. Linden, Garland Publishing.

Ripley Scroll. c. 1700. Watercolor on parchment. Getty Research Institute, J. Paul Getty Trust, Los Angeles (Accession no. 950053).

Roberts, Alison M. 2019. *Hathor's Alchemy: The Ancient Egyptian Roots of the Hermetic Art*. Northgate Publishers.

Robinson, James M., ed. 1988. *The Nag Hammadi Library in English*. Harper & Row.

Rumi, Jalal al-Din. 2004. *The Essential Rumi*. Translated by Coleman Barks. HarperOne.

Sappho. 1958. *Sappho: A New Translation*. Translated by Mary Barnard. University of California Press.

Schiffman, Richard. 2004. "Finding Healing Music in the Heart." *New York Times* (9 November), *www.nytimes.com*.

Shiva, Vandana. 2005. *Earth Democracy: Justice, Sustainability, and Peace*. South End Press.

Sinclair, John, interviewer. 1967. "Sun Ra: An Interview: Part One: Collision of the Suns." *Ann Arbor Sun* (April): 1–3.

Smith, Chuck. 2013. *Forrest Bess: Key to the Riddle*. Foreword by Robert Thurman. powerHouse Books.

Sontag, Susan. 2001. *Against Interpretation: And Other Essays*. Picador.

Space Is the Place. 1974. Directed by John Coney, performance by Sun Ra. Ashimba Films.

Stich, Sidra. 1994. *Yves Klein*. Hayward Gallery. London.

Stockholm Papyrus. c. 3rd century BCE. National Library of Sweden, Stockholm, Sweden.

Szwed, John F. 1997. *Space Is the Place: The Lives and Times of Sun Ra*. Pantheon Books.

Taussig, Hal, et al. 2010. *The Thunder: Perfect Mind: A New Translation and Introduction*. Palgrave Macmillan.

Taylor, Susan L. 2020. "A Love Supreme with Alice Coltrane." *Essence* (29 October), *www.essence.com*.

Teresa of Ávila. 1961. *Interior Castle*. Translated and edited by E. Allison Peers, from the critical edition of P. Silverio de Santa Teresa. Doubleday.

Townsend, William. 2013. *Forrest Bess: Key to the Riddle*. With essays by Robert Gober and Clare Elliott. Menil Collection; distributed by Yale University Press.

Trismosin, Salomon. 2019. *Splendor Solis: The World's Most Famous Alchemical Manuscript*. Watkins.

Van Lommel, Pim. 2013. "Non-local Consciousness: A Concept Based on Scientific Research on Near-Death Experiences During Cardiac Arrest." *Journal of Consciousness Studies* 20, nos. 1–2: 7–48.

Vaughan-Lee, Llewellyn, ed. 2016. *Spiritual Ecology: The Cry of the Earth*, 2nd ed. The Golden Sufi Center.

Viso, Olga M. 2004. *Ana Mendieta: Earth Body, Sculpture and Performance, 1972–1985*. Hatje Cantz Publishers.

Watlington, Emily. 2023. "Trailblazing Trans Artist Pippa Garner on Moving Fluidly Between the Studio and the Body Shop." *Art in America* (17 August), *www.artnews.com*.

White, T. H. 2011. *The Once and Future King*. Ace Books.

Wier, Dennis R. 1996. *Trance: From Magic to Technology*. Trans Media Inc.

Wilde, Oscar. 2005. *De Profundis*. Edited by Robert Ross. Penguin Classics.

Wilson, Peter Lamborn, Christopher Bamford, and Kevin Townley, eds. 2007. *Green Hermeticism: Alchemy and Ecology*. Lindisfarne Books.

The Wizard of Oz. 1939. Directed by Victor Fleming; performances by Judy Garland, Frank Morgan, Ray Bolger, Bert Lahr, and Jack Haley. MGM.

Wolkstein, Diane, and Samuel Noah Kramer. 1983. *Inanna, Queen of Heaven and Earth: Her Stories and Hymns from Sumer*. Harper & Row.

Zosimos of Panopolis. 1937. *The Visions of Zosimos*. Translated and with a prefatory note by F. Sherwood Taylor. *Ambix*, vol. 1, 88–92.

INDEX

ABOUT THE AUTHOR

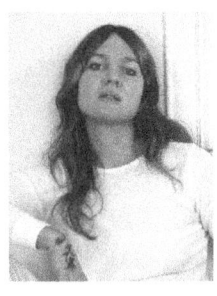 **Eliza Swann** is an interdisciplinary artist, intuitive, writer, and educator based in New York City. They are the author of *The Anatomy of the Aura*, which bestselling author Yumi Sakugawa called "beautiful and life-affirming," and the founder of the Golden Dome School, an alternative school that explores the mystical dimensions of art. *The Alchemical Imagination* draws on Eliza's ten years of teaching alchemy in universities and cultural institutions, including a long-standing popular interdisciplinary art and alchemy course at the Pratt Institute.

Eliza received a BA in painting from the San Francisco Art Institute and an MFA from Central St. Martins in London. In 2023, they were selected as lecturer-in-residence at the Philosophical Research Society and have also been an invited lecturer at Central St. Martins, the San Francisco Art Institute, the Hammer Museum, the Pratt Institute, and the New School. Their writing has appeared in *BOMB*, *Arthur*, *Contemporary Art Review LA*, *Momus*, and *Perfect Wave*. They contributed essays to Taschen's Witchcraft and *A Confluence of Witches*. Their work has been supported by PEN America, the Foundation for Contemporary Art, the Los Angeles Department of Cultural Affairs, the Pratt Faculty Development Fund, the Feminist Center for Creative Work, and the Wassaic Project. As a visual artist, Eliza has exhibited artwork internationally, at the Feminist Center for Creative Work in Los Angeles, California, and, most recently, at the University of California Santa Cruz.

Visit for More Information

www.elizaswann.com

www.golden-dome.org